Whips
to
Walls

Titles in the Series

NEW PERSPECTIVES ON MARITIME HISTORY AND NAUTICAL ARCHAEOLOGY
James C. Bradford and Gene A. Smith, editors

Rivers, seas, oceans, and lakes have provided food and transportation for man since the beginning of time. As avenues of communication they link the peoples of the world, continuing to the present to transport more commodities and trade goods than all other methods of conveyance combined. The New Perspectives on Maritime History and Nautical Archaeology series is devoted to exploring the significance of the earth's waterways while providing lively and important books that cover the spectrum of maritime history and nautical archaeology broadly defined. The series includes works that focus on the role of canals, rivers, lakes, and oceans in history; on the economic, military, and political use of those waters; on the exploration of waters and their secrets by seafarers, archeologists, oceanographers, and other scientists; and upon the people, communities, and industries that support maritime endeavors. Limited by neither geography nor time, volumes in the series contribute to the overall understanding of maritime history and can be read with profit by both general readers and specialists alike.

Whips to Walls

Naval Discipline from
Flogging to Progressive-Era
Reform at Portsmouth Prison

Foreword by Rear Adm. John D. Hutson, USN (Ret.)

Rodney K. Watterson

NAVAL INSTITUTE PRESS
ANNAPOLIS, MARYLAND

Naval Institute Press
291 Wood Road
Annapolis, MD 21402

Library of Congress Cataloging-in-Publication Data
Watterson, Rodney K.
 Whips to walls : naval discipline from flogging to Progressive-Era reform at Portsmouth Prison / Rodney K. Watterson ; foreword by Rear Adm. John D. Hutson, USN (Ret.).
    page cm — (New perspectives on maritime history and nautical archaeology)
 Includes bibliographical references and index.
 ISBN 978-1-61251-445-1 (pbk. : alk. paper) — ISBN 978-1-61251-446-8 (ebook) 1. Portsmouth Naval Prison (Prison : Kittery, Me.)—History. 2. United States. Navy—Prisons—History. 3. Naval discipline—United States—History. 4. Prison discipline—United States—History. 5. Prisons—Maine—Kittery—History. I. Title. II. Title: Naval discipline from flogging to Progressive-Era reform at Portsmouth Prison.
 VB893.W38 2014
 365'.974195—dc23
                                                                                2013042408
♾ Print editions meet the requirements of ANSI/NISO z39.48-1992 (Permanence of Paper).
Printed in the United States of America.

22 21 20 19 18 17 16 15 14   9 8 7 6 5 4 3 2 1
First printing

CONTENTS

Illustrations

FOREWORD

If you have seen the iconic film *The Last Detail*, starring Jack Nicholson, you may think you know something about the Portsmouth Naval Prison. But if you read *Whips to Walls*, by Capt. Rod Watterson, USN (Ret.), you will really know about the prison. And, indeed, you will learn about U.S. Navy history as well as the progressive history of penal theory and practice in the United States. As Captain Watterson explains, this history has been a poorly documented part of American and naval history. Using his knowledge of the Navy—how it runs, how it communicates, its strengths and weaknesses—he very successfully fills that void. This is an eminently readable book that virtually brings to life the ghosts that linger behind the white castle walls that dominate the skyline of the Portsmouth harbor. This is the area where Northwest Passage begins. It is an era full of history that *Whips to Walls* reveals in just the right level of detail.

Captain Watterson and I were stationed together at Portsmouth Naval Shipyard in the mid-1980s. Even then, though long since closed, the prison irresistibly captured your imagination. I well remember taking a call from a representative of the Bureau of Prisons who was looking for a place to house Cuban refugees from the Mariel boatlift. I told him that the Portsmouth prison would not be a good location (I think I actually said "horrible"). It was within the secure industrial area of a nuclear shipyard and, more to the point, it had been closed in 1973 by a presidential administration unhappy with New England without even turning off the water or boarding up the windows. He scoffed and said they would come anyway to inspect, and they did exactly that a few weeks later. Wearing hazmat suits to protect us from the inches thick asbestos, we opened the creaking door and brushed away the cobwebs. Peering into the looming darkness, it took about fifteen seconds for them to agree this wasn't going to suit their needs. But then we spent the next hours simply exploring what seemed like a giant tomb. In many respects it was exactly that. The tomb of a bygone era where desperate and often pathetic men were sent to pay their debt to society. Some literally died there; others only lost their souls and their futures. What tales those walls could tell! But, of course, none of us on that futile inspection knew those stories or the men who lived them. Now, thanks to Rod Watterson, what happened there is known. Importantly, why it happened is told as well.

I have been an observer and student of American, and particularly Navy, justice all my adult life. I have seen the good, the bad, and the ugly. It is a path that has headed inexorably toward more justice, but slowly and not without its setbacks. *Whips to Walls* details that progress in what could by some be viewed as a narrow, confined example, the Portsmouth Naval Prison. But like Moby Dick isn't just the story of a guy and a whale, *Whips to Walls* is much more than it appears to be at first blush (although, to be sure, it is a gripping story even at the narrowest reading.)

It is really two stories. One discusses the end of flogging in 1850 and how the Navy then achieved (or failed to achieve) good order and discipline without the whip. One way was to eliminate the grog ration. Another was a variety of forms of shipboard confinement that met with some, but limited, success. The latter half of the book explores the second story—the early beginnings of formal incarceration starting with the Navy prison system in 1888 and the opening of the Portsmouth Naval Prison in 1908.

It is at this point that the hero of our story emerges. Thomas Mott Osborne was the greatest penologist of his, or likely any other, era. The book involves such notables as President Wilson, several preeminent secretaries of the Navy, Assistant Secretary Franklin D. Roosevelt, and other luminaries, but it is the force of Osborne's personality and his vision that carries the story. He arrived as warden at Portsmouth in 1917 after serving similarly at Sing Sing. He immediately set about to install many of the reforms at Portsmouth that he had experimented with in his prior assignment. Some worked and some didn't, but it soon became clear that then, as now, there is a world of difference between civilian life and the life of a sailor and the sea. That, in and of itself, is a cautionary tale that bears remembering.

Portsmouth Naval Prison was open for business only twenty-five years longer than the length of time it has been closed and shuttered. Warden Osborne served for only three years and left almost ninety-five years ago. And yet . . . and yet, this is a story that needs to be told. Among other perspectives, it tells a tale of pendulum physics, how the pendulum tends to swing too far one way, then too far the other, only to gradually, oh, so gradually, achieve equilibrium somewhere near the center. Ultimately, at its core, it is a human story, as all the best stories are. It is the story of presidents and deserters, secretaries and criminals, and how a prison warden dealt with them all.

Read the story and see if you can hear the cell door clang shut.

—*Rear Adm. John Dudley Hutson, USN (Ret.)*
Judge Advocate General (Navy), 1997–2000

ACKNOWLEDGMENTS

This book has been a long time in the making, and many have contributed to its development. First, I want to thank the members of my master's thesis committee at the University of New Hampshire, Ellen Fitzpatrick, Lucy Salyer, and James Tucker, who got me started on this project. Their comments were extensive, insightful, and helpful. I also want to acknowledge the encouragement and support of my dissertation adviser, Kurk Dorsey, who encouraged me to pursue publication of this material.

The project expanded greatly in scope and research over the years. Many contributed to the success of that research. Archivist Joanie Gearin at NARA Waltham was especially helpful with Portsmouth and Boston Navy Yard records and managing the many carts of boxes and binders that I "mined" during my visits. Charles Johnson and Chris Killillay provided a similar service at the National Archives, Washington, D.C., as did Sarah Hays and Joanne Jones during my visits to the New Hampshire Historical Society Library in Concord, New Hampshire. Lydia Wasylenko at the Syracuse University Bird Library deserves thanks for focusing my efforts with the Osborne family papers. Many others at the Navy Department Library, Navy Yard, Washington, D.C.; and the Library of Congress photographs reading room made significant contributions.

Nancy Mason, special collections assistant at the Milne Special Collections and Archives at the University of New Hampshire, was helpful in locating and reproducing shipyard photographs. Michelle Wright provided the same support at the Library of Congress, Washington, D.C. Gary Hildreth, public affairs specialist at Portsmouth Naval Shipyard, provided access to a video of the interior of the prison and other valuable details. Thanks to Walter Ross and William Tebo, volunteers at the Portsmouth Naval Shipyard Museum, for their energetic support, suspect sea stories, endless unsolicited opinions, and tireless efforts in maintaining a wealth of local naval treasure on a meager budget. Thanks also to the late James Dolph for his support and devoted efforts over many years as director of the shipyard museum. Similar thanks go to Tom Hardiman, Keeper of the Portsmouth Athenaeum, for his support with this and other projects.

Special thanks to my good friend Gary Sabbag, who read the original manuscript and provided important editorial comments and constructive criticism. The short sentences and to-the-point paragraphs reflect his experience as a newspaper editor. I am also most grateful to John Hutson for writing an exceptional foreword. His extensive experience with Navy justice and his personal experience with Portsmouth prison eminently qualified him to take on that task. I am especially indebted to copyeditor Jeanette Nakada, whose contributions refined and improved this work.

I want to thank my wife of fifty-two years, Susan, for proofreading numerous drafts and offering recommendations and encouragement. I am deeply indebted to her for the patience and understanding in granting me endless hours of our retirement time to pursue a dream. Lastly, I want to thank my longtime, loyal project assistant, Molly. Ever present during long hours at the computer, always eager to listen to new ideas, and frequently reminding me, with a nudge of her nose, when it was time for us to balance work with play, she was even more faithful and supportive than the average golden retriever.

Flogging was a weekly, almost daily occurrence. It was almost certain
that somebody would be drunk at evening muster, and the
punishment was flogging at 11:30 next forenoon.

—Cdr. N. H. Farquhar, USN, 1885

During the first day he [a visitor to Portsmouth prison] looked about;
found upwards of 2000 prisoners . . . most of them living in barracks
outside the prison—with no bolts or bars and no wall around the
grounds . . . in short, an unguarded prison run by the prisoners.

—Thomas Mott Osborne, 1925

"Get me out of here quickly," pleaded the warden of Portsmouth Naval Prison in closing a letter to his good friend, Assistant Secretary of the Navy Franklin Delano Roosevelt, in March 1920.[1] Warden Thomas Mott Osborne was highly stressed from being under investigation by naval authorities for the past six months. A special team, headed by FDR, had recently completed an investigation into conditions at Portsmouth prison, which included allegations of widespread sexual depravities and gross mismanagement. Six months earlier, complaints of fiscal mismanagement from a disgruntled ex-prisoner had resulted in a preliminary investigation by the judge advocate general (JAG) that had uncovered far more serious accusations. The JAG recommended the formation of a special team to further investigate the charges. FDR insisted on personally leading that team. The team's recently issued report had absolved Osborne of all blame. Despite the exoneration, Osborne correctly surmised that the powerbase he had enjoyed for the past three years, with the full support of FDR and Secretary of the Navy Josephus Daniels, had been seriously eroded.

Osborne's imminent departure from Portsmouth prison was a replay of his departure from Sing Sing Prison just a few years earlier. In both cases, the most noted prison reformer of his era had conducted successful progressive prison reform programs only to have the programs end in turmoil and controversy. Also with both, an aggressive backlash reversed most of his initiatives shortly after his departure.

Progressive prison reform at Portsmouth Naval Prison during World War I could be viewed as either a success or a failure depending on your point of view. Roosevelt and Daniels could not have been more pleased with the man they had personally selected to turn things around at Portsmouth prison. Osborne opened prison doors and had prisoners guarding and governing themselves. Thousands of young sailors, responding to the humanitarian conditions, were restored to the fleet during wartime. On the other hand, senior officers in the fleet, the recipients of those thousands of restored prisoners, felt they were being inundated with troublemakers and malcontents. Vice Adm. William S. Sims, and other officers, accused Osborne of running a prison at which some prisoners found living conditions more attractive than a sailor's life at sea. These officers considered Osborne an abject failure.

The humanitarian reforms implemented under Osborne were in sharp contrast to the harsh naval punishments exercised during the first half of the nineteenth century under the Articles of War (1800), commonly known as "Rocks and Shoals." The seventy-year journey between these two extremes in naval discipline included the birth and maturation of the naval prison system. The progressive reform experiment at Portsmouth prison during World War I was the capstone of the early years of that system.

During the first half of the nineteenth century, the pendulum of naval discipline was firmly fixed in the hard right position with shipboard flogging being the punishment of choice. The pendulum began to swing toward the center with the abolishment of flogging in 1850. The Navy, having lost this harsh but efficient and effective discipline tool, was forced to substitute less efficient punishments. Various conditions of confinement topped the list of substitute punishments; however, the Navy had essentially no shipboard confinement spaces on its mid-nineteenth-century sailing ships and few cells in brigs and jails ashore. In addition, a ship could ill afford to lose a crewmember to confinement or another crewmember to guard a confined prisoner. All members of the crew were needed to sail and fight a nineteenth-century ship of war.

Faced with a shortage of confinement facilities, the Navy had to improvise. Onboard confinements were often of short durations with accommodations that permitted the offender to continue as a productive member of the crew. For example, a sentence of hard labor during the day and confinement in double irons at night resulted in minimal disruption to the ship's operations. Sentences of minimal onboard confinement with the loss of shore liberty for six months to a year had the same effect. Ship's captains proved to be very innovative with onboard punishments until an adequate number of prison cells ashore became available.

The period between the abolishment of flogging in 1850 and the formal establishment of the naval prison system in 1888 was characterized by a lack of clear guidance on punishments from the Navy Department. Punishments were merely suggested and not mandated. The result was considerable inconsistency in interpretation and application of punishments for the same offense between ships of the fleet. A naval prison system was needed to promote more uniform discipline throughout the fleet.

The Navy's efforts to gain congressional approval and funding for a naval prison in the 1870s were unsuccessful. It was not until the late 1880s that a prison was cobbled out of an existing building at the Boston Navy Yard, and another upgraded from a small Marine barracks prison at Mare Island Navy Yard, that the Navy had the start of a naval prison system. An ever-increasing need for cells, primarily driven by high desertion rates, forced the Navy to continuously expand and upgrade the Boston and Mare Island prisons. In 1908 the Portsmouth Naval Prison was constructed as a more permanent solution to the Navy's long-term prison needs.

The pendulum of naval discipline continued to move slowly past the center position toward the left during the early twentieth century as naval discipline was influenced by the progressive prison reform initiatives gaining favor in the private sector. In 1912 humanitarian considerations and overcrowded naval prisons drove the Navy to a system of disciplinary barracks for military offenders with high potential for restoration. The conditions of confinement in the disciplinary barracks were much less harsh than those in the naval prisons. This was followed in 1915 by an even more humanitarian probation system that eliminated the need for the disciplinary barracks and permitted deserving sailors, convicted of lesser military offenses, to remain in a duty status on their ships at reduced pay.

As a result of the disciplinary barracks and probation system, the naval prisons and prison ships had excess capacity for the first time in their histories. This situation led to a massive restructuring of the naval prison system that eliminated numerous prisons and prison ships. Portsmouth and Mare Island, California, were left as the only stateside naval prisons, with Portsmouth becoming the dominant centerpiece of the entire naval prison system. With the primary focus of World War I being Europe and the Atlantic Ocean, the East Coast became the hub of naval activity and Portsmouth prison became a much larger operation than its counterpart on the West Coast. Portsmouth was the primary focus of the naval prison system when Thomas Mott Osborne arrived on 10 August 1917.

Figure 1, showing the distribution of prisoners in naval prisons from 1914 to 1920, illustrates how dramatically Portsmouth prison dominated the naval prison system during World War I. The prison ship *Southery*, tied at a pier adjacent to Portsmouth prison, and the disciplinary barracks at Parris Island, South Carolina, confined the lesser offenders. Portsmouth and Mare Island confined more serious offenders, and Cavite prison, in the Philippine Islands, provided the same service for the Asiatic Fleet. The most serious offenders, naval criminals, usually numbering fewer than one hundred prisoners annually, were confined in five state prisons. If the U.S. Navy wanted to conduct an experiment in progressive prison reform, Portsmouth prison was the place to do it.

Under the liberal administration of President Woodrow Wilson and the leadership of Daniels and FDR, the pendulum of naval discipline swung even further to the left with Osborne at Portsmouth. Prisoners governed themselves, prison doors were opened, and thousands of supposedly rehabilitated prisoners were returned to the fleet until ship's captains became convinced that too many troublemakers were rejoining the fleet. Osborne restored about the same number of prisoners to the fleet in one year, 1919 (1,563),[2] as the same prison restored during all four years of World

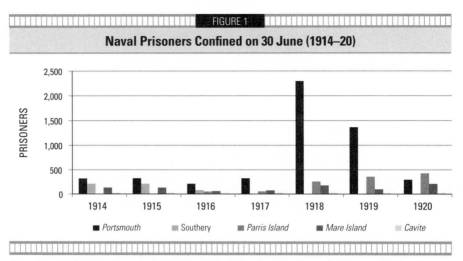

FIGURE 1

Naval Prisoners Confined on 30 June (1914–20)

Legend: Portsmouth, Southery, Parris Island, Mare Island, Cavite

Source: Secretary of the Navy Reports for the Fiscal Years 1914–20. Navy Department Library, Naval History and Heritage Command, Washington Navy Yard, Washington, D.C.

War II (1,576) when the prison and prison population were much larger.[3] The fleet's impression was that Portsmouth prison was fitted with revolving doors. Osborne had driven the pendulum of naval discipline as far left as it could go.

Figure 2, showing the number of prisoners received, confined, restored, and discharged annually at Portsmouth prison from 1916 to 1923, suggests something extraordinary happened during the period that Osborne was the commanding officer of the prison. During World War I, the number of prisoners sent to Portsmouth increased dramatically, and Osborne's reforms just as dramatically increased the number of prisoners rehabilitated and restored to the U.S. Navy and Marine Corps. As impressive as this is, it doesn't begin to tell the story of the controversy and turmoil that accompanied the decision of Daniels and Roosevelt to commission Osborne a lieutenant commander in the U.S. Navy and make him the commanding officer of Portsmouth Naval Prison. The few restorations during the years following Osborne's departure in 1920 are testimony to an immediate backlash to Osborne's liberal reform initiatives. This backlash moved the naval discipline pendulum off its hard left position and caused it to seek the center once again.

The history of naval discipline during the nineteenth century up to the Civil War period has been thoroughly researched and documented by James E. Valle's *Rocks & Shoals: Order and Discipline in the Old Navy 1800–1861* and Harold D. Langley's *Social Reform in the United States Navy, 1798–1862*. These works highlight the cruelties, but also the efficiency and effectiveness, of flogging and the events that led to its abolishment in 1850. Almost equal importance is given to the daily grog ration, the source

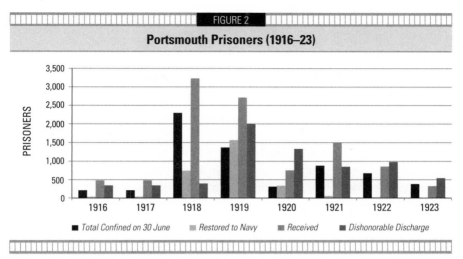

FIGURE 2

Portsmouth Prisoners (1916–23)

Legend: ■ Total Confined on 30 June   ■ Restored to Navy   ■ Received   ■ Dishonorable Discharge

Source: Commanding Officer Portsmouth Naval Prison, *Annual Reports for the Fiscal Years Ending 30 June 1916–1923*, NARA Waltham, RG 181, Portsmouth General Collection.

of most of the Navy's discipline problems, and the events that led to its abolishment in 1862. These works conclude by noting that the Navy faced a serious challenge in its efforts to replace flogging with confinement as its primary discipline tool.

Almost nothing has been written about the development of the naval prison system that eventually solved the Navy's confinement needs. An innocuous memorandum buried in a file labeled "Prisons Miscellaneous, Material Relative to," at the National Archives and Record Administration (NARA) in Washington, D.C., shows how little is known about the subject. Archivist Alma R. Lawrence's 12 April 1945 note, responding to a Chaplain Drury's query about the origin of the naval prison system, professed that her research could not answer his question with any certitude: "Our records did not reveal the exact date when prisons for court-martialed men were established. In 1872 it was recommended that an appropriation be made to build a suitable prison at one of the marine stations. In 1891 there were two naval prisons, one at Mare Island, Cal., the other in Boston Navy-yard. In 1905 mention is made that there was a new naval prison under construction at Portsmouth, N.H."[4]

The first half of this book answers Chaplain Drury's question by filling in many of the details lacking in Lawrence's sketchy response and, in the process, sets the stage for Osborne's arrival at Portsmouth prison in 1917. Much has been written about Thomas Mott Osborne and his unique contributions to progressive prison reform. However, a detailed account of his years at Portsmouth Naval Prison has never been told. The second half of this book tells that story. Most of what is known about the experiment stems from Osborne's own self-promotion in newspapers, speeches, and articles. He was the most noted spokesman for prison reform of his era and was extremely accomplished at public relations. Thus, most of what is known about the Portsmouth experiment, and the little that has been published, originated from him.

This book will show that his views about the time he spent at Portsmouth were somewhat skewed in his favor.

The most comprehensive work on Osborne is Rudolph W. Chamberlain's *There Is No Truce: A Life of Thomas Mott Osborne* (1935); of over 400 pages, fewer than 20 pages are about Osborne's time at Portsmouth prison and no naval records are cited. Osborne's life and his prison reform initiatives are well documented in penal histories; Frank Tannenbaum's *Osborne of Sing Sing* (1933) is one of those works. It too devotes only a few of its 336 pages to Osborne's experiences at Portsmouth. Richard Lewis Alan Weiner's 1981 Harvard history thesis, "Ideology and Incumbency: Thomas Mott Osborne and the 'Failure' of Progressive Era Prison Reform," devotes one sentence to Portsmouth.[5] Geoffrey C. Ward's *A First-Class Temperament: The Emergence of Franklin Roosevelt* (1989) devotes about 15 of 800 pages to the FDR-Osborne relationship. Ward, after labeling Tannebaum's *Osborne of Sing Sing* "a worshipful account of his public career" and Chamberlain's *There is No Truce* a "hugely admiring study," concludes, "Osborne and his curious career deserve a modern, more objective study."[6] This book provides that more modern, objective study of Osborne's life at Portsmouth prison. Neil D. Novello's video *TMO @ the Castle* also presents Thomas Mott Osborne in a very positive light.[7] Another recent work, Rebecca M. McLennan's *The Crisis of Imprisonment: Protest, Politics, and the Making of the American Penal State, 1776–1941* (2008) devotes over 40 of 500 pages to Osborne and his prison reform experiences prior to his arrival at Portsmouth prison. His time at Portsmouth is reduced to the following three sentences containing several errors, for which the corrections are indicated in brackets:

> The U.S. Navy also adopted Sing Sing-style reforms in its military prisons. Following Osborne's resignation from Sing Sing in 1916, his old comrade from the Tammany battles—Franklin D. Roosevelt, now Woodrow Wilson's Secretary of the Navy [Assistant Secretary of the Navy] appointed him warden of the Naval Prison at Portsmouth, New Hampshire. Lieutenant-Colonel [Lieutenant Commander] Osborne proceeded to remodel the prison along the same lines as Sing Sing, organizing the 6,000 [2,500] servicemen-prisoners into a self government league and removing [some of] the Marine guards from the prison.[8]

This account of Osborne's tenure at Portsmouth, as with the others described earlier, is typically brief and lacking understanding of the naval prison environment. The most comprehensive of the local histories of Portsmouth Naval Prison, Robert J. Verge's *A History of the U.S. Naval Prison at Portsmouth, New Hampshire* (1946), devotes only four of seventy-seven pages to the Osborne years.

Tannenbaum, Chamberlain, Weiner, and McLennan stressed Osborne's contributions to progressive reform outside the U.S. Navy. Ward touches on Osborne's time in the Navy with few details. Verge stressed Osborne's naval experience without mentioning his previous involvement with prison reform at Auburn or Sing Sing prisons. All the works are quite complimentary of Osborne and his reform efforts, and rightfully so, because he was a remarkable man of great accomplishments. None of these sources, however, explore Osborne's Portsmouth experience in any depth or context. This book provides a detailed analysis of Osborne's years at Portsmouth.

It is not obvious why Osborne's years at Portsmouth have received so little attention from historians while the rest of his life has been the subject of considerable study. The Osborne years at Portsmouth Navy Yard are well documented by a plethora of official naval correspondence at the National Archives and Record Administration (NARA) in Waltham, Massachusetts. Naval correspondence can be extremely confusing with seemingly endless endorsements and strange addresses unless one is familiar with the Navy Department and the naval system of correspondence. Tracing through such correspondence can be a discouraging exercise that may have made the investigation of Osborne's civilian life a more attractive exercise for researchers. The other possibility is that, perhaps, previous historians found little of importance in Osborne's years at Portsmouth prison. This book argues strongly to the contrary.

Osborne wrote several books, but none adequately address his time at Portsmouth. His two longest works, *Within Prison Walls* (1914) and *Society and Prison* (1916), were written before he went to Portsmouth. In 1924 Thomas Mott Osborne wrote *Prisons and Common Sense*. This book draws heavily on his experiences at Sing Sing, Auburn, and Portsmouth prisons to expound on his theories of penal reform and especially his concept of prisoner self-government: the Mutual Welfare League. Regarding his time at Portsmouth Naval Prison, Osborne wrote, "If time allowed, it would be well to describe in detail the working of the League in the Naval Prison at Portsmouth, for in many ways this has been its most interesting expression. . . . Some day the story may be written; in the meantime I can only say that the fundamental principles of the League, learned at Auburn and emphasized at Sing Sing, were thoroughly and brilliantly vindicated at Portsmouth."[9] Osborne undoubtedly would have written more about his years at Portsmouth, but he died two years after the publishing of *Prisons and Common Sense*.

This book tells the story that Osborne hoped would be written some day: a detailed account of his tenure as commanding officer of Portsmouth Naval Prison (1917–20); however, contrary to his belief, the fundamental principles of his penal reform initiatives will not be thoroughly and brilliantly vindicated by this account. As with so much of Osborne's innovative work in prison reform, success or failure resides in the eye of the beholder.

The following chapters focus on three primary themes: (1) the evolution of naval shipboard discipline after flogging, (2) the origins and maturation of the naval prison system, and (3) the evolvement of progressive prison reform in our national and naval prisons, with the Osborne years at Portsmouth prison the shining example. The themes often overlap and elements of each theme frequently occur concurrently, making a straightforward chronological history of each theme a challenge. The book is organized as follows:

Chapter 1 provides an overview of nineteenth- and early-twentieth-century prisons and reform movements, the context for subsequent chapters. The nation's prisons were evolving during the first half of the nineteenth century when flogging was the discipline tool of choice in the Navy. The nation's prisons continued to evolve through the last half of the century concurrent with the Navy's search for a prison system. The two prison systems, national and naval, and their reform movements, eventually merged at Portsmouth during World War I. Chapter 1 establishes the historical framework of national prisons and prison reform through which the remaining chapters pass en route to the rendezvous with Osborne in the latter half of the book.

For purposes of this book, the Navy's prison system is considered to have developed in six phases between 1850 and 1920 (figure 3, USN and USMC Enlisted Men [1880–1939], helps define these phases). Although the total number of naval prisoners, not the total number of personnel in the Navy and Marine Corps, dictated the need for cells, the number of courts-martial prisoners was a fairly constant percentage of the Navy's personnel during the latter half of the nineteenth and the early twentieth centuries. Thus, figure 3 provides a rough picture of the Navy's evolving need for confinement cells.

The need for cells was primarily driven by prisoners convicted of desertion in its various forms. In *Rocks and Shoals*, James E. Valle says, "Desertion was rife in the Navy throughout the nineteenth century. . . . It averaged about 10 percent per year throughout the nineteenth century."[10] Chapter 5 shows that the desertion rate was slightly higher at the end of the century, averaging about 12.5 percent between 1887 and 1902. Later chapters show the desertion rate remained consistent during the early years of the twentieth century. Fairly consistent desertion rates as the Navy grew in numbers meant increased desertions and an increased need for confinement facilities.

Chapter 2 covers phase 1 of the development of the naval prison system—it reviews the highlights of flogging and its immediate aftermath during which the Navy struggled to find suitable substitute punishments. This chapter, a capsule summary

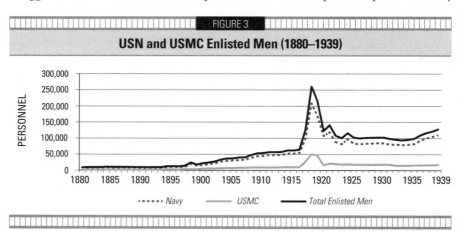

FIGURE 3

USN and USMC Enlisted Men (1880–1939)

······ Navy   ——— USMC   ▬▬▬ Total Enlisted Men

Source: George T. Davis, *A Navy Second to None: The Development of Modern American Naval Policy* (New York: Harcourt, Brace, 1940), 469–72.

of events during this period, sets the stage for the following chapters, which deal with the increasing need for confinement cells and facilities. James E. Valle's *Rocks & Shoals: Order and Discipline in the Old Navy (1800–1861)* and Harold D. Langley's *Social Reform in the United States Navy, 1798–1862* provide a comprehensive treatment of the flogging era.

This book discusses few incidents in Civil War prison history, which is a colossal study unto itself, a history that has been covered in detail by many works. This study of the development of the U.S. naval prison system does not suffer for lack of Civil War coverage—the naval prison narrative, which began in the early 1850s with the abolishment of flogging, made essentially no progress until the early 1870s when the Navy first identified a need for a state-of-the-art prison system. Prior to 1870 the narrative involved the lack of a uniform system of shipboard discipline and sporadic prisoner confinements in various Navy yards, stations, and ships—all issues not appreciably affected or altered by the Civil War.

Phase 2 (1862–88) is covered by chapters 3 and 4, a phase during which commanding officers employed innovative onboard punishments that primarily involved various conditions of confinement. Shipboard punishments were supplemented by whatever shore confinement facilities were available at various Navy yards and stations. During this phase, the Navy's changing regulations governing punishments were inconsistently interpreted and applied by commanding officers of ships of the fleet. The phase also includes the Navy's early and unsuccessful efforts to obtain congressional approval and funding to build its own prison as the Army did at Fort Leavenworth in 1874.

During phase 2 the U.S. Navy was small in numbers (see figure 3). George T. Davis, *A Navy Second to None*, has this to say about the decline in the size of the Navy after the Civil War: "During the Civil War the government built up a first-class Navy, in total tonnage as well as in quality. . . . After the war the Navy entered a period of decline in size, power, and relative position. Retrenchment was normal after a long and exhausting conflict. . . . A hiatus of shipbuilding, experimentation, and public interest in naval affairs occurred. . . . Congress failed to appropriate money and the country refused to listen [to the warnings of President Grant and Secretary of the Navy George M. Robeson]."[11] During this era Congress was not inclined to fund the building of ships or an increase in personnel for the U.S. Navy. It was even less interested in funding a naval prison.

As might be expected, the number of courts-martial prisoners confined annually during this period was small, never exceeding one hundred prisoners. However, these prisoners were distributed between fifteen different commands in various Marine barracks, Navy yard jails, naval station guardhouses, eleven different ships, and one state prison. During the 1870s, this hodgepodge assortment of confinement facilities caused the Navy to begin to campaign for a prison to consolidate and standardize prison operations. Although initially unsuccessful, the Navy's persistent efforts were eventually rewarded with the establishment of the Boston and Mare Island prisons in the late 1880s and the construction of Portsmouth prison in 1908.

The post–Civil War Navy continued to decline until 1883 when a modicum of a revival of interest occurred. Davis wrote, "March 3, 1883, became a significant date in the history of the American Navy. The bill of that date hastened the process of writing off obsolete ships. . . . This law also definitely provided for the construction of the first ships of the new Navy."[12] Little or no growth occurred in naval personnel during the 1880s (see figure 3). There was, however, a spark of interest in upgrading the Navy's capabilities that would burn brighter in the next decade. The Navy's need for prison cells grew as the Navy added ships and personnel.

Chapter 5 covers phase 3 (1888–1908), which began when existing buildings at the Boston and Mare Island Navy Yards were converted into prisons about 1888, to consolidate prisoners and establish the Navy's first prison system. The Navy grew during the latter half of the 1890s with a spike for the Spanish-American War (1898–1900) (figure 3); it expanded even more after the turn of the century under the influence of the renowned naval strategist Alfred Thayer Mahan and his disciple, President Theodore Roosevelt. In the decade after the Spanish-American War, American naval policymakers, according to Davis, "boldly selected a new place in the rank of naval powers and decided to build and maintain a fleet second to none but that of Great Britain." An increase in naval personnel accompanied the new commitment to the American fleet. The Boston and Mare Island prisons struggled during this phase with haphazard and piecemeal expansions to accommodate an increasing demand for prison cells. Phase 3 lasted until Portsmouth Naval Prison was built and commissioned in 1908 as a more permanent solution to the Navy's long-term prison needs.

Chapter 6 covers phase 4 (1908–14) and includes the early years of Portsmouth prison and a massive naval prison reorganization in 1914 that left Portsmouth the dominant centerpiece of the Navy's entire prison system. During these years, the Navy experimented with innovative concepts for the confinement of those prisoners with high potential for restoration. These concepts included the establishment of disciplinary barracks, detention ships, and a probation system. Phase 5, covered by chapter 7, begins with the 1914 reorganization and concludes in 1917 with the start of World War I. Near the end of this phase, the Naval Act of 1916 was passed to provide the United States with "a Navy second to none."[13]

The remaining chapters of the book cover phase 6 (1917–1920), the World War I progressive reform experiment at Portsmouth prison and its decline. Chapters 8 and 9 backtrack a little to develop the careers of Daniels and Osborne up to the eve of World War I. Chapter 10 through the conclusion chronicle events at Portsmouth under Osborne and his successors.

As suggested by the enormous spike in figure 3, the Navy's enlisted population peaked during World War I—as did its need for prison cells. The naval prison system was suddenly overwhelmed and in need of even more radical planning and innovative thinking to survive. The timing could not have been better for Lt. Cdr. Thomas Mott Osborne to arrive at Portsmouth prison. The fleet needed sailors and Osborne was eager to work his restoration magic. Rarely have a man and his moment met under more favorable circumstances.

National Prison Reform
(1790–1917)

While society in the United States gives the example of the most extended liberty, the prisons of the same country offer the spectacle of the most complete despotism. The citizens subject to law are protected by it; they only cease to become free when they become wicked.

—Alexis de Tocqueville, 1832

This overview of the evolution of national prisons and prison reform will serve as a framework for the study of the development of the naval prison system. Prison reform in the United States ebbed and flowed during the nineteenth century before progressive reform took root late in the century and continued through the first few decades of the twentieth century. Thomas Mott Osborne and Portsmouth Naval Prison played important roles in the progressive prison reform movement. Penal historians frequently cite Osborne's work at Portsmouth prison as this nation's most ambitious attempt at progressive prison reform.[1]

This chapter also examines the early history of New Hampshire state prison, an adjunct to Portsmouth prison during Osborne's tenure at Portsmouth. Many of the more hardened criminals were sent to the state prison at Concord, only forty miles from Portsmouth. The Concord prison was one of four state prisons to fill this role for the U.S. Navy during World War I. Portsmouth quickly assumed the dominant position among naval prisons after its commissioning in 1908, and the New Hampshire state prison acquired the same distinction among the state prisons.

NATIONAL PRISONS

The first prisons in the United States were small and hastily assembled to briefly house prisoners awaiting judgment under harsh penal codes. Judgment was often a death sentence or some other form of corporal punishment. The first American penitentiary is believed to have been Philadelphia's Walnut Street jail, established in 1790. With time, prisoner confinements replaced corporal punishment for the more serious offenses. Isolated cells and solitary confinements often offered little improvement over the previously administered corporal punishment.

By 1830 the penal codes had become less severe, and longer confinements were more popular. Penitentiary confinement was widely promoted as being a more humane punishment than corporal punishment. Corporal punishment, however, remained the foundation of naval discipline during the first half of the nineteenth century; flogging was the Navy's answer to discipline problems. During this period, civilian prisons grew in number and the construction of elaborate penitentiary systems became the rule for the remainder of the nineteenth century. Penal historian D. J. Rothman wrote, "The penitentiaries of the nineteenth century were architectural testaments to American pride and ingenuity. Awesome in size and elaborate in design, inside and outside, the penitentiaries were to resolve newfound social ills and restore order and proper social organization."[2] Portsmouth prison, although not opened until 1908, resembled the typical nineteenth-century prison. It was elaborate in design and awesome in size (see photo 2).

Osborne's early description of Portsmouth prison in a letter to Secretary Daniels painted a dismal picture of the prison and penitentiary life that is reminiscent of nineteenth-century prison conditions, "It is at the prison that we find the senseless and degrading system which breeds criminals . . . everything that was dry and mechanical in military discipline had been added to everything that was most revolting and medieval in our worst state prisons. . . . The place is a perfect mass of useless iron and steel— an arsenal of worse than useless weapons. . . . The Naval Prison is conducted upon a system so bad that it is hard to see how it could well be worse."[3] Much of Osborne's career as a prison reformer, and especially his tenure at Portsmouth Naval Prison, was a response to what he perceived to be outdated nineteenth-century prison practices.

Long-term penitentiary confinement carried with it a different form of cruelty and inhumanity. In *American Penology: A History of Control*, Blomberg and Lucken wrote, "The lofty objectives of the penitentiary were to be achieved through strict rules of obedience, routine, silence, labor, separation, and surveillance."[4] Rules of separation and silence quarantined the offender from society and fellow inmates. In addition, these institutions did not hesitate to employ harsh measures in the face of even the slightest acts of disobedience. Breaches of the code of silence were often met with severe punishments such as the iron gag, whipping, the ball and chain, suspension in the air by toes or thumbs, the stretcher, and sweat boxes.[5]

During the second quarter of the nineteenth century, prison debate centered on two U.S. prison systems, the Pennsylvania and the Auburn [New York] systems. A common characteristic of both systems was the rehabilitation of prisoners through an ideal prison routine and the "perfecting influence of bell-ringing punctuality and steady work habits . . . rules of silence, the lock step, and long periods of isolation."[6] In the Pennsylvania system, offenders lived and worked in silence and isolation. In the Auburn system, prisoners worked in silence but together. Debate about the merits of penitentiaries in the United States centered on these two harsh and cruel prison systems. The Pennsylvania system of total isolation was widely adopted in Europe and the United States between 1830 and 1850. After 1850, fearing that too many offenders were going insane as a result of continuous isolation, many states abolished routine solitary confinement and followed the more humane Auburn system.

The first prisoners arrived at Auburn prison in April 1817 and provided manpower to work on the prison, which opened in 1823. The philosophy of the prison was total domination of the inmate's body, mind, and spirit, achieved through a powerful control system, robotlike routine and regimentation, absolute silence at all times, and swift punishments for violation of the rules. Although more humane in comparison with the Pennsylvania system of total isolation, it fell far short of the standards advanced by progressive reformers later in the century: "In 1819 [in New York], flogging of prisoners was authorized (up to 39 lashes) in the presence of at least two of the inspectors. Silence was kept on pain of swift punishment—inmates were flogged for talking, and flogged again for denying it. . . . In 1845, Auburn administered 173 whippings for attempts to communicate."[7] The 173 whippings administered at Auburn in 1845 may seem excessive, but the U.S. Navy admistered far more whippings that same year under the "Rocks and Shoals" discipline system. Whippings were outlawed in national prisons in 1847, three years before flogging was abolished in the Navy in 1850.

The Auburn system required prisoners to "lockstep" when moving in groups. While in lockstep, prisoners shuffled along with one hand on the shoulder of the next man and with their heads turned toward the guard so he could see any lip movements.[8] Lockstep was the hallmark of the robotlike control procedures implemented at Auburn and other late nineteenth-century prisons. The Auburn system was also characterized by the productive employment of prisoners in prison shops, albeit in silence, to make everything from nails and barrels to wagons and sleighs. Profits from the sales of these products were returned to the prison's coffers.[9] For reasons of absolute control and profitability, the Auburn prison system became the prison system of choice in the United States. Visitors from all over the United States and Europe visited Auburn prison to observe the latest in state-of-the-art prison administration.

The well-publicized historical visit of Alexis de Tocqueville to the United States (1831–32) included an evaluation of American prison systems. His much-quoted book, *Democracy in America,* was the prime product of his visit. The second product of his visit, *On the Penitentiary System in the United States and Its Application in France* (1833), reports extensively on the Pennsylvania and Auburn systems: "We have every reason to believe that the system of perpetual and absolute seclusion there [Philadelphia prison] in full vigor, will prove less favorable to the health of the prisoners than the Auburn system . . . it must be acknowledged that the penitentiary system in America is severe. While society in the United States gives the example of the most extended liberty, the prisons of the same country offer the spectacle of the most complete despotism. The citizens subject to law are protected by it; they only cease to become free when they become wicked."[10] Tocqueville had accurately assessed the severity of the United States penitentiary punishment, the relative merits of the two prison systems, and the eventual preference for the Auburn system.

Thomas Mott Osborne had a connection to the Auburn prison that started when he was a child and continued throughout his life. He was born at Auburn, New York, in 1859, twenty-seven years after Tocqueville's visit. As a child he often passed by the same Auburn prison that Tocqueville had visited. His early interest in prisons and prison reform was the result of a childhood curiosity about happenings behind the walls of Auburn prison. In *Within Prison Walls* (1914), Osborne discussed his childhood recollections about Auburn prison: "Many years back, in my early childhood, I was taken through Auburn Prison. It has always been the main object of interest in our town. . . . No incident of childhood made a more vivid impression upon me. The dark, scowling faces bent over their tasks, the hideous striped clothing, . . . the horrible sinuous lines of outcast humanity crawling along in the dreadful lock-step; the whole thing aroused such a terror in my imagination that I never recovered from the painful impression."[11] Later in life, assignments as chair of the New York State Commission on Prison Reform (1913–14) and warden at Sing Sing Prison (1915–16) kept Osborne close to his roots and Auburn prison.

By 1850 numerous legislative reports and commissions had conceded penitentiaries did little more than incapacitate prisoners. Facilities such as Auburn prison had ceased to attempt to rehabilitate prisoners and had instead defaulted to a custodial role. Conditions worsened and the likelihood of recidivism was far greater than the likelihood of rehabilitation. Attempts to rehabilitate prisoners were resisted; prison admissions increasingly included more serious offenders and foreign-born inmates. These conditions only heightened the indifference of prison officials to the inhumane treatment of prisoners.[12]

Much of the increase in serious crime was attributed to foreigners. In 1860 foreign-born inmates represented 44 percent of New York prisoners, 40 percent of Massachusetts prisoners, and 46 percent of Illinois prisoners. Foreign languages and customs were communication barriers between prisoners and prison administrators, which discouraged attempts at reform and rehabilitation. Similarly, a high percentage of foreigners in the U.S. Navy during the same time frame also contributed to harsh, if not inhumane, treatment of seamen.

The seriousness of prosecuted crimes increased during the nineteenth century. Although a wide range of behaviors was considered criminal in colonial America, the majority of those crimes were not serious by today's standards. According to Bloomberg and Lucken, the most frequently prosecuted crimes in colonial America were fornication, lewd behavior, drunkenness, petty theft, assaults, and Sabbath violations. Violent crime became more prevalent by midcentury.[13] Between 1830 and 1836, 70 percent of the one thousand prisoners who entered the Auburn penitentiary were guilty of grand larceny (409) or crimes of violence (269), including murder, assault, burglary, and robbery.[14] Eric C. Monkkonen noted that the highest murder rate in the history of the city of Philadelphia was recorded in 1850, 20 per 100,000.[15] Prison officials were less inclined toward humane treatment for murderers and rapists than their predecessors had been for the colonial unfortunates found guilty of drunkenness and petty theft.

An 1867 report to the New York legislature, *Report on the Prisons and Reformatories of the United States and Canada,* disappointedly concluded that penal institutions no longer made rehabilitation the central goal.[16] Instead, long-term penitentiary confinement had become the norm. About this time the U.S. Navy began to seriously consider a naval prison system. Reacting to a severe shortage of confinement facilities, and aware that the Army was actively seeking congressional funding for a prison at Fort Leavenworth, Kansas, the Navy sought its own prison. In late 1872 Secretary of the Navy George M. Robeson commissioned Lt. Col. J. L. Broome, USMC, to inspect a number of the nation's northeast prisons "for the purpose of collecting such information as may be useful to the Bureau of Yards and Docks in enlarging the means of security and humanely [confining] the court martial prisoners of the Navy."[17] The roots of the Navy's prison system reach back to Broom's inspection of northeast prisons in 1872.

At the time, the three building blocks of the naval prison system were a shadow of what they would become. At Mare Island Navy Yard, a future naval prison was a small Marine barracks brig. At the Boston Navy Yard, another future naval prison was a granite storage building. And the future site of the Portsmouth prison was a vacant lot on Seavey's Island, which the Navy purchased in 1866, to enable the Navy yard to expand from Dennett Island.

Lieutenant Colonel Broom's "Report of Examination of the Prisons and Prison Systems at Albany, Auburn, and Sing Sing, N.Y.; Boston, Mass.; Wethersfield, Conn.; and Philadelphia, PA." provides valuable insight into existing conditions at those prisons. The report is especially useful because it provides an update to Tocqueville's earlier observations (1832) of the Auburn and Pennsylvania (Philadelphia) prison systems. Also, it provides Broome's first-hand observations of several other northeast prisons (Albany, Sing Sing, Boston, and Wethersfield, Connecticut) that will play key roles in later discussions in this book.[18]

At each prison Broome evaluated a long list of prison attributes including design, security, profitability, cell dimensions, weekly menus, exercise programs, punishment practices, overall cleanliness, prisoner clothing, heating systems, quality of ventilation, prisoner appearance, restrictions on prisoner movement and communication, work programs, daily schedules, possibility of escape, religious services, writing privileges, visitor policy, bathing frequency, and library content. As a general rule, he found all the prisons had high security and moderate-to-aggressive work programs. He was most disturbed by grossly undersized cells, inadequate heating systems, poor ventilation, excessive restrictions on prisoner movement and speech, oppressive working conditions, and extremely harsh punishment for those who broke prison rules. Conditions had changed little since Tocqueville had visited the Auburn and Philadelphia prisons forty years earlier. Progressive prison reform had not made much progress in the nation's prisons by 1872. The following paragraphs highlight some of Broome's observations.[19]

Broome considered the Albany prison, which housed 534 males and 92 females, to be a harsh environment with some cruel and inhumane elements. He observed the lockstep reported earlier by Tocqueville firmly enforced. "I saw the prisoners coming in squads from their workshops formed in single ranks, marching to their cells (where they eat all their meals) in the lock-step, each man with one hand on the shoulder of the man preceding him and his night-bucket on the left arm, with his head bent down and turned to the right." He found prisoners "working so violently . . . and so rapidly as to excite my surprise that human beings should be compelled to work at so rapid and tiresome rate." The prisoners were making shoes under the watchful eyes of a prison official, whose duty was to ensure the prisoners maintained the furious pace. When finished with one piece, the prisoner was required to fold his arms and remain looking down until the next piece arrived at his station or be subject to punishment. As Tocqueville had observed, the prisoners worked in groups, but maintained complete silence.[20]

At the Boston prison, where there were 556 males confined, Broome was struck by the improved appearance of the prisoners as compared with what he had observed at Albany, where the prisoners had a "blanched complexion and dejected appearance." At Boston "they nearly all had a cheerful appearance" and were permitted to "walk with their heads erect and their hands by their sides." He did find considerable fault with the lack of ventilation in the extremely small cells. He found conditions at Boston to be an improvement over those at Albany, but still considered it "an inhumane place of confinement for the court-martial prisoners of the Navy."[21]

At Auburn, Broome noted that most of the 1,119 male prisoners had blanched complexions and that the lockstep previously observed at Albany was enforced. However, more freedom of body movement was allowed at the worksites, where the work pace was much more reasonable than at Albany. He was particularly disgusted with the bed-bug-infested cells, where the walls were covered with blood spots from the bugs squashed there by the prisoners. Although told that the only punishment inflicted on prisoners was confinement to a dark punishment cell on bread and water, he subsequently learned that "paddling" also occurred in the punishment cells. This punishment was administered by hoisting the prisoner to his toes by and lifting him with leather straps tied around his wrists and run through a block and tackle attached to an eye in the ceiling of the cell. In this suspended position, and with his trousers lowered, the man was beat on the buttocks with a "stout stick about the length of a man's arm, four inches broad at one end and about an inch thick." A prisoner was also observed wearing a "heavy iron basket on his head . . . night and day . . . clasped around the neck with an iron collar." (For Osborne demonstrating a similar head cage restraint, see photo 3.) Broome also considered confinement conditions at Auburn too severe for naval prisoners.[22]

The conditions at the Wethersfield, Connecticut, prison, home to 175 males and 9 females, resembled those at Albany; Broome observed prisoners moving in lockstep, working at an accelerated pace, and taking meals in their cells. The prison had 9 "United States prisoners," which were probably military prisoners serving extended sentences for more serious crimes. At Sing Sing, which confined 1,076 males and 103 females, paddling was very much in vogue. In this case, the prisoners were "triced up" by their thumbs using fishing line. Head cages weighing up to eight pounds were also a common form of punishment.[23] The distinctive characteristic of Albany and the other New York prisons was that, unlike the Pennsylvania prisons, prisoners did not spend most of their time in isolation. As noted, however, there was no shortage of harsh treatment at the New York prisons.

The Philadelphia physical prison and prison system were quite different from the others. Physically the prison design was one with wings extending out from a central building. The prison administration stressed prisoner separation and isolation. As described by Broome, "This prison is constructed on a different plan from any prison in the United States, and the system with it is also different, being called the solitary or separate system in contradistinction of the congregate system which applies to all prisons in the United States except those of Pennsylvania. The cells of this prison are built in . . . blocks or corridors radiating from a center building of an octagonal shape forty feet in diameter." Based on the number of cells reported, the capacity of the prison appeared to be about five hundred prisoners. The separation of prisoners included Sunday worship for which the prisoners remained in their cells and listened to a minister preaching from the central building. There was limited congregational activity that permitted some prisoners to work in the shops, but many prisoners also performed daily work assignments in their cells. The only punishment allowed was confinement in dark cells on bread and water. There was no evidence of the paddling or head cage punishments found at other prisons. In fact, there was no evidence of any form of corporal punishment.[24]

Each of the prisons had its own kind of hell. The separation and isolation practices at Philadelphia caused prisoners considerable mental anguish. At the New York state prisons, even though corporal punishment was forbidden by law, it found its way into the punishment cells. Broome quoted a New York prison inspector who summarized well that state's negative attitude about the possibility of prison reform, "Men who come to State prisons are criminals sent here for violation of the laws of the land, and cannot be entirely governed by moral suasion or kindness any more than they could be so compelled before their imprisonment."[25] Broome's observations confirmed that "moral suasion" and "kindness" were definitely in short supply at Albany, Auburn, and Sing Sing prisons.

Overall, Broome was shocked at the conditions he observed and did not consider any of the harsh prison environments to be satisfactory models for a naval prison. He obviously thought that such harsh conditions would be excessive punishment for naval prisoners, a large percentage of whom were often guilty of only violating naval regulations. As will be reiterated throughout this book, naval prisoners fell into two categories: offenders of naval regulations (AWOL, desertion, drunkenness, disrespect to an officer, etc.) and criminals guilty of civilian crimes (theft, assault, embezzlement, murder, etc.). The former were often misguided young sailors and the latter were frequently hardened criminals. The Navy's challenge was to find suitable confinement facilities for each within the same prison system.

Flogging had been a one-size-fits-all punishment that was often prescribed for both types of offenders. Timely flogging prevented any concerns about the possible inappropriate confinement of misguided sailors with hardened criminals. The abolition of flogging presented the Navy with a dilemma that would complicate its efforts to establish a naval prison system for many years: the need to segregate prisoners according to the seriousness of their offenses. The confining of serious criminals in state prisons went a long way toward resolving the problem, but many of those prisoners passed through naval prisons en route to state prisons.

Young sailors guilty of moral offenses were considered criminals and confined, as such, in state prisons or naval prisons along with hardened criminals. Naval regulations grouped naval prisoners convicted of scandalous conduct and homosexual crimes with prisoners convicted of more serious crimes; both were required to be separated from the other prisoners. Osborne, who took issue with the separation of prisoners, believed all prisoners entered his prison with an equal opportunity to prove themselves worthy of parole. At Sing Sing and Portsmouth he was much more tolerant of prisoners convicted of homosexual crimes than his superiors and society in general.

The Auburn prison system continued its notoriety for harsh treatment of prisoners throughout the latter half of the nineteenth century. The prison had the dubious distinction of introducing the electric chair in 1890. On August 6, 1890 William Kemmler, convicted of murder during a bar room brawl, was the first victim of this new form of execution. His last words, to a guard fumbling with the straps were, "'Take your time and do it right.'"[26] Fifty-four men and women died in Auburn's chair [the last in 1963], including Leon Czolgosz, the assassin of President McKinley. Massachusetts, Ohio, and New Jersey quickly followed New York's lead with the electric chair, and by 1926 nineteen states had adopted its use.[27]

About the time that the electric chair was introduced at Auburn, Thomas Mott Osborne was a young man recently graduated from Harvard (1884). He returned to his Auburn roots to become involved in New York politics. After an unsuccessful run for lieutenant governor of New York in 1894, Osborne became mayor of Auburn in 1902. He was well aware of the oppressive treatment of prisoners at Auburn prison. His long association with family and friends who were staunch supporters of social reform fueled his desire to improve conditions at the local prison.

In the late nineteenth century, managerial and budget concerns increasingly dictated penitentiary operations. Fiscal considerations ultimately forced relaxation of the rules of separation at the Pennsylvania prisons and the other prisons, where it was practiced to a lesser degree. The pendulum quickly swung to the other extreme with overcrowded prisons being the result. Blomberg and Lucken noted, "Not only were cruel punishments being routinely administered within overcrowded prisons, but administrative corruption was also running rampant. Bribery of guards by inmates was not uncommon."[28] Clearly, American prisons were ripe for reform.

By the turn of the century, sweeping social, political, and economic change affected many segments of American society. Progressives focused on the plight of America's cities and the urban afflictions of poverty, disease, overcrowded slums, and crime. Prison reform was a logical extension of these progressive concerns. Social scientists argued that the less fortunate and criminally wayward were not to be punished for presumed moral failings, but ought to be socially and economically rehabilitated.[29] Progressive prison reform programs were to be tailored to each inmate's individual needs so as to give him the maximum opportunity for rehabilitation. Progressivism struggled to get a foothold in the U.S. Navy, especially in the naval prison system, until Daniels, FDR, and Osborne arrived on the scene.

The progressive prison reform movement included the gradual restricted use of the death penalty. Michigan abolished the death penalty in 1847, followed by Rhode Island in 1852 and Wisconsin in 1853. This was the same era of increased social liberalism that saw mounting congressional pressure to eliminate flogging in the Navy. The trend toward restricted use of the death penalty continued throughout the nineteenth and early twentieth centuries. By 1925 fourteen states had abolished the practice. However, six of those states restored it, with four of the restorations occurring between 1913 and 1917 when national security concerns were heightened during World War I. Thus, in 1925 eight states had abolished the death penalty while forty states still retained it.[30]

Meanwhile the death penalty was an authorized, but seldom used, naval discipline tool. In 1896 twenty-five offenses were subject to the death penalty under military code and twenty-two under the naval code.[31] Daniels, who strongly opposed capital punishment, took pride that the death penalty was not exercised on his watch. On 11 July 1919, a *Christian Science Monitor* article stated that under Daniel's tenure naval discipline had been "maintained without the necessity of inflicting the extreme penalty in any case." Daniels said of this accomplishment, "Several times there were acts for which capital punishment seemed the only sentence possible . . . but a way had been found to serve justice without imposing it."[32] This is not to imply that Daniels' avoidance of capital punishment was unusual. James E. Valle noted, "Although the twenty-two crimes that were punishable by death were still enumerated as late as 1949, the Navy probably refrained from executing anybody at least since the Civil War."[33] A sentence of confinement for life in a civilian prison was far more likely than a death penalty for a deserving naval prisoner.

By the early 1900s the seeds of reform had taken root at Auburn prison. The strict rules of silence, the lockstep, and the zebra-striped inmate uniforms were all on their way out.[34] A few years later, Thomas Mott Osborne continued to improve conditions for prisoners as state commissioner for prison reform and then warden of Sing Sing Prison. In the process he pushed the boundaries of progressive reform far beyond anything previously conceived. Rules of silence, lockstep, and zebra-striped uniforms were one thing. Prisoner self-government, open cells, and prisoners guarding other prisoners were something else entirely. Penal scholars generally agree that the heyday of progressive prison reform coincided with the Progressive Era of social and political activity in the United States, making it a "turn of the century" movement between 1880 and 1920. The Osborne years at Portsmouth prison (1917–20) were at the end of the progressive prison reform era.

In addition to more humane treatment of prisoners, David J. Rothmam says progressive prison reform included innovative approaches to "probation, parole, and the indeterminate sentence."[35] Osborne invoked all these innovations and more at Portsmouth prison. He considered all prisoners who arrived at Portsmouth prison to be serving indeterminate sentences, no matter what sentences had been assigned by the naval courts and authorities. All prisoners were eligible for timely probation and parole through compliance with the rules of the Mutual Welfare League. Rothman added, "We know surprisingly little about the origins and initial consequences of these [progressive] procedures; how they were conceived, how they were translated into practice, and how they actually worked."[36] These areas will be explored in the chapters that follow.

NEW HAMPSHIRE STATE PRISON

New Hampshire state prison was one of the state prisons used to confine naval prisoners classified as criminals. The conditions of confinement were more severe at the state prison, making the threat of transfer a motivator for continued good behavior of prisoners at Portsmouth. When Portsmouth prison opened in 1908, the prison at Concord had no naval prisoners. By 1912 it had more naval prisoners (61) than the other two state prisons combined (57).[37] In 1916 Concord had 101 of the 208 naval prisoners in state prisons.[38] This trend continued until the end of World War I when the prisoner population at Portsmouth was greatly reduced and it was no longer necessary to house prisoners at the state prison. All the naval prisoners at Concord were transferred to Portsmouth prison on 31 December 1918. The New Hampshire state prison was an integral part of the naval prison system during Osborne's experiment in prison reform at Portsmouth.

Figure 4, showing the number of naval prisoners confined in state prisons on 30 June between 1914 and 1920, illustrates the important role that the New Hampshire state prison played as part of the naval prison system during this era. The other state prisons that confined naval prisoners were located at Wethersfield, Connecticut, San Quentin, California, Atlanta, Georgia, and the Eastern State Penitentiary of Pennsylvania. The latter was discontinued for confinement of naval prisoners in 1917. The Georgia prison began confining naval prisoners in 1919.

The New Hampshire state prison was opened in November 1812. By 1818 the existing 36 resident cells were already overloaded and unable to contain the inmate population, which had risen to 87. As with most prisons of that era, expansion was required to keep up with increasing prisoner confinement needs. In 1831, after a special committee of the legislature noted instances of crowding including as many as 8 men to a cell overnight, another wing was added with an additional 120 cells. The number of prisoners continued to climb, reaching a high of 233 in 1877, at which time the prison was again expanded.[39] The prison population continued to grow through the end of the nineteenth century and into the beginning of the twentieth century, reaching 256 in 1896 and 337 in 1914.

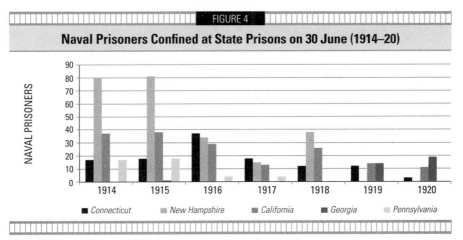

FIGURE 4

Naval Prisoners Confined at State Prisons on 30 June (1914–20)

■ Connecticut   ■ New Hampshire   ■ California   ■ Georgia   ■ Pennsylvania

Source: JAG Reports, in Secretary of the Navy Reports for Fiscal Years 1914–20. Navy Department Library.

Consistent with the trend previously noted for national prisons, the percentage of foreign-born prisoners in New Hampshire increased significantly during the last half of the nineteenth century. The mill towns of New Hampshire experienced much immigration during the late nineteenth and early twentieth centuries that populated the state with many different nationalities, including Italians, Irish, Greeks, Poles, and French-Canadian Catholics. Many of these immigrants apparently ran afoul of the law and swelled the population of the state prison at Concord. The relative percentages of foreign-born prisoners increased from about 10 percent in the 1850s to 30 percent by the turn of the century. The state prison confined many foreign-born minorities, but few blacks. Black convicts at the New Hampshire prison rarely amounted to more than a few individuals each year.[40]

Deaths during confinement at the state prison were more common than one might expect. The highest numbers of annual deaths were reported in 1878 and 1879, with twelve deaths in each of those years. This represented approximately 5 percent of the prison population. In 1878 seven of the twelve deaths were owing to phthisis, more commonly known as consumption or tuberculosis.[41] Again in 1879 seven of the twelve deaths were because of phthisis. Prison authorities noted, "As usual, all of these men [who died of consumption] brought the seeds of the disease with them and, finding a congenial soil for development, the end was, in each case, very rapid."[42]

The prison was apparently ill equipped to handle such diseases. Not until 1911 was the need identified for better hospital accommodations and "a ward, where men suffering from communicable diseases may be segregated, particularly with tuberculosis which presents itself at times."[43] In the late nineteenth and early twentieth centuries, medical care at the state prison was marginal at best and death was a much too frequent occurrence. Portsmouth Naval Prison, on the other hand, had a shipyard hospital located nearby with medical services immediately available for the treatment of prisoners.

The annual prison reports contain much evidence of the harshness of prison life consistent with the observations of Tocqueville and Broome. Punishments included confinement to "the dark cell, with rations of bread and water."[44] Prisoners were required to keep their eyes cast down when they were not in their cells. When the latter punishment was considered for revision in 1891, the governor's council decided against it because there were too few officers watching over too many desperate characters.[45] In 1916 New Hampshire remained one of only four states that persisted in the "antiquated method of feeding their prisoners in their cells."[46] The state prison converted to dining hall feeding of prisoners only after a survey of all the other state prisons revealed the pros and cons of such an arrangement. Adopting the proven successes of other state prisons would become the modus operandi for the advancement of progressive reform at the New Hampshire state prison.

Following the lead of the Auburn prison system, the state prison made productive use of prison labor. The annual report of 1887 notes, "There is a mighty moral force in industrial labor, and it affords lessons of reformation which cannot be overlooked. . . . While the convict may in some sense feel that the labor he performs is a part of his sentence, yet the influence will contribute to his health, happiness, and reform."[47] In addition to the prisoner's health, happiness, and reform, the prisoner's industrial labor also contributed to profits that could be applied to prison expenses.

As late as 1918 a system of silence was maintained in the shops at the state prison. The warden spoke out against that system in his biennial report. "I am in favor of abolishing the system of silence among the men in the shops and elsewhere. A small beginning has been made and this should be extended until orderly conversation is permitted among men without restriction. This is rapidly becoming the rule at penal institutions in other states, and we should keep abreast of the times."[48]

During the same timeframe, at Portsmouth prison any rules of silence between prisoners were long gone. Prisoner work parties were venturing out beyond prison walls to shipyard worksites and interacting not only with each other, but other shipyard workers. In 1918, when the warden at the state prison was considering relaxing the longstanding system of silence, as had already been done at most other state prisons, the prisoners at Portsmouth were governing themselves under Osborne's Mutual Welfare League, traveling outside the prison walls to perform plays, living in unlocked cells, and guarding each other. Whatever the measurement standard, the conditions of confinement were considerably better for prisoners at Portsmouth than at the state prison. The threat of transfer to the state prison was a motivator that kept Osborne's prisoners in line at Portsmouth prison.

NAVAL PRISONERS AT NEW HAMPSHIRE STATE PRISON

Confinement of military prisoners to the state prison started in June 1865 when the prison "was constituted by the authorities at Washington, a military prison."[49] During the next two months about fifty men were sent to Concord with sentences ranging from two to ten years. By September 1865 all but eleven of the military prisoners had been discharged. The warden's annual report noted that military prisoners were not fiscally attractive because "most of the men were released by the President before their labor could be made profitable."[50] In addition, several had "severe cases of chronic complaints; they have required large quantities of costly medicines."[51] The dissatisfaction that state prison officials voiced about the unprofitability of military prisoners in the 1860s would be repeated with the military prisoners relocated from Portsmouth prison during World War I.

No other military prisoners appeared at the state prison after the Civil War until after Portsmouth prison opened in 1908. Sixty-two naval prisoners were confined there in 1911 and in 1913 the naval prisoner population jumped to ninety.[52] Portsmouth prison was quickly overloaded after opening in 1908, and it appears that many excess prisoners, not necessarily hardened criminals, were sent to the state prison. The biennial report for fiscal years 1912/13–1913/14 indicates that the sixty to ninety naval prisoners confined during that period were, for the most part, junior enlisted men who had committed the crimes of theft or "scandalous conduct."[53] This was a marked departure from the situation during World War I when only the most hardened criminals and prisoners convicted of morality offenses were confined at the state prison.

In 1913 the New Hampshire legislature passed an act proposing a minimal reimbursement to prisoners for services rendered. The reimbursement was to be taken "out of such money as may be available for current running expenses of the state prison."[54] However, legislators quickly determined that the sixty to ninety U.S. Navy prisoners then in confinement should not share in the compensation because it would cause an additional tax burden to state citizens.[55] The governor's committee ultimately decided that no prisoners should receive the proposed per diem. The committee felt that the ten dollars and new suit provided upon release "constitutes a sufficient concession to . . . these abnormal men."[56] In 1913 prison authorities in the state of New Hampshire were not about to give concessions to "abnormal" men. A few years later, Osborne was breaking down all barriers at Portsmouth prison to prove his inmates "normal" and deserving of maximum concessions.

The 1914 consolidation of naval prisons and World War I swelled the inmate population at Portsmouth and heightened the need for additional capacity at the state prison. For the total number of naval prisoners confined at state prisons during 1915 and 1916, see table 1; see figure 4 for numbers of naval prisoners confined annually on 1 July (1914–20). Table 1 highlights the naval prisoner activity at Concord and the important role that the state prison played in the naval prison system immediately prior to Osborne's arrival at Portsmouth. The Concord prison was more active than its counterpart on the West Coast and far more than the other two state prisons on the East Coast.

State prison authorities considered naval prisoners a poor fiscal investment. For example, a decrease in prison earnings of approximately $4,000 between 1915 and 1916 was attributed to an unpopular and comparable reduction in the board received from the federal government for the naval prisoners.[57] The confinement of naval

Table 1	Naval Prisoners Confined Annually at State Prisons (1915–16)	
	1915	*1916*
Concord, NH	101	57
Wethersfield, CT	17	43
Eastern, PA	19	19
San Quentin, CA	71	58

Source: Annual Report of the Judge Advocate General for the Fiscal Year 1915, 23; Annual Report of Secretary of the Navy for the Fiscal Year 1915. Navy Department Library.

prisoners was a fiscally unattractive proposition for state prison authorities during World War I, just as it was in 1865 when the first military prisoners were confined at the prison. Officials at the state prison were eager to transfer all naval prisoners back to Portsmouth in late 1918 when cells became available.

While at the state prison, the prisoners were administered by state authorities but remained under the jurisdiction of the commanding officer of Portsmouth prison. Prisoners who exhibited good behavior and proper performance of duties could earn a transfer to the Portsmouth prison. It was common knowledge among the prisoners that they could get a "square deal" under Osborne at Portsmouth, while confinement at Concord involved harsher treatment and less opportunity for rehabilitation. Osborne took maximum advantage of this arrangement between the prisons, and the absolute authority that he enjoyed, to reward good prisoners with the "carrot" of reassignment to Portsmouth. At the same time, the threat of a transfer from Portsmouth to Concord was a "stick" that encouraged good behavior at Portsmouth.

For most of the nineteenth century the national prisons were typically harsh environments with little concern for prisoner welfare or rehabilitation. The prisons gradually expanded and adjusted operations to meet and reflect society's needs, which were increasingly influenced by the Progressive movement. Initially the progressive prison reforms implemented at national prisons found little application in the U.S. Navy, which had no prison system. These reforms peaked during the early years of the naval prison system. The two would meet and thrive under Thomas Mott Osborne at Portsmouth prison. Having presented the advancement of national prisons, let us now turn to the concurrent evolution of naval discipline and the naval prison system.

2

The End of Flogging
(1850–62)

We are, therefore, in our opinion, without sufficient suitable penalties to enforce the discipline of the service and punish petty officers. . . .
It cannot be doubted that the law, in its present shape, is insufficient and unsuited service.

—Commo. Charles Stewart, USN, 1851, president of Navy Board
to Investigate Status of Naval Discipline

The abolishment of flogging in 1850 changed everything in terms of naval discipline and the naval system of punishments. Flogging had been the cornerstone of naval discipline before 1850; its abolishment set off a long and complicated period of adjustment for the Navy during which brigs, jails, prison ships, naval prisons, state prisons, and disciplinary barracks all played important roles at one time or another. The immediate, but problematic, solution was to confine naval prisoners to tight quarters on board nineteenth-century sailing ships or to the few cells available ashore at various Navy yards and stations.

FLOGGING

To understand the acceptance—if not the popularity—of flogging in the old Navy, it is necessary to appreciate the typical old Navy sailor and the challenge that a seagoing captain faced in trying to control an unruly crew of one hundred or more of these individuals. In his 1885 prize-winning essay for the U.S. Naval Institute *Proceedings*, "Inducements for Retaining Trained Seamen in the Navy, and Best System for Rewards for Long and Faithful Service," Cdr. N. H. Farquhar described a typical nineteenth-century "Poor Jack": "In days gone by, Poor Jack was pitied by everybody. He was considered an amiable, good-for-nothing fellow; on shore, harmless; a drunkard, and the victim of pimps, runners and prostitutes. . . . His normal condition on shore was a state of intoxication. A few days sufficed to spend the money saved by years of toil and exposure, and before he realized it he found himself once more enlisted, with no money, and at least three months in debt. During a cruise, if he was given liberty, he was expected to go on a spree or debauch. . . . The men could, as a rule . . . neither read nor write."[1]

A quick, efficient, effective, and visible punishment system was needed to keep Poor Jack in line and to constantly remind his shipmates that their misconduct would reap the same rewards. Prior to 1850 flogging was the Navy's choice of punishment to do just that. According to Commander Farquhar, "Flogging was a weekly, almost daily occurrence. It was almost certain that somebody would be drunk at evening muster, and the punishment was flogging at 11:30 next forenoon."[2] Despite its cruelty, flogging was a respected and expected discipline tool (see photo 4).

Given the circumstances, could the Navy have devised a better punishment system? Naval discipline historian James E. Valle answers in the negative, "Probably not . . . when the personal and moral habits of the largely illiterate, polyglot, and destitute social underclass that furnished the bulk of the crews for warships are taken into account, could any other system but one of drastic and immediate physical punishment have worked, particularly for officers not extraordinarily gifted with the talents for leadership."[3] Flogging was a good fit in the old Navy where unruly sailors served under commanding officers who were more taskmasters than gifted leaders.

Flogging with a cat-o'-nine-tails was authorized under the "Rules for Regulation of the Navy of the United Colonies," promulgated in December 1775 and subsequent revisions, until it was abolished in 1850. A cat-o'-nine-tails "consisted of nine small hard, twisted cords of cotton or flax about eighteen inches long, which was fastened to a wooden handle. At the end of each cord was a hard knot or a pellet of lead."[4] For very minor offenses, lashes might be assigned with the "colt" rather than the "cat." The colt was a small, hard, twisted rope about the diameter of a man's forefinger and approximately three feet in length. Both hurt.

There were limits to the number of lashes that a commanding officer of a ship or a court-martial could prescribe for punishment. Naval regulations directed that "no commander shall inflict any punishment upon a seaman beyond twelve lashes upon his bare back with a cat of nine tails; if the fault shall deserve a greater punishment, he is to apply to the Commander in Chief of the Navy in order to the trying of him by a court-martial."[5] In the case of a trial by court martial, a man could be flogged with a cat-o'-nine-tails up to one hundred lashes.

Flogging was quick and efficient punishment, as well as a frequent reminder to the crew of the need for absolute shipboard discipline and compliance to orders. Shipboard confinement, on the other hand, took up valuable onboard space, required the involvement of other crewmembers to guard or service the prisoner, was unhealthy at best, and resulted in the loss of an able-bodied seaman when every hand was needed to operate the ship. "A Plea in Favor of Maintaining Flogging in the Navy," written by an anonymous naval officer in the 1840s, laid out the case against confinement very well:

> Extra labor, ordinary confinement, solitary confinement, bread and
> water diet, are plans that do not suit well on shipboard. . . . Ordinary

confinement, such as practiced, is scarcely a mode of punishment at all. The offender hears and sees most of what is going on, is relieved from work, his pay is not stopped, and he is snug between his blankets while others who have done no wrong are exposed to the weather and deprived of sleep upon their watch. . . . Solitary confinement is not practicable on board ship, from the want of room. If cells were built in the hold for the purpose, they would take up space required for storage, and at the same time [were] totally destitute of ventilation and reeking with a foul atmosphere. Above the hold, the accommodations for the crew and for the battery preclude the erection of anything of the kind. . . . That ship cannot be ready for emergencies of any kind which has a score or two of her crew laid by the heels in stocks. . . . Every man should be at all times at his post. . . . This end would not be gained by throwing offenders into confinement.[6]

On 24 February 1845, Secretary of the Navy Thomas W. Gilmer, responding to a House of Representatives inquiry as to what punishment, if any, might be substituted for flogging, expressed sentiments similar to those quoted above and wrote, "I am not aware of any mode of punishment that can be substituted . . . without serious injury to the discipline and efficiency of the service."[7] Furthermore, the secretary added, "I confidently believe that it is not regarded as a personal degradation by the great body of seamen in the Navy, but that they consider it as necessary to preserve discipline, to ensure the safety of the ship, and to secure a faithful performance of duty by all hands on board."[8] Flogging appeared to enjoy considerable support and popularity throughout the Navy, except from those being flogged.

Even though many congressmen and civilians found the practice abhorrent, flogging was passionately defended by most naval officers. These same officers may have agreed with the critics' assertion that flogging was a cruel and inhumane punishment; however, they argued for its continuance because they knew of no disciplinary substitute able to provide the same tight control over crews highly populated by ruffians, thugs, and foreigners. The more responsible crewmembers, who rarely if ever saw the lash, also supported the practice to keep their unruly shipmates toeing the line. The supporters of flogging were equally as passionate about its continuance as critics were about its abolishment.

Congressional pressure mounted for the abolishment of flogging as the result of newspaper articles, citizen petitions, and especially Herman Melville's *White Jacket, or the World of a Man-of-War* (1850), in which he vividly described flogging abuses in the U.S. Navy. In 1848, after the Senate had rejected the most recent antiflogging amendment, it passed a resolution designed to gather more data to bolster future attempts to abolish flogging. The resolution called "on the Secretary of the Navy to submit copies of the reports of punishments inflicted on the various ships of the naval force."[9] Subsequent resolutions called for more data for later years to better quantify the extent of flogging on board naval ships. A review of one of those reports dated 28 July 1848 gives valuable insight into the type and frequency of offenses for which flogging was routinely administered. Fourteen ship commanding officers reported 446 punishments for various periods averaging about two and one half months. This was an average of about 13 floggings per month per ship. The following table shows the most common offenses that resulted in flogging. The table is not precise in that the offenses were not reported in common categories, but were instead described in terms chosen by each commanding officer; also, offenses were frequently combined (drunk and disorderly, insolent and drunk, drunk and fighting, etc.), making an exact count impossible. In table 2, the first offense of a compound offense is the one counted. Though lacking exactness, the table does provide an overall picture of discipline problems on board a mid-nineteenth-century U.S. vessel of war.

Except for skulking and many of the more minor "other" offenses, the most common punishment for the above listed offenses was the maximum allowed, twelve lashes with the cat-o'-nine-tails. Punishments for a few of the "other" offenses included twelve lashes with the cat for using profanity in the wardroom, twelve lashes for spitting on a man, ten lashes for urinating in a spit box, and on three occasions, three lashes on commodore's orders with no offense specified.

Consistency of punishments between ships of the fleet was not a problem when flogging was in vogue. Twelve lashes with the cat-o'-nine-tails was the consistent

Table 2	Offenses Resulting in Flogging (1848)
Offense	*Number of Cases*
Drunkenness	125
Disobedience	74
Fighting (40), Striking (12), Drawing Knife (3)	55
Insolence & Insubordination (26) / Disrespect (8)	34
Neglect of Duty (32), Sleeping on Post (4)	36
Desertion / AWOL (18), Remained Ashore (7)	25
Smuggling Liquor	19
Gambling	13
Conduct, Seditious (5), Mutinous (2), Disorderly (5)	12
Stealing	8
Skulking	7
Indecency (2), Filthiness (1), Disgraceful Conduct (2) Attempted Sodomy (1)	6
Language, Seditious (2), Improper (1), Profane (1)	4
Others	28
TOTAL	446

Source: S. Exec. Doc. 69, 30th Cong., 1st Sess., Report of the Secretary of the Navy, communicating copies of returns of punishments in the Navy in compliance with a resolution of the Senate (July 28, 1848).

answer for most discipline problems. Chapter 3 addresses the inconsistency of ship-board punishments among ships after flogging was abolished and suggests the incon-sistency as one reason for a naval prison system.

For very minor offenses, lashes might be prescribed with the "colt" instead of the "cat." Minor offenses could indeed be very minor. For example, on 31 December 1847 William J. Smith, the wardroom cook on the *Marion*, received twelve lashes with the colt for "bad cooking." That same day, two others received six lashes with the "colt" for "cutting up swabs" and seventeen others received nine to twelve lashes with the "cat" for various offenses. Three days later, on 3 January 1848, seventeen *Marion* seamen received twelve lashes and five seamen a lesser number with the cat for "drunkenness and desertion." Forty-two of the *Marion*'s crewmembers were flogged in a period of three days. It appears that Commo. L. E. Simonds was determined to whip his crew into shape, or at least until their attitude and behavior improved.

From 1865 through World War I, desertion and AWOL accounted for well over half the offenses with the other half consisting mostly of fraudulent enlistment, theft, assault, and scandalous conduct. This is in stark contrast to offenses listed in the above table—drunkenness, disobedience, fighting, insolence, and neglect of duty dominated the Navy's discipline problems at the mid-nineteenth century.

Two primary factors contributed to the change in discipline problems between 1865 and World War I. The first factor was the abolishment of the daily grog in 1862. Drunkenness topped the list of offenses in table 2, and many of the other offenses on the list were rooted in excessive drinking. Eliminating the daily ration of alcohol solved many of the Navy's discipline problems. The second factor was the eventual recruitment of higher-quality seamen. The Navy had changed from wooden sailing ships to steel-hulled, engine-driven vessels, and a more technically competent sailor was needed to operate the ships.

Recruitment of a higher-caliber sailor solved many—but by no means all—of the Navy's discipline problems. Whereas drunkenness had essentially disappeared from the list of offenses by World War I, there was a noticeable increase in the number of reported morality offenses. Many of Osborne's challenges during his time at Ports-mouth prison involved large numbers of prisoners committed for sodomy or scandal-ous conduct who were required to be confined separately from other prisoners. Table 2 shows few cases that fall into that category, with only a broad interpretation of the offense. The word "sodomy" appears only once in the 1848 report and that was a case of "attempted sodomy." Even if it is assumed that the reported cases of indecency (2), filthiness (1), and disgraceful conduct (2) may be describing homosexual activity, only 5 of the 446 offenses appear to have involved such actions.

Harold D. Langley, who conducted a much more extensive review of the con-gressional requested punishment data, found similar vague descriptions and low num-bers of homosexual crimes. He found one instance in which two men were punished "for a crime hardly ever committed" and for which the writer would not "sully this page by describing it."[10] Langley says that discharge from the service, after punish-ment, was often a consequence for such crimes.[11] Valle draws similar conclusions,

"The extent and nature of homosexual activity in the Old Navy is one of the major question marks in its social history. Precise evidence in the form of records, documents, and statistics are almost wholly lacking."[12] For the few cases in which records were kept, Valle says:

> In those cases where homosexual activity . . . was officially reported, . . . a court-martial was held . . . the officers betrayed their disgust and loathing for the duty assigned them by simply refusing to grapple with the issue of homosexuality. They either voted to acquit without waiting to hear much of the evidence, or they found the defendant guilty of some other charge. . . . Consequently, no one Navy man was ever convicted of homosexuality by a formal court-martial [in the old Navy].[13]

In the mid-1840s, morality offenders were quickly flogged, released from the naval service, and soon forgotten.

In *The Story the Soldiers Wouldn't Tell: Sex in the Civil War* Thomas P. Lowry notes, "No soldier was disciplined for homosexuality because the term was not introduced until 1895." However, he wrote of three pairs of U.S. Navy sailors courts-martialed for offenses with homosexual connotations in 1865. One pair was charged with "improper and indecent intercourse with each other"; another with "what was indecent, immoral and a violation of nature"; and the last with "an unnatural crime."[14] These charges were a little more precise than those described earlier. Portsmouth prison data show that the reporting of homosexual crimes during World War I was much more precise and far more prevalent. Punishment was usually confinement for several years with hardened criminals, segregated from other prisoners, and followed by a dishonorable discharge.

The congressional inquiries into flogging in the late 1840s that led to the data presented in table 2 were repeated with heightened interest until flogging was finally abolished a few years later. The congressional act that abolished flogging on 28 September 1850 was the culmination of a campaign that had begun twenty years earlier.

THE ABOLISHMENT OF FLOGGING

The abolition of flogging in the Navy was part of a rising tide of social rejection of all forms of violent punishments during the first half of the nineteenth century. Myra C. Glenn in her study "The Naval Reform Campaign Against Flogging: A Case Study in Changing Attitudes Toward Corporal Punishment" argues that the naval reform campaign against flogging was "part of a broad spectrum of transatlantic reform which sought to limit, if not abolish, a range of violent, punitive practices . . . the flogging of convicts, children, and slaves, as well as seamen."[15] She notes that these protests "occurred concurrently with Anglo-American campaigns against slavery, capital punishment, dueling, war, and cruelty to animals."[16] Some of Osborne's relatives, including Lucretia Coffin Mott and William Lloyd Garrison, were among the most active social reformers of that era. (Chapter 9 investigates their contributions to various social reform agendas as well as their influence on young Osborne during his early years in Auburn, New York.)

The motivation for the abolishment of flogging came primarily from citizens and legislators of northern states and not from any humanitarian movement within the Navy. Portsmouth, New Hampshire, had strong spokesmen for more compassionate treatment of sailors long before Osborne arrived at Portsmouth prison. One of the most ardent spokesmen was Levi Woodbury, who practiced law in Portsmouth before serving as secretary of the Navy from 1831 to 1834.[17] Woodbury introduced some of the Navy's earliest attempts to moderate flogging and the onboard consumption of alcohol. His circular of 26 September 1831 encouraged commanding officers to make use of "pecuniary fines, badges of disgrace, and other mild corrections, rather than the humiliating practice of whipping."[18] It would be another twenty years before the humiliating practice was eliminated.

Recognizing the direct correlation between drinking and punishments, another Woodbury circular of 5 June 1831 promised an equal value in pay to any sailor who voluntarily relinquished his spirit ration.[19] This offer was met with little enthusiasm. Sailors were reluctant to accept the offer because punishment for a minor offense was often the suspension of the grog ration for some period of time and, without that option, flogging was the next alternative. It was far better to have a grog ration that could be taken away than not have one and be flogged.

Representative John P. Hale, also from New Hampshire, introduced an amendment to an appropriations bill in 1843 to abolish flogging. The bill passed the House of Representatives but was rejected in the Senate. Hale had access to firsthand knowledge about flogging through his brother-in-law, Thomas Lambert, who was a seagoing naval chaplain from 1834 to1854. Lambert, who studied law under Levi Woodbury in Portsmouth, New Hampshire, received his chaplain appointment when Woodbury was secretary of the Navy.[20] The Portsmouth, New Hampshire, area was well represented in the antiflogging movement through the efforts of Hale, Woodbury, and Lambert.

Chaplain Lambert served on several ships, including the *Brandywine, United States,* and *Constitution.* He sailed the world—Brazil, Chile, Peru, Egypt, Greece, Athens, Malta, Spain, and France—with plenty of opportunities to observe a captain's iron hand of discipline, which was almost always the lash. Several incidents involving Lambert highlight the cruelty and capriciousness of nineteenth-century naval discipline.

Lambert experienced the extreme harshness of naval discipline when he was counsel for a murder case while on the frigate *United* States. In a 15 July 1837 letter to his mother, postmarked Port Station in the Mediterranean Sea, he wrote, "I have been engaged for a fortnight in a Court Martial as counsel for a man who is on trial for murder."[21] He described it as a "very tedious and disagreeable trial" for which he could "hardly predict the result." He concluded, "It is my impression that they cannot hang him on the evidence." Leaving his mother in suspense, there was no mention of the trial in later letters.

Valle treated the trial in far more detail in *Rocks and Shoals*. According to Valle, SM John Herring had accidentally killed Thomas Hyland, rated as a Boy, during a shipboard fight. In Herring's defense, Lambert, after invoking a "series of legal techni-calities" to delay the proceedings, sought to avoid the death penalty by arguing "there had been no previous bad feeling between the two men and that Herring was drunk when he made his fatal attack." Putting on his chaplain's hat, Lambert "penned a long defense memoranda citing the evils of alcohol and the base passions it aroused" and warned the court members not to make a decision they might regret for the remain-der of their lives and of which "heaven may not approve." The charge was reduced to manslaughter; the punishment assigned was a staggering four hundred lashes—later reduced to three hundred lashes with the additional specification that Herring be flogged 'round the fleet at Port Mahon and his sentence read on each vessel. A pun-ishment of three hundred lashes, when the maximum number permitted by naval regulations was one hundred, is testimony to the absolute authority of the captain and courts-martial on distant stations, as well as the lack of compliance with existing reg-ulations. Chaplain Lambert was obviously pleased that he had achieved his goal and avoided the death penalty for his client. Seaman Herring may have been less pleased.[22]

Langley suggests Hale learned about the abuses of flogging from his chaplain brother-in-law because "they were on close terms and corresponded with each other."[23] However, a review of Lambert's surviving correspondence at the New Hampshire Historical Society finds that none of his letters to Hale and others address flogging—as determined by reading his marginally legible handwriting on yellowed nineteenth-century paper.[24] An incident involving a horserace, a court-martial, and letter writing gone wrong may have dissuaded Lambert from writing about flogging and other matters that challenged authority. The incident has the appearance of a convoluted comedy of errors, but it is really a disturbing example of mid-nineteenth-century naval discipline gone awry.

This time Lambert was a principal and not a counsel. He was charged by the commander in chief of the Mediterranean Squadron, Commodore Elliott, of "writ-ing an anonymous and disrespectful letter [to the secretary of the Navy] impugning his [Elliot's] conduct in a dispute with Lt. Cdr. Charles G. Hunter." The commo-dore had previously ordered Hunter's court-martial for "disrespect and treating with contempt his superior officer." The charge stemmed from a letter Hunter wrote to the secretary of the Navy claiming he had been treated in a humiliating manner by the commodore after a dispute over whose horse had won a race. Lambert's anony-mous letter to the secretary of the Navy had aggressively defended Hunter and rec-ommended that Elliott be court-martialed when the ship returned to the United States. The letter found its way to Elliott, who deduced the author. Confronted by a court of inquiry, Lambert admitted writing the letter; however, the court of inquiry was "unable to form any opinion or make a recommendation for a court-martial." Lambert escaped any consequence for his controversial letter writing, but the expe-rience may have discouraged him from writing about controversial subjects—such as flogging—in future letters.[25] However, his return visits to Portsmouth during his twenty-year naval career would have given him ample opportunities to relate his experiences to John Hale, who lived in Dover, New Hampshire.

John Hale continued to lead the congressional efforts to abolish flogging, which peaked during the first six months of 1850 when the Senate received 271 anti–corporal punishment petitions "demanding the abolition of the naval lash."[26] In 1850 the now Senator Hale introduced the amendment to an appropriations bill that ended flogging in the Navy.[27] The bill passed in the Senate by the narrowest of margins, twenty-six to twenty-four, and was signed into law by President Millard Fillmore on 28 September 1850. The voting pattern underscored the sectional over-tones of the anti–corporal punishment campaign. "Twenty-four of the twenty-six senators who voted to abolish corporal punishment in the Navy came from northern states while the other two senators came from the border states of Missouri and Kentucky (Thomas Hart Benton and Joseph R. Underwood, respectively)."[28] Langley attributes most of the credit for the abolishment of flogging to Senator Hale. He wrote, "Many men participated in the crusade against flogging, but all of their efforts would have been in vain without [Hale's] leadership and support in the Congress."[29]

After President Fillmore signed the bill abolishing flogging, the Navy Department was frustrated in its attempt to find a suitable substitute punishment to enforce shipboard discipline. Secretary of the Navy Will A. Graham immediately established a board under Commo. Charles Stewart to review the status of naval discipline and recommend actions to be taken. Stewart, one of the more senior officers in the Navy, with service that reached back to the War of 1812, was an excellent choice to head the board because he was one of only a few naval officers who had "urged a change in the naval regulations governing flogging and grog."[30] Senator Hannibal Hamlin (D-Maine) invoked Stewart's name in his appeal for support for the antiflogging amendment, "Some of the oldest and most valiant of the Navy officers, among them Commodore Charles Stewart, feel that this relic of barbarism should be swept away."[31] With the abolishment of flogging, Stewart had gotten the change to naval regulations he wanted. Now he and his board would have to deal with the aftermath and the unintended consequences of that legislation.

Despite Stewart's personal objections to flogging, the board's report of 1 January 1851 laments its passing, concisely summarizes the current unsatisfactory state of naval discipline, and accurately forecasts the changes needed to restore it. The report takes the form of providing answers to five questions posed by the secretary of the Navy. The questions and a synopsis of the answers provide a revealing snapshot of the unsettled state of naval discipline at the time:[32]

1. *"Whether, in the present state of the law, there are sufficient and suitable practices provided to enforce the discipline of the service and punish petty officers?"*

   As a precursor to answering the question, the law prior to the abolition of flogging was restated, "By the act of better government of the Navy approved 23d April 1800, penalties are provided for offenses of every grade—from the most aggravated, for which a court-martial is obliged, on conviction, to pass sentence of 'death,' to the lightest, which may be punished at the discretion of the captain. . . . The punishments specified are death, cashiering with incapacity to join the service again, cashiering, dismission from the Navy, suspension, reprimand, forfeiture of pay and subsistence, confinements, lashes with the 'cat-of-nine-tails.'" The elimination of the cat-o'-nine-tails left limited remaining options. The historical importance of the loss of that option was emphasized: "It has been, and is still considered, the only punishment that can be brought to bear with effect upon the petty officers and seamen at sea, because [it is] the only one that can be inflicted in so summary a way as not to deprive the ship of a part of the physical force provided for her navigation and preservation."

After reviewing the options remaining and noting the impracticality of shipboard confinement, the board concluded, "But now the law is deprived of this coercive measure [flogging], and nothing has been substituted for it. *We are, therefore, in our opinion, without sufficient suitable penalties to enforce the discipline of the Navy* [emphasis added].

2. *"What summary punishments may be inflicted by the commander of a ship at sea"?*

"*Strictly speaking, no summary punishment can be inflicted by a commander of a ship of war at sea* [emphasis added]. He may, at once, and summarily, place a man in confinement, but the confinement, to become a punishment, must be continued, and so ceases to be summary; and if there should be many cases, which there undoubtedly would be in a protracted cruise, the force of the ship might so be reduced as to put at hazard the honor of the flag and endanger the safety of the ship."

3. *If the law be insufficient or unsuited to the service, what legislation is required to render it effectual?*

"*It cannot be doubted that the law, in its present shape, is insufficient and unsuited the service* [emphasis added]." The board, in one final attempt to continue flogging, albeit in a reduced and limited fashion, recommended that flogging be authorized "to a certain extent . . . by a general or summary court." This proposal went no further.

4. *Granting that the prohibition against flogging shall be continued by Congress, what substitute or mode of government can be most advantageously adopted?*

"In such case, nothing remains but to devise, digest, and frame a system combined of rewards for good conduct and such punishment for bad conduct as may not contravene the law. As preliminary to this, it is believed that a small addition to the wages of seamen, accompanied by great care at the recruiting offices in the selection of men for the service, would do much to elevate the general character of that class of persons in the Navy." The board recommended a system of good and bad conduct discharges as a basis for rewarding the good performers with reenlistment opportunities and bonuses and keeping out of the service the "litigious, insubordinate, or troublesome." It was also suggested, "Such as did not work with alacrity might be punished by reductions to inferior rates, and by badges denoting them as sluggards, or employment of extra or scavenger duties. . . . Such as refused to work at all might be confined on bread and water for such time, and in such secluded place, as in the opinion of the surgeon would not be seriously injurious to health."

5. *"Are there any other particulars besides those already specified, in which the laws for the government of the Navy require amendment?"*

The board recommended that a previously drafted act (1832) to revise and amend the act for the better government of the Navy, which was never approved by Congress, be resurrected and updated to incorporate the "late legislation and present state of the Navy."

The board's report shows that the Navy, within a few months after the abolishment of flogging, had a clear understanding of the changes needed to restore discipline. To the Navy's credit, it recognized that extensive and timely changes were needed to improve the lot of the sailor. Changes were initiated that otherwise may have taken many years to effect. Some of those changes were made in a few years, others required decades to implement. Honorable discharges of seamen, reenlistment bounties for those honorably discharged, and improved leaves of absence were addressed within a few years by An Act to Provide a More Efficient Discipline for the Navy (1855). Although the Navy did not immediately recognize the need for a naval prison system, decades of struggling with confinement needs would lead to that conclusion.

In his 9 January 1851 letter to the president, which forwarded the board's report, Secretary of the Navy Will A. Graham solicited Fillmore's help to urge Congress to pass recommended legislation to establish new and effective discipline guidelines for the fleet. To stress his point that the Navy was searching for an adequate substitute for flogging, the report summarized punishments assigned to persons brought to trial before courts-martial since the date of the act abolishing flogging. In a New York trial, one ordinary seaman found guilty of drunkenness and mutinous conduct was sentenced "to be confined in the cells in the Gosport [in Portsmouth, Virginia] Navy yard for the term of one month on bread and water." Another found guilty of disobeying an order was sentenced to "wear a ball and chain for two months, to be made a scavenger to the marine barracks at the Gosport Navy yard, and, further, to be confined in the cells there from sunset till sunrise every day during that period." At Norfolk, twenty-four courts-martial prisoners sentenced to confinement were transferred from *John Adams* to the receiving ship *Pennsylvania* for safekeeping. Thus within months after the abolishment of flogging, the Navy was exploring the use of Navy yards, marine guards, work parties, and prison ships to accommodate confinement sentences.[33]

A subsequent 22 December 1851 report from Graham to the Senate provided evidence of the discontent and frustration experienced by commanding officers attempting to maintain discipline at sea without the option of flogging. A common thread throughout the commanding officers' reports was the ineffectiveness and futility of confinement as a substitute punishment. Cdr. James T. Gerry of the receiving ship *Ohio* spoke to the triviality and inefficiency of confinement as a punishment on vessels at sea. "Confinement is a trifling punishment to such persons [badly disposed persons on board ship], and while they enjoy a respite from work, innocent men actually suffer by having the onus of extra duty imposed upon them. The efficiency of the vessel is also materially injured by the confinement of men whose constant drilling is indispensable to constitute a well regulated man-of-war."[34] However, Gerry did note, "On board this receiving ship, I have facilities for the punishment of delinquents by solitary confinement, which cannot exist in cruising vessels, the same room being occupied as store-rooms."[35] Another commanding officer noted, "There is no place on a ship-of-war, where a man can be confined for punishment, without seriously injuring his health."[36] Confinement on a naval vessel at sea was clearly not an acceptable punishment option in the 1850s.

Even more damning of confinement as a punishment was Lt. John Manning of the brig *Bainbridge,* who reported from Montevideo that offenders were going unpunished because all hands were needed to sail the ship: "So far as the law will allow, I have tried all kinds of punishment. And I feel it my duty to state that I do not think discipline can be maintained in our service, unless by flogging. The [attached] punishment roll is small, because in vessels of our tonnage while at sea, we cannot spare the men from deck, and I have therefore been obliged to let many offenders pass unpunished."[37] Commanding officers of ships at sea were left with few options to maintain discipline. There was an increasing need to find spaces or cells where prisoners could be confined.

The sentences that resulted from an attempted mass mutiny on the frigate *Independence* at anchor in New York Harbor in August 1854 highlighted the Navy's need for cells. Most of the recaptured men received punishments involving confinement in the cells at the New York Navy Yard. Two others, OS Frank Dynes and David Hazard, the latter found guilty of drawing a knife on a midshipman, were sentenced to terms in the penitentiary of the District of Columbia. Five years earlier, the deserters would have been flogged—end of story. In this case, numerous jail cells at the New York Navy Yard were occupied and steam packet transport to Washington, D.C., had to be arranged for Dynes and Hazard so they could serve their sentences. Naval discipline quickly became much more complicated and time consuming with the abolishment of flogging.[38]

Some congressional support for flogging continued for several years after its abolishment. One of its strongest supporters, Senator Stephen Mallory of Florida, later secretary of the Confederate Navy, argued in January 1852 that restoration of flogging was "absolutely necessary for proper order and discipline in the Navy" and that its need was "fully answered by the daily experience [on board ships] of a thousand years."[39] He took strong issue with the way flogging had been abolished, "by a proviso in an appropriation bill passed by a narrow margin at the end of a session."[40]

On 20 January 1852, the *New York Times* reported, "The Senate will talk a long time about it, but they will not repeal the law [abolishing flogging]. And even if they should so vote, the House of Representatives would veto their action."[41] The newspaper reporting was accurate. Congressional efforts to resurrect flogging slowly subsided as the Navy adjusted to the new shipboard reality of life without flogging.

The abolishment of flogging had widespread repercussions in the fleet, but none more immediate or threatening than an incident on the frigate *Brandywine*. The ship returned to New York Navy Yard in November 1850 from the Brazil Station, "where she cruised for more than three years protecting United States interests in the region."[42] The crew was unaware that flogging had been abolished. Upon learning that Congress had put an end to the dreaded punishment, a mass desertion ensued. New York Navy Yard commandant W. D. Salter described the chaotic scene that took place at his yard, "The day before her arrival, (the law not being known on board) punishment with the cat was inflicted, and the men were in a good state of discipline until the vessel hauled into the wharf, when a change took place immediately on the men being informed of the recent act of Congress, which showed the inefficiency of the law for the government of the navy, as they now stand. The crew of the frigate *Brandywine* were [*sic*] in a state of open mutiny on the arrival of that ship."[43] Salter advised Secretary of the Navy Graham in a 10 December 1850 letter, "In consequence of two or three hundred men having left the ship [*Brandywine*], it was not possible to have the crew exercised at quarters."[44] With a complement of 480 officers and men, it was Salter's estimate that about half the *Brandywine* crew had mutinied.

Capt. Charles Boarman, *Brandywine*'s commanding officer, reported to his superior, Commodore Storer, that he had been powerless to prevent the mass desertion, "They were noisy and insolent to the officers, and in some cases assaulting violently with dangerous weapons the master-at-arms and the sergeants of marines. On our arrival at our berth on the yard, when the steamers cast off, a rush on the part of a large number of the men was made to get into the shoreboats to quit the ship—in which many succeeded, in spite of every effort that was made to prevent it; and I am convinced nothing short of a very considerable destruction of life could have checked them."[45] Storer also attributed the mutiny to the recent act of Congress. In his 7 December 1850 letter to Secretary Graham he wrote, "I am constrained to think that their [the *Brandywine* crew] recent improper behavior is in a great measure to be ascribed to their having learned the recent abrogation of whipping."[46]

Those of the *Brandywine* crew who remained "drew up a letter of thanks to Hale for his efforts in abolishing the cat-o'-nine-tails. This letter, signed by the nine seamen on behalf of all, was delivered to Hale by one of the crew."[47] The *Brandywine* incident reveals the troublesome state of naval discipline a few months after flogging was abolished. Ship crews gave thanks, but they also rebelled and left ship's commanding officers bewildered and powerless to deal with unprecedented insubordination. Flogging was gone and also, possibly, good order and discipline on the Navy's ships.

On at least two occasions (*Carrington vs. Stinson* and *Barnet vs. Luther*) shortly after flogging was abolished, seamen brought libel suits against officers to test the full intent of the new law. The seamen had not been flogged, but they had been struck by officers in some other manner. In the first case, a cook was kicked and struck by an officer for not preparing coffee as quickly as expected. In the second case, a captain struck a seaman with a rope for insubordination and grumbling. In both cases the courts found that the act abolishing flogging did not apply and that the actions were justified. The act abolishing flogging did just that and no more. The law had been changed, but the courts still recognized the need for strict shipboard discipline.[48] With time, the act abolishing flogging was fully accepted by the Navy. In late 1854 Secretary of the Navy James C. Dobbin said that he was "far from recommending the restoration of flogging" because recent experience "justified its abrogation."[49] Dobbin did, however, see the urgent need for some substitute discipline that would incorporate a system of rewards as well as punishments.

Dobbin recognized that the Navy would be well served and punishments reduced with a recruitment process able to screen out troublesome individuals, especially if that process included the ability to prevent the reenlistment of men who had previous bad conduct records in the Navy. The latter was a widespread problem over which the Navy had little control. The rewarding of good behavior with good conduct discharges was thought to be a good first step toward gaining control of the problem. Increased pay and improved leave and liberty policies were also needed if the threat of withholding these was to be an effective discipline tool.

Legislation passed on 2 March 1855 began to address these issues. An Act to Provide a More Efficient Discipline for the Navy provided for honorable discharges of seamen, reenlistment bounties for those honorably discharged, and leaves of absence. It also established a system of summary courts-martial for minor offenses. Regarding honorable discharges, the act read, "It shall be the duty of every commanding officer of any vessel of the Navy, on returning from a cruise, to forward, immediately on his arrival in port, to the Secretary of the Navy, a list of the names of such of the crew who enlisted for three years as, in his opinion, on being discharged, are entitled to an 'honorable discharge.' As a testimonial of fidelity and obedience; and he shall grant the same to such, according to the form to be prescribed by the Secretary of the Navy."[50] The honorable discharge along with reenlistment bonuses and leaves of absence were important steps toward achieving improved retention and recruitment of personnel.

The act gave the commanding officer another shipboard discipline tool by creating the summary courts-martial for those cases that he thought were deserving of more punishment than he was authorized to dispense: "Summary courts-martial may be enacted upon petty officers and persons of inferior ratings, by the commander of any vessel in the Navy to which such persons belong, for the trial of offenses which he may deem deserving of greater punishment than the commander of a vessel himself is by law authorized to inflict by his own authority, but not sufficient to require trial by court-martial."[51] No sentence of a summary court-martial could be carried into effect without the approval of the commanding officer. Commanding officers would make innovative use of this new discipline tool, but the lack of adequate shipboard confinement facilities would continue to limit its effectiveness.

As previously noted, the sailor's daily ration of onboard spirits, and even larger consumption ashore, was the source of many of the Navy's discipline problems. For that reason, the initiatives to abolish flogging were often accompanied by proposals to limit or prohibit spirits on board naval vessels. If flogging could be abolished, sailors would be more inclined to accept a monetary reimbursement as a substitute for their daily ration of grog. From there, the abolishing of onboard grog was thought to be only a matter of time. With the demise of flogging in 1850, these forces worked as predicted and, on 1 September 1862, Congress abolished the onboard spirit ration. This law abolished grog for the enlisted men, but it did not end the wardroom and captain's wine messes; these were abolished on 1 July 1914 when Secretary of the Navy Josephus Daniels issued General Order 99. For this reason, and others to be discussed later, Daniels was not popular with many senior naval officers during his time as secretary of the Navy.

With both flogging and the daily grog ration a thing of the past, naval discipline entered a new era. However, the Navy was still left with the challenge of finding an effective long-term substitute punishment for flogging. Its abolishment had left a huge hole in naval discipline that took many years to fill. The long-term solution involved increased benefits to attract a higher-caliber recruit and, at the same time, create opportunities to withhold or reduce those benefits as a form of punishment.

ATTRACTING A HIGHER-CALIBER RECRUIT

In his 1885 U.S. Naval Institute *Proceedings* article, Commander Farquhar wrote, "The dregs of all countries seem to get into our service. The character of the men now obtained is somewhat improved over former years, but there is still room for much improvement."[52] Farquhar argued for better pay to attract a better sailor because, at present, "only those remain in the Navy who cannot better themselves elsewhere."[53] According to Farquhar, one "Poor Jack," accused by his commanding officer for drunkenness, reportedly responded, "The cardinal virtues of human nature were not to be expected at $20 per month."[54] The Navy apparently got what it paid for.

There were early attempts in 1840 to recruit apprentices in order to get a better class of men for the Navy, but they failed within a few years. The program attracted higher-quality young men at first with the promise that strong performance might lead to promotion to the rank of midshipman with the potential of joining the officer ranks. However, lacking the support of the older naval officers, relatively few were promoted, and many disappointed apprentices merely served their three years' obligation and left the Navy or deserted.

An incident in 1842 involving a mutinous midshipman contributed to the lack of fleet support for the program. Midn. Philip Specer and two others serving on the Navy brig *Somers* were hanged for suspected mutiny during a training cruise. "The scandal that erupted tarnished the old method of training midshipman and led to the establishment of a more formal curricular system."[55] The incident led to the establishment of a training school at Annapolis in 1845 that became the U.S. Naval Academy.

The establishment of the academy was a major step toward improved selection and training of midshipmen. However, little or no progress had been made toward the recruitment of a higher caliber sailor.

Farquhar credits Rear Admiral Shufeldt, chief of the Bureau of Equipment and Recruiting, with initiating the recruitment reforms needed in the 1870s: "Under his able administration the apprentice system was revived, and through his energy and perseverance in a few years there were more than 1,000 on the books, and a fleet which formed a large part of our Navy was constituted for them. The whole condition of the sailor was so much improved . . . and punishments became very much less. And, for the first time in the history of the Navy, men were classified and given privileges according to their conduct. An attempt was also made to give uniformity in punishments."[56]

Immediately before Shufeldt's initiatives, a sailor's life was so unattractive that the Navy had to recruit 4,000 men annually to maintain a naval force of 8,000 men, an annual waste of 50 percent. By comparison, the waste in the British Navy was 13 percent; meaning only 2,500 persons had to be recruited annually to keep up an average of 18,000 seamen. Farquhar attributed the success of the British system to two factors. First, "the class who are entered are bettered in their lot by going into the Navy"; and second, "a faithful service until 38 years of age is rewarded by a comfortable pension to retire upon."[57] Improving the lot of the sailor was immediate fertile ground for the U.S. Navy. Comfortable pensions would take awhile.

With the inducements of improved pay, more liberty, and better living conditions, the Navy gradually attracted young American men with better habits and less need for discipline. Better recruitment of intelligent young Americans reduced the need for large numbers of illiterate and troublesome foreign seamen to crew the Navy's ships. Fewer discipline problems were a natural by-product of better recruiting practices and the improved lot of the sailor. The Navy slowly evolved into a career worth having rather than a place to dump the dregs of society.

Currently the nation's prisons confining 2.3 million Americans are typically overcrowded and costly to maintain. Curiously, these conditions, and concern for prisoner welfare, prompted Peter Moskos to build a case for the return to flogging with *In Defense of Flogging* (2011). Moskos contends that years of incarceration are much crueler and damaging to the prisoner than an immediate flogging. He maintains, "Given the choice between five years in prison and ten brutal lashes," the lashes would be the more popular choice of prisoners.[58] His proposal for a return to flogging will never come to pass, but it does suggest the nation's current colossal prison system is an unintended consequence of the abolition of corporal punishment in the nineteenth century. The remaining chapters consist of a study of the Navy's efforts to manage and control the unintended consequences of the abolition of flogging. Abolishment set the Navy on a new discipline course that quickly led to innovative shipboard punishments and, eventually, to a costly and often overcrowded naval prison system.

3

Shipboard Punishments Post Flogging
(1862–88)

At the present time punishments for the same offense differ as widely
as the station separating ships from each other.

—Rear Adm. W. S. Schley, 1886, Chief of the Bureau of Equipment and Recruiting

The legislative changes that restored proper discipline in the Navy evolved over the latter half of the nineteenth century. Extensive changes were needed because the rudimentary *Naval Regulations* established in 1800 had remained virtually unchanged for over half a century. James E. Valle summarized the chaotic nature of the naval justice system, "The justice system which evolved within the United States Navy between 1800 and 1861 was in retrospect something of an anomaly.... Its basic organic law, the Articles of War of 1800, was sketchy and rudimentary; and its body of statutory law resided in a state of confusion bordering on chaos, as repeated attempts to reform the *Naval Regulations* collapsed in the face of congressional indifference prior to 1862."[1] The changes urgently needed to *Naval Regulations* would come in bits and pieces, so ill defined and broadly interpreted that, for a period of time, punishments for the same offense varied widely among ships.

On 6 December 1858, Secretary of the Navy Isaac Toucey, responding to congressional direction, provided a draft of *An Act for the Better Government of the Navy* that was eventually passed in 1862. The act limited commanding officers and summary courts-martial to the following punishments:

Commanding officers:

1. Reduction of rating.

2. Confinement with or without irons, single or double, not exceeding ten days and with restraint of person, but not so as to be injurious to health.

3. Solitary confinement on bread and water not exceeding five days.

4. Solitary confinement not exceeding seven days.

5. Deprivation of liberty on shore.

6. Extra duties.

Summary courts-martial:

1. Discharge from the service with bad conduct discharge, but the sentence not to be carried into effect in a foreign country.

2. Solitary confinement in irons, single or double, on bread and water, or diminished rations, provided no such confinement shall exceed thirty days.

3. Solitary confinement in irons, single or double, not exceeding thirty days.

4. Solitary confinement not exceeding thirty days.

5. Confinement not exceeding two months.

6. Reduction to next inferior rating.

7. Deprivation of liberty on shore on foreign station.

8. Extra police duties, and loss of pay, not to exceed three months, may be added to any of the above-mentioned punishments.

The above listing will be compared with a sampling of actual shipboard punishments recorded in quarterly reports of punishment from various ships. The confinement punishments rarely exceeded the maximum number of days authorized, as there was little incentive for commanding officers to assign long shipboard confinements. The most serious abuse of the system involved the deprivation of liberty: no limits were specified as to maximum number of days liberty could be suspended. It was not clear if the punishments could be combined, except for the last summary court-martial punishment, which stipulated that "extra police duties and loss of pay may be added to any of the above punishments," implying that this was the only combining of punishments allowed, and this interpretation eventually prevailed. However, the examples that follow show a plethora of combined punishments.

INCONSISTENT PUNISHMENTS BETWEEN SHIPS

Commanding officers prescribed shipboard punishments tailored to their own sense of justice, which was often tempered by personal prejudices and the ship's needs. Commanding officers with wide-ranging personalities and beliefs, operating different types of ships under various conditions in waters all over the globe, had different prejudices and needs. It is not surprising that the new regulations would be loosely interpreted in accordance with local needs, resulting in inconsistent punishments for the same offense throughout the fleet.

From 1862 to 1889 the conduct and shipboard punishment of seamen, as well as concern for their welfare and treatment, were under the cognizance of the Bureau of Equipment and Recruiting. For most of that period, the bureau was more concerned with equipment than with its obligations to seamen under the recruiting half of its title. During the same period, the JAG was responsible for maintaining the records of the relatively few courts-martialed prisoners. After 1888 the worlds of shipboard punishments and prison confinements began to merge with the consolidation of naval prisoners at Boston and Mare Island prisons under the jurisdiction of the JAG.

Near the end of the bureau's tenure for personnel matters, the chief of the Bureau of Equipment and Recruiting Rear Adm. W. S. Schley raised concerns about the lack of a uniform system of punishments for minor shipboard offenses. In his 1886 annual report to the secretary of the Navy, Schley pleaded for a uniform system of punishment for these offenses. Schley wrote, "At the present time punishments for the same offense *differ as widely as the station separating ships from each other* [emphasis added]."[2]

He expressed hope that "after a great number of years with the great number of reports of punishment made quarterly it would seem possible to so classify them . . . so that the offense should be punished alike in every ship of the Navy . . . [to] secure for the enlisted men a punishment for minor offenses prescribed by *unbiased judges* . . . to secure them against the effects of *hasty judgment*, as might occur now [emphasis added]."[3] The following examples from the quarterly reports of punishments referred to by Schley validate his concerns about the inconsistent application of punishments from ship to ship. Using Rear Admiral Schley's words, the examples show many opportunities for hasty judgments by biased judges.

The quarterly report of punishments submitted by Cdr. S. P. Carter, commanding officer of the side wheel gunboat *Monocacy*, for the quarter ending 30 June 1867 is the first of several examples that illustrate Schley's concerns. The ship was on patrol duty for the Asiatic Squadron at the time. Following is a list of all crew members punished during the quarter; except for the punishments for drunkenness, these punishments are less harsh and less hasty than other examples that follow. Codes summarize individual discipline cases. Notable items for subsequent comparisons and discussion are in italics.[4]

SM = Seaman, OS = Ordinary Seaman, LM = Landsman, LP = loss of pay, DI = double irons

- William Frazier, SM, disorderly conduct, confined DI 5 days
- Robert Robertson, OS, disorderly conduct, confined DI five days, LP 1 month, *deprivation of liberty 1 year*
- Charles Landale, SM, *smuggling liquor*, confined DI 10 days, LP 1 month, *deprivation of shore liberty 1 year*
- John Morris, Marine, insolent & disorderly conduct, confined DI 10 days, *deprivation shore liberty 2 months*
- John Morris, 2nd, LM, fighting, confined DI 5 days
- James Thoner, Coxswain, leaving ship w/o leave, confinement DI 10 days
- Thomas Daly, SM, disorderly conduct, in sentry's charge 4 days
- Bartholomew Gaffney, Marine, *smuggling liquor*, confined DI 10 days, *LP 5 months, deprivation of shore liberty for 1 year*

- George Perkins, SM, leaving ship w/o leave, confined 2 days

- John Muldone, Marine, insolence to captain of the Guard, confined 2 days

- John Smith 1st, SM, stealing, confined DI 3 days, reduced to next inferior rating, LP 1 month, 2 months extra police duty

- William Frazier, SM, drunkenness & fighting, confined DI 4 days

- Patrick Mannan, LM, drunkenness & fighting, confined DI 4 days

- Robert Robertson, OS, drunkenness & fighting, confined DI 4 days

- George Williams, Marine, stealing, confined DI 10 days

- James Downing, LM, fighting, confined DI 8 days

Perhaps showing a personal bias, Commander Carter dealt with the offense of smuggling liquor more severely than any of the other offenses. The punishments he assigned for smuggling liquor were also harsher than those assigned by other commanding officers for the same offense. In Bartholomew Gaffney's case, confinement in double irons for ten days, loss of five months' pay (when the maximum allowed was three months), and deprivation of shore liberty for one year was probably more than enough punishment to dissuade him from future attempts to smuggle liquor on board the *Monocacy*. Commander Carter was able to accommodate confinements on board his ship for short periods of time, frequently in double irons. Loss of pay and loss of shore liberty for up to one year were reserved for the more aggravated offenses. The *Monocacy* did not have any punishments for this quarter requiring long confinements at a shore Navy yard or station. This was fortunate because the closest brig was probably an ocean away at Mare Island. Navy yard brigs frequently received prisoners from ships unable to accommodate long confinements.

The side wheel steamer *Michigan's* quarterly report of punishments for the same 1867 quarter as the *Monocacy* example shows further how punishments varied from ship to ship. The *Michigan* was operating in the Great Lakes at the time; following is but a sampling from the *Michigan's* report, which included several dozen punishments.[5]

SM = Seaman, OS = Ordinary Seaman, DI = double irons, SI = single irons, HL = hard labor, B&W = bread and water, SC = solitary confinement

- Lewis Monnor, SM, refusing to obey orders, 4 days DI at night, HL during the day

- John Randall, SM, skulking, 4 days DI at night, HL during the day

- Bernard Conway, Marine, using threatening language, 3 days SI during day, DI at night

- Michael Owens, SM, insolence to superior officer, 5 days DI at night, HL during the day

- *Andrew Gunther, OS, insubordination and assault of superior officer, confined in DI, May 26, 1866, tried by court martial and sentenced May 31, 1866, to 30 days SC in DI, B&W every other day*

- Michael Owens, SM, neglect of duty, 5 days DI at night, HL during the day
- Thomas Kane, Marine, neglect of duty, 4 days DI at night, HL during the day
- Thomas Kane, Marine, disobedience of orders, 3 days DI at night, HL during the day
- Otto Bechtold, SM, skulking, 4 days DI at night, HL during the day

The commanding officer of the *Michigan* displayed more imagination with punishments than did his counterpart on the *Monocacy*. This imagination may have been motivated by the *Michigan's* size: about half that of the *Monocacy*, 685 tons compared with 1,370 tons, making it more of a challenge to find confinement space on the small ship. Punishments of hard labor during the day and double irons at night were to the benefit of the ship. These punishments, instead of reducing the size of the crew, effectively increased it by requiring more work (hard labor) from offenders during the day. To achieve this end, "police duties" had to be interpreted as hard labor—they did not appear anywhere on the menu of punishments. In the case of OS Andrew Gunther, his services were lost for the maximum allowable thirty days in solitary confinement, but the ship's provisions were extended because he was put on a diet of only bread and water every other day. Given the choice, Gunther might have chosen flogging.

Cdr. G. R. Goldsborough's *Shenandoah* report for the quarter ending 30 September 1867 cited about forty punishments. Many involved fighting ashore while on liberty in Japan, punished by confinement in double irons for as little as twenty-four hours. Following is a wide range of offenses for which confinement in double irons for forty-eight hours was apparently a "one size fits all" punishment on the *Shenandoah*.[6]

- Samuel Little, nurse, *furious fighting and killing a Japanese*, paid widow of the deceased 50 dollars, DI for 48 hours
- Winfield S. Wyman, unknown rate, *smuggling liquor on board*, DI for 48 hours
- Henry Peterson, landsman, AWOL, DI for 48 hours
- James Watson, unknown rate, ill treating an inhabitant on shore, DI for 48 hours

Killing a Japanese citizen, smuggling liquor on board, going AWOL, and ill treating an inhabitant on shore were all assigned the same punishment: double irons for forty-eight hours. Smuggling liquor on board the *Shenandoah* was treated far less severely than on the *Monocacy*, where the punishment was confinement in double irons for ten days, loss of pay for five months, and deprivation of shore liberty for one year. Standards were definitely needed to ensure consistency of punishments.

Lt. Cdr. A. R. Gates on the screw steamer *Chocura*, operating with the Gulf Squadron, made frequent use of solitary confinement and bread and water punishments. Examples from his report of punishments for 1 April 1866–30 June 1866 include[7]

Disrespect to superior officer—confinement DI 5 days, B&W

Filthiness—5 days cleaning bright work on the quarterdeck

Fighting—confinement DI 3 days on berth deck, B&W

Disorderly conduct—confinement DI 3 days, B&W

AWOL—reduction to next inferior rating, LP 2 months

AWOL—3 months loss of liberty, LP 2 months

Breaking leave (absent several days)—reduction to next inferior rating, loss of liberty 4 months, extra duty 3 months, LP 1 month

Breaking leave—SC DI 5 days, B&W

AWOL—SC 15 days, extra duty 2 months

Sleeping on watch—SC DI 3 days, B&W

This quarterly report had an unusually high number of AWOL and breaking leave offenses. Lieutenant Commander Gates credited the wide range of punishments for the same apparent offense to various lengths of unauthorized liberty in New Orleans. It is noteworthy that those guilty of breaking leave (absent several days) received an illegal combination of punishments. Apparently some members of the crew had difficulty returning to the ship after an evening in a good liberty port. Gates convened summary courts-martial for the more aggravated AWOL cases, resulting in solitary confinement for a few sailors. He reported, "The large number of punishments during the last quarter is owing in a great measure to the fact that this vessel was under repairs and alongside the levee at New Orleans during nearly two months of the time. Those men tried by Summary Court Martial for breaking leave and AWOL were absent from the ship some days, the other marked for the same offense were only absent some hours."[8] The wide range of punishments included the cleaning of quarterdeck brightwork for the offense of filthiness; a punishment most appropriate for a filthy sailor.

An 1870 quarterly report of punishments for the store ship *Jamestown*, operating out of Honolulu, includes the following punishments:[9]

Attempted desertion—confinement DI 10 days

Gross carelessness—confinement DI 10 days

Fighting—SC, B&W 5 days

Shirking duty—SC, B&W 5 days

Theft—14 nights confinement

Insubordination—SC, B&W 5 days

Disrespect of officer—confinement DI 10 days

Disrespect of officer—5 SC, B&W 5 days

Assault—4 nights confinement DI

Disobedience of orders—confinement DI 5 days (watch below)

Gross carelessness—confinement DI 5 days (watch below)

Overstaying liberty—*confinement DI from 5 PM till reveille (numerous cases from 9 to 14 nights)*

Deserting ship—10 days confinement DI 10 days

Profane language—confinement DI 2 days, confinement DI 20 nights

A large store ship with a displacement of 1,150 tons apparently had more spaces available for confinement than warships, making solitary confinement more of an option. Work during the day and confinement in double irons from 5 p.m. until reveille was another innovative punishment that reduced the impact to ship's operations—the punishment for the many crewmembers who overstayed liberty in Honolulu.

Examples from the quarterly report of punishments (first quarter 1874) for the screw sloop of war *Wachusett* under Cdr. B. B. Taylor show a tendency toward confinement in double irons for most offenses, sometimes for hours instead of days; little use was made of the nighttime-only confinements popular on other ships. [10]

Leaving boat w/o permission—DI 5 days

Drunk and refusing duty—DI 5 days

Drunk and disorderly—*DI 18 hours*

Drunk on duty—*DI 6 hours*

Insolence to an officer—DI 3 days

Disobedience of orders & insolence—DI 5 days

Disobedience of orders—DI 2 nights, DI 5 days

Ashore w/o leave—DI 2 days

Drunk & disorderly—DI 3 days

Ashore w/o leave—DI 24 hours

Striking corporal of the guard—DI 10 days

Insolence to boatswain mate—12 hours sentry's charge

Attempting to smuggle liquor—*DI 8 days*

Disrespect and insolence to an officer—DI 10 days

At the time, *Wachusett* was laid up at the Boston Navy Yard, so the commanding officer did not need to be as innovative with his punishments. The last highlighted example shows punishment for attempting to smuggle liquor that is far less severe than the *Monocacy* example discussed earlier.

As the years went on, commanding officers increasingly relied on punishments involving loss of pay and liberty to maintain discipline. A summary of punishments (the quarter ending 31 December 1875) for the torpedo boat USS *Alarm*, under the command of Lt. Cdr. W. B. Stoff, shows a total of eleven punishments. Nine punishments involved confinement in double irons (2 to 8 days), another nine involved loss of pay (1 to 3 months), and five involved loss of liberty (44 days to 2 months).[11] This example illustrates a recommendation made by Commo. Charles Stewart's board twenty-five years earlier; as pay and liberty improved, they were increasingly withheld as punishment.

The Regulations for the Government of the Navy of the United States (1876) were the next attempt to improve the lot of the sailor and promote discipline and punishment consistency throughout the fleet. The regulations provided guidance for rewards and punishments, significantly different from what was being practiced in the fleet at the time. Section I (Rewards) outlined a system for the granting of liberty based on classes of conduct. First-class men were allowed evening leave plus twenty-four-hour shore leave twice a month. Second-class men were allowed twenty-four-hour shore leave once a month; third-class, once every six weeks; and fourth-class, once every two months. Circumstances permitting, no one of the ship's company was to be deprived of liberty on shore for more than three months, unless under sentence of court-martial. If followed, this regulation would prevent the abuses of this form of punishment noted in the preceding examples.

Section II (Punishments) provided general guidance that encouraged lenient and more compassionate treatment of offenders than had been the case previously.

1. First offenses, when not of a grave nature, should generally be considered leniently.

2. All minor punishments are to be discontinued on Sunday and punishments shall not be inflicted on Sunday.

3. Cells for the confinement of prisoners are not to be less than 6 ½ feet long and 3 ½ feet broad, with the full height between the decks, and are to be properly ventilated.

4. Confinement in coal bunkers or other close places is forbidden.

5. The use of irons is to be avoided as much as possible, and the gag is not to be used under any circumstances.

The primary purpose of the *Regulations* was to promote consistency of shipboard punishments by order of the commanding officer, by providing a list of fifteen *suggested* [emphasis added] punishments (coded A–O) for forty-four specific offenses (coded No. 1–No. 44). The suggested punishments were far more lenient than those being practiced in the fleet. For example, the suggested punishment for absence without leave (No. 1) was deprivation of liberty on shore (Code N), which the *Regulations* limited to three months except for sentences of courts-martial. Being drunk at sea or on duty (No. 11) was to be punishable by Code M (reduction in rate) *or* Code O (extra duties). The suggested punishment for returning from leave drunk (No. 12) was "None." Nonconfining punishments were suggested for thirty-two of the forty-four categories of offenses, including neglect of duty, lying, malingering, spitting on deck, being habitually dirty or slovenly, etc. From these examples, it is clear that sailors were spending much more time in confinement and irons than was the intent of the Department of the Navy.[12]

Confinement and irons were reserved for the more serious offenses listed below. Asterisks indicate those offenses for which solitary confinement was a *suggested* option.

No. 10   ★Disobedience of orders

No. 14   ★Smuggling liquor

No. 15   ★Trafficking in liquor

No. 20   ★Gambling

No. 21   ★Misbehavior at Divine service

No. 22   ★Making noise on deck, aloft, or at quarters

No. 35   ★Cursing others, or using obscene language

No. 36   ★Striking inferiors or equals

No. 37   ★Fighting

No. 38   Quarreling with words or using provoking language

No. 39   Smoking out of hours or in improper places

No. 40   Having lights after hours

For offenses involving liquor (highlighted on several of the earlier examples), smuggling liquor (No. 14) or trafficking in liquor (No. 15), the suggested punishment was Code A (solitary confinement; five days or less; no irons; bread and water). As shown in those examples, the actual punishments for liquor-related offenses far exceeded the suggested punishment.[13]

Application of the shipboard punishments specified in the 1876 regulations was problematic. The most obvious problem was that punishments were suggested and not mandated. Commanding officers were free to continue to liberally interpret or deviate from the suggestions. In his U.S. Naval Institute *Proceedings* article (1888), Commander Farquhar noted the shortcomings of the 1876 regulations: "If these had the authority of law, or were mandatory instead of suggestive, they might have been beneficial to the service, but in their present yielding form they are virtually void. The Navy is not governed by suggestions, but by commands." Despite good intentions and considerable effort, the Navy Department had done little to promote consistency of punishments.

The *Regulations* provided similar coded suggestions for offenses to be punished by summary courts-martial. The actual punishments prescribed by these courts were often more severe than suggested in the regulations. A common error was combining parts of several sentences into one sentence, when police duties and loss of pay were the only authorized additions to a sentence. In his *Proceedings* article "Naval Law and Naval Courts" (1897), 1st Lt. Charles H. Lauchheimer, USMC, noted this error: "Any one of the seven punishments may be given, but when given it must be given in its *entirety*, to which, however may be added extra police duties and loss of pay as authorized in the eighth clause of the Article. As a familiar illustration, the second clause of Article 30 provides for a punishment of 'solitary confinement, not exceeding thirty days, in irons, single or double, on bread and water or on diminished rations.' Courts frequently award the solitary confinement on bread and water, but do not include in the sentence '*in irons*,' single or double, which is part thereof, and as a consequence such sentences are, whenever practicable, disapproved by the Department."[14] The Navy Department absurdly rejected sentences for minor noncompliance with the rules, when major noncompliance and inconsistent application of the rules ran rampant in the fleet.

An 1888 *Alliance* quarterly report shows punishments that reflect correct interpretation of the regulations. Various conditions of confinement were assigned with extra police duties and loss of pay added as authorized in the regulations.[15]

1. Absent from ship w/o permission—SC 30 days, B&W, full rations every 3 days, LP 3 months, extra police duties 3 months

2. Possessing liquor—DI 20 days, extra police duties 2 months

3. Liquor on board—reduced in rate from Master at Arms to LM, LP 2 months, extra duty 3 months

4. Leaving ship w/o permission—30 days B&W, full ration every 3 days, LP 3 months, extra police duty 3 months.

Despite this example, it was a constant struggle to achieve consistency of punishments throughout the fleet.

In the opinion of Commander Farquhar, "The punishments [suggested in the 1876 regulations], in most cases, are disproportionate to the offense."[16] He offered the following example to make his point: "For example, absence without leave, and leaving a boat or working party, offenses akin to desertion, are punished only by deprivation of leave on shore, and it may happen there is no opportunity to give leave. So also, making false charges, lying, being dirty and slovenly, being drunk, spitting on decks, are punished alike by extra duties. While smoking out of hours or in improper places [is punished] by confinement in irons, single or double, not exceeding ten days."[17] Farquhar was quite clear about his feelings on the subject: "With all due respect, I must say that nothing could be more unjust. Can it be possible that it is a more serious matter to smoke out of hours than to lie, to get drunk and therefore unfit for duty?"[18]

Farquhar commented further on the inconsistent application of punishments by various commanding officers, using the offense of drunkenness as an example: "There are many officers in the Navy who look upon drunkenness as natural to a sailor, and therefore should not be severely dealt with. . . . There are others who look upon this as one of the worst crimes and think no punishment too severe. And so with many other misdemeanors. Yet these commanders are both sincere in their convictions."[19] He concluded, "I do not believe this code is strictly carried out on any vessel of war now in commission."[20] Without the option of confinements to a naval prison system, commanding officers would continue to improvise with shipboard punishments to suit their needs.

Over time the Navy helped its cause by improving the living conditions and privileges of sailors. The *Regulations* spoke to a radical shift in the Department of the Navy's attitude toward its sailors. The Navy sought to make men feel at home and contented on their ships. "The surest way to make men contented on shipboard, and attached to the service, is to make them feel that our ships of war are their homes, and to make it apparent to them that their interests will be well cared for while they remain in the Navy."[21] This Navy policy regarding personnel matters was new, and many commanding officers still had their roots in the old Navy where a ship of war did not necessarily offer the comforts of home.

HINTS OF PROGRESSIVISM IN THE U.S. NAVY

The stirrings of progressivism outside the Navy gradually found their way into some Navy circles. From 1862 to 1889 the Bureau of Equipment and Recruiting was responsible for the conduct of seamen, and the bureau chiefs occasionally attempted to highlight and gain support to correct conditions in the fleet that contributed to an excessive number of military offenses. High desertion rates were of particular concern to Rear Admiral Shufeldt, then captain, who became chief of the Bureau of Equipment and Recruiting in 1875. During his tenure he actively campaigned for better treatment of seamen with the goal of reducing the high desertion rates. Commander Farquhar thought highly of the admiral: "Besides being a man of great intelligence, [he] is a great philanthropist and humanitarian."[22] Humanitarians were in short supply in the naval officer corps at the time.

After no mention of the subject in his predecessor's reports of 1873 and 1874, Shufeldt suggested in his 1875 report that better treatment of men might result in fewer desertions: "The time has come when something besides coercion must be used to improve the *morale* of the Navy; educate the man for the service and give him inducements to remain in it, by consulting his wants, both mental and physical. The records of this bureau prove that the fear of punishments does not deter men from deserting; take away the provocation for deserting and this demoralizing crime will diminish; if it then ensues, punish it with the rigor of military law."[23]

Continuing with his theme of more humane treatment of sailors, Shufeldt's 1876 report challenged the typical severity of courts-martial sentences: "I do earnestly ask your consideration of the laws which govern our courts-martial in the punishment of enlisted men in the Navy. The Department is constantly occupied in mitigating or modifying sentences, which, although honestly rendered, and in accordance with law, are almost uniformly found to be not only too severe on the man but injurious to the service. An intelligent revision of the naval code would not only harmonize it with the spirit of the age. . . . The letter of the law is too severe for practice, and the spirit inconsistent with modern ideas of right and justice."[24] His contention that naval law was inconsistent with society's "modern ideas of right and justice" was right out of the progressives' playbook.

Shufeldt's 1877 report noted, for the first time, great inconsistency in the administration of punishments: "These records exhibit, however, a great want of uniformity in the manner of punishing offenses, not only in different vessels of the same squadron, but in the same vessel at different times. Offenses are often punished without any apparent regard to the amount of criminality involved, particularly in the case of desertion."[25] Ten years later, the chief of the Bureau of Equipment and Repair, Rear Adm. W. S. Schley, would make the inconsistencies of shipboard punishments one of the hallmarks of his administration. Schley's emphasis of the subject would contribute to the first naval prisons being established a few years later.

Shufeldt, also concerned about the problem of drunkenness in the Navy, sought mitigated punishment for intoxicated men by requiring medical officers to treat and recommend confinements for offenders: "I am of the opinion that if intoxicated men were turned over to the medical officer for medical treatment, and only confined upon his recommendation, punishment would be very much lessened and some of the very best men in the service would be saved to usefulness instead of spending months in the 'brig,' and perhaps years in the penitentiary, for offenses, which when sober they would never dream of committing."[26] Shufeldt, much as Thomas Mott Osborne thirty years later, was quick to give the sailor the benefit of the doubt and provide him with every opportunity to make good. That said, Shufeldt was more of a realist who, as a very cost-effective measure, was also quick to recommend removal and discharge of the relatively few chronic offenders of naval discipline:

> On board of most ships of war, however there are always a few men who, in the course of a cruise, exhibit uniform bad conduct. With such men, punishment seems to have no beneficial effect, while their example is a constant provocation to others to do wrong. These should be discharged by sentence of summary court-martial, properly approved, wherever the ship on which they are serving may be found. The cost of transportation to the United States would be more than saved in the increased efficiency of the crew. They are known as Uncle Sam's hard bargains, and two or three of them can keep a ship in a constant state of turbulence and discontent.[27]

Shufeldt, unlike Osborne, was not inclined to restore "Uncle Sam's hard bargains" to their ships where they could keep it "in a constant state of turbulence and discontent."

Had Shufeldt continued in the job, the treatment of seamen and naval prisoners might have made significant advances. This was not to be the case. Shufeldt's replacement, Rear Adm. Earl English (1879–83), did not continue the campaign for improved treatment of seamen.[28] English's replacement, Rear Adm. W. S. Schley, after a slow start, did take a more active interest.[29] Beginning in 1886 Schley resurrected concerns for the treatment of prisoners, which had been largely ignored since Shufeldt's departure seven years earlier. He wrote, "The Bureau would respectfully invite your attention to the need for some uniform system relative to punishment of men for the minor offenses committed onboard ship. Under the present system, . . . there is much vagueness and great latitude of action permitted."[30] Schley recommended that the conduct reports of recent years be reviewed and "a suitable punishment prescribed for each offense in accordance with the law." His goals were to achieve "greater uniformity in the means of preserving discipline" and "secure to the men of the service similar punishments for similar offenses." Emphasizing the importance of the issue, he wrote, "The Bureau holds this matter to be one of vital concern to the best interests of the service, as it will secure for the enlisted men a punishment for minor offenses prescribed by unbiased judges and will tend to secure them against the effects of hasty judgment, as might occur now."[31]

Schley assumed the role of spokesman for achieving discipline through rewards instead of punishments. His 1888 report noted the need for better treatment of enlisted men in order to attract a higher class of person to the naval service. "The number of men enlisting under continuous service is large yearly, but there yet remains much to be desired in the increase of the class. My own impression is that more attention to the comfort of men, more regard to their future and more consideration of their privileges when abroad in service are the means by which men are to be made more contented, efficient and attached to their profession." He was especially critical of unfair and inconsistent treatment of minor shipboard offenses, especially when left to the total and absolute discretion of the commanding officer. "My own impression is that men never dislike a 'taut ship' if the officers are just. . . . But, as judgment is so variable, we find the greatest variety in the treatment of the minor offenses on board different ships . . . punishment inflicted when an officer is excited is apt to be unfair, but it is much more unfair to the man when the punishment of offenses committed by him is left to the absolute discretion of commanding officers."[32] Schley was convinced of the need for mandated rules for the treatment of minor offenses that would eliminate the unfair and inconsistent punishments frequently cited and illustrated previously.

It had been almost forty years since the abolishment of flogging. During those years, several attempts had been made by the Navy Department to improve the lot of the sailor and gain control of naval discipline and punishments. Three significant acts had been passed toward that end—*An Act to Provide a More Efficient Discipline for the Navy* (1855), *An Act for the Better Government of the Navy* (1862), and *The Regulations for the Government of the Navy of the United States* (1876). These acts laid the groundwork for transforming the Navy and naval discipline, but there was still much to be done, including the establishment of a naval prison system to ensure consistent treatment of naval prisoners.

4

Origins of the Naval Prison System
(1870–88)

Prior to the year 1888, naval prisoners undergoing sentences of courts-martial
were either accommodated in improvised prisons at the several naval
stations, or were sent to state institutions intended for criminals proper.

—Capt. S. C. Lemly, USN, 1898, LL.D., Judge Advocate General, USN, 1892–1904

The first naval prisons were established at the Boston and Mare Island Navy
Yards in the late 1880s. About that time the primary responsibility for the
confinement and treatment of naval prisoners transferred from the Bureau
of Equipment and Recruiting to the JAG. Below is a review of JAG's early involvement with courts-martial prisoners before the establishment of naval prisons, and the
Navy's early, unsuccessful attempts to gain congressional support and funding for a
naval prison during the 1870s. The next chapter discusses the launching of the first
naval prisons at the Boston and Mare Island Navy Yards. The Navy's ongoing quest
for a naval prison system, and the JAG's eventual assumption of responsibilities for
that system, is a major theme of the balance of this volume.

GENERAL COURTS-MARTIAL PRISONERS CONFINED (1875–91)

Naval lawyers were not needed to interpret the simple codes that governed the early
Navy. Naval discipline, in particular, was self-explanatory with little need for discussion or explanation. During the Civil War, Secretary of the Navy Gideon Welles
named a young assistant U.S. attorney in the District of Columbia, Nathaniel Greene,
to present the government's case in complicated courts-martial. By an act of 2 March
1865, the president was authorized to appoint a solicitor and naval judge advocate
general (JAG) on a year-to-year basis. In 1870 Congress transferred the billet to the
newly established Justice Department with the title of naval solicitor. Col. William
Butler Remey, USMC, was the first uniformed chief legal officer of the Navy. In
1878 he convinced Congress that the Navy needed a permanent uniformed JAG. The
billet was established on 8 June 1880 with responsibilities for all matters related to
courts-martial. Colonel Remey served in the billet until 1892 when he was relieved

by Capt. Samuel Conrad Lemly, USN. Lemly, who held the position until 1904, presided over the formative years of the naval prison system.[1] Lemly's observations and correspondence are the basis for much of the discussion in this book about the origin of the naval prison system.

In 1880 the duties of the newly created JAG included the maintenance of a register of prisoners under sentence of general court-martial. The locations of confined courts-martialed prisoners between 1875 and 1890 are summarized in table 3, based on that register.[2] During that period, fifteen different commands reported the confinement of prisoners in various Marine barracks, Navy yard jails, naval station guardhouses, eleven different ships, and one state prison at Wethersfield, Connecticut. Captain Lemly described well the ad hoc nature of naval prisoner confinements prior to 1888: "Prior to the year 1888, naval prisoners undergoing sentences of courts martial were either accommodated in improvised prisons at the several naval stations, or were sent to state institutions intended for criminals proper."[3] The 19 May 1897 *Boston Daily Globe* made a similar observation: "Before the naval prison was established at the Charlestown [Boston] Navy Yard, the wicked were kept in cells in the barracks on the various stations."[4]

The early use of Marine Corps barracks cells at various stations for the confinement of naval prisoners was addressed in a 19 October 1868 letter from the commandant of the Marine Corps, Brig. Gen. J. Zeilen, to Secretary of the Navy Gideon Welles. The letter confirms the Navy's growing need for cells and recommends that the station brigs, which were originally intended solely for Marine Corps prisoners, be enlarged to accommodate courts-martialed sailors as had been directed by the Navy Department:

> I would also suggest that a small appropriation be made to enlarge the places of confinement at the barracks of the principal northern stations. When constructed these places of confinement were intended for the uses of the marine corps alone, but the department having directed them to be used also for the confinement of sailors sentenced by naval courts-martial to solitary confinement, it has been found there is not a sufficient number of cells at some of the stations to admit of solitary confinement, and, in some instances, two men have to be placed in the same apartment, thus failing to carry into full effect the sentence of the court.[5]

The Navy's use of station brigs for the confinement of courts-martialed sailors increased by the mid-1870s, as shown in table 3. Another obvious conclusion from table 3 is that the Navy did not have a lot of courts-martial prisoners before the late 1880s. The total number of courts-martial prisoners climbed from about twenty in the late 1870s to about ninety in the late 1880s. Several factors contributed to the low numbers of courts-martial prisoners confined to the facilities listed in table 3. The total number of enlisted men in the Navy and Marine Corps during the 1880s remained low and fairly constant—at about eight thousand men (see figure 3)—as did the number of courts-martial prisoners In addition, with the advent of the

Table 3

Court-Martial Prisoners Confined (1875–90)

	1875	1876	1877	1878	1879	1880	1881	1882	1883	1884	1885	1886	1887	1888	1889	1890
Boston Navy Yard			2	4	5	8	14	6	5	7	2	5	14	71	59	56
New York Navy Yard		2	9	5	16	23	20	19	20	40	11	25	20	2	7	17
Portsmouth Navy Yard												2	2			
Mare Island Navy Yard	1	15	8	4	8	19	11	16	6	2	11	14	17	19	22	18
Washington, D.C., Navy Yard			1						1	1	2					
Pensacola Navy Yard									1							
USNA Annapolis								1				1				
Wethersfield State Prison				8	9	1		3	3	2			2	2		
Norfolk Navy Yard			1	2			1			1	7	3	1			
North Atlantic Station										1						
Sitka, Alaska										6						
South Atlantic Station						2	1									
European Station						2	2									
Pacific Station							5									
Asiatic Station							6	2								
TOTAL	1	17	21	23	38	55	60	47	36	60	33	50	56	94	88	91

Note: Until the converted storehouse became a prison on 12 September 1888, prisoners at the Boston Navy Yard were held at the Marine barracks. In 1878, 1882, and 1889 a single prisoner was held there on *Wabash*. In October 1878, all naval prisoners at the New York Navy Yard were moved from the Marine barracks to the Cobb Dock prison. Marine prisoners remained at the Marine barracks. In 1877 four prisoners there were on *Colorado*. At Mare Island, all prisoners were confined at the Marine barracks before it evolved into a naval prison in 1888, while prisoners at USNA were confined to the Marine barracks. At the Norfolk Navy Yard, a single prisoner was at the Marine barracks in 1877 and 1891, while two prisoners passed through the barracks between the years 1884 and 1887. Two prisoners were confined to the Navy yard jail in 1888 while ten prisoners served sentences on *Franklin* at times between 1884 and 1887. The North Atlantic's single prisoner was confined to *Galena*, while the six prisoners in Sitka, Alaska, were kept at the guardhouse. The *Shenandoah* and *Marion* each confined a single prisoner in 1880 for the South Atlantic Station, with the *Marion* holding another in 1881. *Trenton* housed two prisoners for the European Station during 1880, while *Nipsic* and an unknown ship each held one prisoner in 1881. *Alaska* and *Adams* held prisoners for the Pacific Station, while the six prisoners held in the Asiatic Station in 1881 were held in an undesignated area (two prisoners were confined to *Monocacy* a year later). Most sentences ranged from one month to one year, the exception being Wethersfield State Prison, where sentences varied from one to ten years, averaging about three years.

Source: Register of Prisoners Under Sentence of General Court-Martial ("Court-Martial Prisoners"), Jan 1877–June 1892, NARA Washington, D.C., RG 125, Records of the Office of the Judge Advocate General (Navy), Entry 32, Single Bound Volume.

summary court-martial, most offenses could be handled shipboard, where the long-standing naval tradition of absolute rule by a ship's captain continued to prevail. Discipline problems were limited to the boundaries of the ship as much as possible. Flogging had been a most convenient tool for that purpose, but commanding officers continued to restrict discipline to the bounds of the ship with innovative punishments.

A shortage of cells ashore, and the often long prisoner transport required to reach those cells, discouraged their use except for extreme cases. As more cells became available in the late 1880s, more prisoners found their way to those cells. Whereas the number of courts-martial prisoners increased annually by only dozens—to less than one hundred—in the fifteen-year period between 1875 and 1890, the number of courts-martial prisoners increased by hundreds, and reached well over one thousand prisoners, twenty years later. Did the numbers expand because of a radical increase in the number of discipline problems in the fleet, or because the availability of cells ashore relieved commanding officers of the need to maintain a self-contained ship-board discipline system? The answer is probably a little of both with the end result being an ever-increasing need for cells. As predicted in *Field of Dreams*, "If you build it, they will come." And come they did—in droves.

Most prisoner confinements (1875–90) were at Boston, New York, and Mare Island Navy Yards, with New York the most active site from the mid-1870s until the mid-1880s. Before October 1878 New York prisoners were confined at the Marine barracks alone; after that date, Marine prisoners were confined at the Marine barracks and naval prisoners at Cob Dock prison. In 1878 the three prisoners at the Norfolk yard were transferred to the New York yard; it appeared New York was ready to assume the position as the dominant naval prison site on the East Coast. However, the Boston yard assumed that role in 1888 because a suitable building with the poten-tial for expansion was available. Prior to 12 September 1888, Boston prisoners were confined at the Marine barracks; after that date they were confined at the new naval prison converted from a Navy yard store building. Mare Island, which continued to evolve and expand to serve both the Asiatic and Pacific fleets, assumed a similar role on the West Coast. In 1888 five prisoners were transferred from New York to Boston, beginning the consolidation of naval prisoners that would continue until Portsmouth prison opened in 1908.

Except for Wethersfield, Connecticut, state prison, the sentences for prisoners assigned to the fifteen sites (summarized in table 3) were generally one year or less. The sentences at Wethersfield, where the more serious offenders were imprisoned, varied from one to ten years and averaged about three years. The only other excep-tion was Mare Island, where sentences of two or three years occasionally occurred; Mare Island, the only continental naval confinement site on the West Coast, appar-ently had to accommodate longer sentences than the other Navy yards. At the turn of the twentieth century, a small prison was established at Cavite in the Philippine Islands to better serve the needs of the Asiatic fleet.

Sentences served on board prison ships at distant commands were always less than one year and usually one to three months. Prisoners assigned longer confinements were returned to the states to serve those sentences at one of the Navy yards or state prisons, as designated by the secretary of the Navy. In the case of the Asiatic Fleet, that jail was often thousands of miles away at Mare Island Navy Yard. On the East Coast, the jails were closer, but it remained a challenge to match prisoners to available cells. For example, a 14 July 1879 letter from the commandant of the League Island Navy Yard, Capt. T. Crosby, to Secretary of the Navy R. W. Thompson reports the transfer of SM Andrew Parker from the USS *Constitution* to the commandant of the New York Navy Yard for confinement in that yard's jail in accordance with the terms of his sentence by general court-martial.[6] Seaman Parker was one of the sixteen prisoners confined at the New York Navy Yard in 1879.

The JAG's role with regard to courts-martialed prisoners changed considerably from 1875 to 1890. In the early 1880s, the JAG merely collected reports from the many commands holding courts-martialed prisoners and maintained a status of those prisoners. With the assignment of Boston and Mare Island as naval prison sites in 1888, the JAG's role expanded to include prison inspection, upkeep, and administration, as well as concern for the treatment and welfare of the prisoners. The haphazard and sporadic courts-martial prisoner assignments (table 3) explain the Navy's desire to have a prison system consolidated to a few prisons, if not to a single prison.

THE CAMPAIGN FOR A NAVAL PRISON

The Navy's campaign for a naval prison followed fresh on the heels of the Army's successful efforts that resulted in the opening of Fort Leavenworth prison in 1874. The Army also faced the challenge of finding suitable confinement facilities for its prisoners after the abolishment of flogging in the Army in 1812. Congress passed laws in March and April 1812 that forbade punishment by flogging in the militia and Army, respectively. As a substitute the Army punished men by "cobbling" or paddling them with a board or a strap. And despite the prohibition, corporal punishment was inflicted, especially in out-of-the-way posts.[7] Almost sixty years after abolishing flogging, the Army finally achieved the cornerstone of its modern military prison system: Fort Leavenworth prison. Curiously, the Navy opened its marquee prison at Portsmouth in 1908, about sixty years after the abolition of flogging in the Navy. Having witnessed the Army's success, the Navy began its own campaign for a similar prison in the 1870s. We will now review the Army's efforts to gain congressional support for Fort Leavenworth, then review the Navy's early efforts to gain similar approval for its own prison.

After the Civil War the Army sought a prison system that would permit the separation of criminals from those guilty of lesser military offenses, take advantage of prisoner labor as was happening in civilian prisons, and incorporate programs to reform prisoners. Secretary of War William W. Belknap's 13 January 1870 letter to the House of Representatives discussed the Army's need for a military prison system and proposed a law to establish such a system. He described the unsatisfactory conditions that existed in the Army's guardhouses: "The usual punishments are hard labor, with ball and chain, in charge of the guard, and confinement in one guardhouse without discriminating between men of different characters . . . the men sleep on the floor without tables or other comfort. . . . Their clothes become shabby, and often ragged. . . . They perform nothing but menial service . . . few are ever sent to state prisons because the law limits confinement in them to those convicted of certain felonies."[8] The Navy was experiencing similar conditions in its local jails and brigs.

As deplorable as conditions were in the Army's guardhouses, Belknap's primary motivation was to create the opportunity to reform prisoners: "This system of punishments which has been for many years in practice fails to reform men, but tends to degrade them more and more; and by throwing hardened and desperate criminals in close contact with young and thoughtless soldiers, subjects the latter to contamination by precept and example."[9] The secretary thought that the solution to these problems was to build three or four military prisons at various locations around the country. His proposal provided some support for the Navy with the stipulation "that on application of the Secretary of the Navy, . . . the Secretary of War may direct naval convicts to be received at any military prison for the execution of their sentence."[10] The Navy apparently made little use of this provision as it was committed to getting its own prison.

The Army's drive for military prisons was strengthened in the summer of 1871 when a board of officers visited British military prisons in Montreal and Quebec "to examine and report on the system of Army prisons, Army prison discipline, and military punishment adopted in the British service with a view to the adoption of a system for the U.S. Army."[11] Impressed with what they saw, the board members concluded, "No one can witness the British System without being fully convinced of its entire superiority over ours. . . . The evils of our own methods have been pointed out, and it is hoped that our service may be strengthened by their abandonment, and the adoption of a system more in consonance with the humanity and enlightened views of the present age."[12] Progressivism, with its concerns for humanity and its "enlightened views of the present age," had gained a foothold in the U.S. Army. The board's report was forwarded to the House of Representatives on 16 January 1872, with another recommendation to establish military prisons. The Navy also began to investigate prisons about the same time. The Army's research, however, would bear fruit much sooner than the Navy's.

The secretary's proposed bill became law on 3 March 1873, and the first military prison opened at Fort Leavenworth, Kansas, in late 1874. In his report for 1876, Secretary of War J. D. Cameron stated, "This prison has now completed the first year of its existence as a distinct institution, and the result confirms the wisdom of the plan of confining prisoners serving long terms in one place, and utilizing their labor for the benefit of the Government."[13] In 1895 Fort Leavenworth became a U.S. penitentiary under the newly formed Federal Prison System.[14] In 1906 Fort Leavenworth was reactivated for confinement of Army prisoners, and the following year the prison on Alcatraz Island, which first housed prisoners in the early 1850s, was upgraded and commissioned as part of the military prison system. While the Army's prison system was maturing in the late nineteenth and early twentieth centuries, the Navy struggled with a few inadequate prisons, cobbled from existing Navy yard buildings.

About the time the Army was launching Fort Leavenworth, the Navy began building a case for its own prison. Toward that end, Commo. C. R. P. Rodgers investigated the British Lewes prison in April 1871. Unlike the U.S. Navy, the much larger Royal Navy had anticipated its prison needs even though flogging was not abolished in the Royal Navy until 1881. Lewes prison had been used as a marine barracks until 1862 and then converted into a royal naval prison. Coincidently, and on a much smaller scale, in the early 1860s the Marine barracks brig at Mare Island Navy Yard had also been converted to a confinement facility for naval prisoners. Rodgers' report on Lewes prison may have inspired the Navy to expand the converted Marine brig at Mare Island into a full-scale naval prison later in the century. Rodgers' report about Lewes also noted prisoners "are employed during working-hours in making mats, gaskets, fenders, and other rigger's work, which is paid for by the dock-yards at a fair valuation."[15] Gaining useful work from the prisoners at the Boston, Mare Island, and Portsmouth Navy Yard prisons would become an important feature of the U.S. Navy prison system.

Rodgers commented positively on the apparent health of the prisoners, the cleanliness of the prison, and the exercise program for the prisoners at Lewes. However, the confinement conditions were more severe than those anticipated for the Navy's prisons. At Lewes, Rodgers observed that the 150 prisoners "work in perfect silence, and when not at work, at school, or at chapel, are kept in solitary confinement. Its silence, hard work, and inexorable discipline, *render it a terror to the men of the fleet*" [emphasis added]. The Navy's prisons, especially Portsmouth Naval Prison under Osborne, would never earn the "terror of the fleet" reputation of Lewes, a prison that apparently retained some of the worst elements of the Auburn and Pennsylvania systems. Despite the severity of what he saw, Rodgers was favorably impressed and concluded, "If a similar prison could be established for our Navy, it would, in my opinion, be of the highest advantage to our discipline."[16]

The 1872 annual report of Secretary of the Navy George M. Robeson endorsed Rodgers' report and made an urgent plea for a naval prison to be located on one of the Marine stations.

> Corporal punishment having been happily abolished in the Navy and punishment by fines being in great degree inapplicable, only imprisonment remains to be awarded by courts-martial as the punishment for enlisted men convicted of offenses not deserving severer punishment. But the Navy has no proper prison to carry out such sentences. At our marine barracks are to be found a few cells, barely sufficient for the police and discipline of the marine garrison, and *wholly unfit for the confinement of convicts sentenced to protracted imprisonment* [emphasis added]. These cells are our only resource where men under sentence are brought from our squadrons and stations. They are so insufficient in number and in accommodations that it often becomes necessary to

place two men in one cell, and to expose the prisoners to rigors against which humanity protests. We are sometimes compelled to discharge old prisoners to make room for the newcomers.[17]

Robeson's statement lends credibility to the earlier hypothesis that commanding officers were improvising with shipboard punishments because the Navy's facilities were, he argued, "wholly unfit for the confinement of convicts sentenced to protracted imprisonment." Rodgers was also concerned about the unhealthy conditions at the few facilities the Navy did have. He wrote, "The ventilation and dryness of the cells are necessarily defective; and there is no means of employing the prisoners so as to diminish their expense to the Government, and to the improvement of their health, their morals and their decency." He concluded his push for a naval prison with the recommendation that "a moderate appropriation be made to build a suitable prison at one of our marine stations, where the necessary guards and medical attendance may be had without expense" so that "we may be able to give that care to the well-being and improvement of our prisoners which modern civilization everywhere demands."[18] The old Navy had been little concerned about the demands of modern civilization; the Navy of the 1870s was being gradually influenced by the reform movements gaining ground throughout all of society.

One year after Rodgers' inspection of Lewes prison, Lt. Col. J. L. Broome, USMC, made his grand tour of northeast prisons in late 1872. Broome's report reinforced Rodgers' conclusion about the need for a naval prison (see chapter 1).

Robeson made another plea for a naval prison in his 1873 annual report, this time suggesting one of the Navy yards as a prison site: "A proper naval prison at one of our Navy-yards is greatly needed . . . [current condition of] confinement produces indecency and vicious habits, and I cannot too strongly urge an ample appropriation to remedy such a *crying evil*" [emphasis added].[19] According to Robeson, prisoners were crowded into brigs and jails "in a manner contrary to the humane spirit of the age, and ruinous to that hope of reform, which well-regulated prisons encourage. Two men are of necessity placed in a cell not large enough for one, badly ventilated and drained, and generally insecure."[20] Using Robeson's words, the Navy's punishment system was a crying evil twenty-three years after flogging had been abolished; it would remain so for another fifteen years until the Boston and Mare Island prisons were established.

It is not surprising that the Navy's campaign for a prison in the early 1870s fell on deaf ears in Congress. The economic panic of 1873 limited Navy appropriations, to the great concern of President Grant, who warned, "Unless early steps are taken to preserve our Navy, in a few years the United States will be the weakest nation upon the ocean."[21] Congress was not about to fund a naval prison if it could not find money to fund the building of urgently needed ships. It would be another ten years before Congress made any serious commitment to fund a new Navy and fifteen years (1888) before the Navy had a makeshift prison system. It would be thirty-five years before Portsmouth prison was built and the Navy could claim a first-rate prison system of its own. Until then the Navy struggled to make do, as best it could, with existing resources.

5

Makeshift Naval Prisons
(1888–1908)

There are two naval prisons, one at Mare Island, Cal, the other in Boston
Navy-yard. Extensive repairs and alterations have been made on each.
That in Boston occupies part of a building originally built for a storehouse,
and is in my opinion unsuitable for the purpose. A regular prison should
be built on Seavey Island, a part of the Portsmouth, N. H., Navy-yard.

—Secretary of the Navy Benjamin F. Tracy, 1891

Having been unsuccessful in gaining congressional backing for the construction of a naval prison, the Navy decided to take matters into its own hands in the late 1880s. It adapted existing buildings at Boston and Mare Island to suit its prison needs. Future intent was to confine all naval courts-martialed prisoners at those two sites. A consolidated and coordinated naval prison system would replace the ongoing random and chaotic confinement of prisoners. Similarly, assigned punishments would become more consistent and treatment of prisoners more uniform.

Capt. S. C. Lemly, judge advocate general, USN (1892–1904), played an important role in the early development of the naval prison system. In an era when advancements in rank were difficult to obtain, President Benjamin Harrison appointed Lieutenant Lemly to the position of Navy JAG, with the rank of captain, in December 1892. It was reported that the appointment met with "widespread satisfaction in naval circles" because he was so well qualified for the position, having "presided over nearly all naval courts since 1882."[1]

Lemly was an especially strong spokesman for naval prisons and an advocate for fair treatment of naval prisoners. His address to the Annual Congress of the National Prison Association of the United States in October 1898 is rich in its description of the early history of prisons, especially the Boston prison. During his address, Lemly noted that there were only two naval prisons in 1898, "one at the Navy yard, Boston, Massachusetts, the other at the Navy yard, Mare Island, California,"[2] with Boston being the larger. Discussing the origins of those prisons, he described how the Navy had converted an existing building at the Boston Navy Yard into a prison and then incrementally expanded it over the next ten years: "In that year [1888], one of the stone buildings at the Navy yard, Boston, was converted into a prison, and with the gradual improvements made from time to time since, has gradually developed into what I believe to be, on a small scale, a very credible institution."[3] (Photo 5 shows the building that was the Boston prison.)

A 19 May 1897 *Boston Daily Globe* article made observations similar to Lemly's about the origin of the Boston prison, noting that it confined courts-martial prisoners from all over the East Coast as well as prisoners from foreign stations: "Six or seven years ago, it was decided to take the easterly end of the equipment building, which is a huge three story structure of rough granite . . . and transform it into a jail. . . . Charlestown [Boston Naval Prison] receives general court martial prisoners from Norfolk, League Island, Brooklyn and Portsmouth Navy yards, besides such as are brought here from foreign stations."[4] A few years earlier, these four Navy yards, cited for contributing prisoners to the Boston prison, would have confined those prisoners in local brigs.

Both the Boston and Mare Island prisons were marginal facilities when opened in 1888. In his annual report for FY 1889, the chief of the Bureau of Yards and Docks, now Rear Adm. N. H. Farquhar, noted that both prisons were undersized and in need of improvements from the start. Then-Cdr. N. H. Farquhar had written in 1885 the prize-winning essay regarding the need to recruit higher-quality seamen; in his 1889 report, he wrote, "The naval prison at Boston Navy-yard is one of the store-houses altered for the purpose. It is too contracted, and should be replaced by a building built for the purpose. It is being improved in light and ventilation. That at Mare Island was built for the purpose, but it is also too contracted. It is now being enlarged and improved."[5]

The Boston prison was not replaced immediately as recommended by Farquhar. Instead, it and the Mare Island prison were frequently and haphazardly modified and enlarged to meet the Navy's expanding need for cells. Farquhar would, a few years later, become a strong advocate for the construction of a prison at Portsmouth Navy Yard to replace the Boston prison. The Boston and Mare Island prisons were the cornerstones of the naval prison system from 1888 until the commissioning of Portsmouth prison in 1908.

High desertion rates drove the need for expanded prison facilities. As previously noted, the Navy's desertion rates remained fairly constant at about 10 percent for most of the nineteenth century and increased to about 12 percent around the turn of the twentieth century. The high rates persisted despite the Navy's best attempts to bring desertion under control.

DESERTION

At the turn of the twentieth century, the U.S. Navy was growing in numbers of enlisted men and also in the numbers of deserters. During the first fifteen years of operation of the Boston and Mare Island prisons, enlisted men increased from about 8,000 to over 20,000 and annual desertions increased in roughly the same proportion

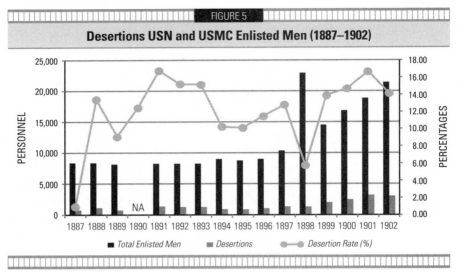

FIGURE 5

Desertions USN and USMC Enlisted Men (1887–1902)

Source: H.R. Doc. No. 2, 58th Cong., 2nd Sess. (1903) Annual Report of the Navy Department for the Year 1903, Miscellaneous Reports, 10.

from about 1,000 to 3,000 (see figure 5). For the period shown, the desertion rates averaged about 12.5 percent—a rate that drove the Navy's increased need for confinement spaces.

The high desertion rate was the subject of continuing debate in the Navy and a topic of much discussion in Congress. The debate centered on whether the carrot or the stick was the best approach to lower the desertion rate. One school of thought argued that pay increases and improved amenities would make sailors less inclined to desert. Others maintained that the punishment for desertion should be made more severe, to serve as a deterrent to those who might be considering desertion. The debate continued for several years with no clear preference emerging for either the carrot or the stick.

An 1890 U.S. Naval Institute *Proceedings* article by Lt. Alexander McCrack expressed the Navy's frustration about the causes and proposed cures for high desertion rates: "The subject of desertion from the army and navy has been discussed by many persons, and the causes assigned for desertion, with the methods proposed for its prevention and punishment, have been almost as numerous as the number of writers. . . . It is idle to write of the evils of desertion and its punishment when wholesale amnesties to deserters are made."[6] Making the point that the number of desertions was much higher than the number of deserters, McCrack highlighted the problem with fraudulent enlistments and repeat deserters: "If desertion ended a man's connection with the navy the latter would be the gainer, but unfortunately the deserter thinks it is quite the proper thing to go to another ship, re-enlist under a different *alias,* stay in the new ship long enough to once more become a factor of discontent and disorganization, and then desert again, and so on. Men who have been dishonorably discharged adopt the same course."[7]

McCrack attributed the Navy's inability to protect itself from repeated desertions to the lack of a personnel identification system. He suggested that a permanent marking of offenders might be a useful identification tool; however, he noted, "The 49th Article for the Government of the Navy forbids the branding, marking or tattooing on the body" for such purposes.[8] Lacking other alternatives, McCrack argued, "There is one system for identifying persons that was inaugurated in Paris in 1882, and which has given such excellent results that it is now used throughout France and is being generally adopted in Europe and the United States, viz. the *Anthropometrical System* of M. Alphonse Bertillon."[9] The identification of a person by the Bertillon system relied on the measurements of eight key body parts: (1) length and width of the head, (2) length of the left middle and little fingers, (3) length of the left foot, (4) length of the left forearm, (5) length of the right ear, (6) height of the figure, (7) length of the outstretched arms, and (8) length of the trunk. That the Bertillon personnel identification system was even considered is testimony to the seriousness of the Navy's problems with repeated desertions. The Bertillon system was never adopted because photography and fingerprinting became the mainstays for prisoner identification a few years later.

In response to a 1903 congressional inquiry into the Navy's high desertion rates, Secretary of the Navy William H. Moody stated that the primary reasons given for desertion, as determined by a comprehensive survey of deserters, included dissatisfaction with food, sleeping accommodations, liberty, and officer attitude toward the crew. Moody believed that unstated causes included the "naturally restless spirit of young men, who irrespective of conditions desire change, disappointment of the recruit who anticipates an easy and leisurely time at sea [and finds otherwise], . . . distaste for the military or mariner life."[10] Moody thought that the desertion rates were high because of increased recruitments from interior states, where the new recruits had no previous experience with either the military or mariner life. The secretary reported a number of actions under way to reduce desertions, including increased pay, better living conditions, improved liberty, and the opening of commissioned ranks to warrant officers.[11] These actions, unfortunately, did not have any appreciable positive effect on the desertion rate.

In his U.S. Naval Institute *Proceedings* (1904) article "Desertion and Its Prevention," Capt. A. S. Williams, USMC, argued in favor of the stick—more severe discipline for deserters.[12] He claimed that the desertion rate was high because violators were "treated with such leniency" that conviction was not a deterrent to others. Williams concluded, "The military offense of desertion, despite its increasing prevalence, is apparently not considered a serious offense by those in authority." He thought that the current maximum punishment for desertion—two years confinement, loss of pay, extra police duties, and dishonorable discharge—was appropriate, but its application was not. With good behavior, the two-year sentence was routinely reduced to sixteen months during which time the prisoner "is allowed many privileges, such as visitors, tobacco, books, etc., and is in few ways worse off than his honorable late companion serving at some remote naval station or isolated post." Worse yet, the overflow from naval prisons went to prison ships, where confinement, Williams maintained, "amounts to restriction and nothing else." Williams' description of a prison ship ridicules it as an element of naval discipline: "Imagine a well-found, roomy, well-lighted and heated ship, with Navy standards of cleanliness, delightfully situated climatically, and you have the prison ship . . . the 'silent system' cannot be enforced. . . . Well fed and happy, the sight of these prisoners loafing in the sun while they work, so demoralized the crews of ships that commanding officers have asked that while at Portsmouth, N.H., their ships be not moored in the vicinity of the U.S.P.S. *Southery*."[13] The *Southery*, moored at Portsmouth in 1904 to accommodate excess prisoners from the Boston prison, would play an increasingly important role in the naval prison system. Clearly, Williams thought that the Navy was coddling deserters on *Southery* and the other prison ships instead of disciplining them.

Williams' recommendations included more aggressive prosecution of offenders, longer prison confinement, sentencing of prisoners to "hard labor" instead of "police duties," and wearing of "distinctive prison clothing" instead of uniforms. He thought the prison to be constructed at Portsmouth would offer opportunities for more formal and stricter confinement conditions. "This state of affairs, it is hoped, will be of short duration, for money has been appropriated to build a modern prison where work, silence, and isolation can be carried out." Many of Williams' recommendations would be implemented at Portsmouth when it first opened, but Williams would most definitely have been disappointed with the confinement conditions at the new modern prison fifteen years later under Thomas Mott Osborne.

About the time Williams was arguing for stiffer punishments for desertion, the Navy continued to go in the other direction. In 1903 the punishment for some deserters was moderated even more by drawing a distinction between deserters and stragglers. Stragglers were defined as men who returned to the Navy voluntarily or were returned to the Navy by officials in less than three months. Stragglers were subject to a summary court-martial with sentences not to exceed three months' confinement with loss of pay and a bad conduct discharge. Deserters were subject to a general court-martial with sentences, during peacetime, of confinement not to exceed two years, loss of pay, and a bad conduct discharge. The more lenient policy with regard to stragglers reduced, but by no means solved, the Navy's need for more cells.[14] The new prisons at Boston and Mare Island would remain undersized as long as the Navy was unable to bring desertions under control.

Desertion rates continued to average above 10 percent. Not having had much luck with the carrot, the JAG, Capt. E. H. Campbell, USN, took the other tack in 1908. He was convinced desertion rates remained high because "men desert without regard for the consequences, and apparently without considering them, partly because they have not been sufficiently impressed with what the punishment for the offense is, but largely because the punishment is not sufficiently severe to have the requisite deterrent effect."[15] Campbell's reasoning and recommendations for more severe punishments were much the same as those presented by Capt. A. S. Williams, USMC, four years earlier. Not only had the Navy not adopted Williams' recommendations, it had, in some cases, reduced the maximum confinement for desertion from two years to one year. According to Campbell, a confinement sentence of one year also applied to much lesser offenses, which included sleeping on watch, leaving station before being regularly relieved, negligence or carelessness in obeying orders, selling clothes, and lewd or indecent behavior. He argued that the Navy would never be able to deter young sailors from considering desertion if it continued to minimize its seriousness by grouping it with these lesser offenses for punishment purposes.

Noting that the Navy's desertion rate was two or three times higher than the Army's, Campbell recommended the Navy adapt the Army's much sterner punishments for desertion, with maximum confinements from one year to five years depending on the circumstances. The desertion rate percentages for the Army and Navy between 1902 and 1907 were:[16]

	Army	Navy
1902	5.0	10.4
1903	7.1	12.3
1904	6.6	11.4
1905	6.8	7.9
1906	7.4	9.0
1907	5.6	9.0

The Navy's desertion rate was improving, but still much too high for the JAG's purposes. In 1907 about 50 percent of the convictions for naval offenses were for desertions (1,054 of 2,101).

By 1918 the maximum allowed punishments for desertion in its various forms were gradually increased to the following:[17]

Absent from station and duty without leave or after leave has expired

■ Officer: Dismissal

■ Enlisted man: Confinement for six months and dishonorable discharge

Desertion (in case of surrender to naval authorities), after thirty days

■ Officer: Dismissal

■ Enlisted man: Confinement for eighteen months and dishonorable discharge

Desertion (in case of apprehension by or delivery to naval authorities) (1) if less than six months in the service, (2) if more than six months in the service

■ Officer: Dismissal and imprisonment for four years

■ Enlisted man: (1) Confinement for two years and dishonorable discharge, (2) confinement for two and one-half years and dishonorable discharge

Desertion from a ship about to sail on an extended cruise

■ Officer: Dismissal and imprisonment for three years

■ Enlisted man: Confinement for three years and dishonorable discharge.

Aiding or enticing others to desert

- Officer: Dismissal and imprisonment for four years
  Enlisted man: Confinement for one year and dishonorable discharge

Attempting to desert

- Enlisted man: Confinement for six months

Throughout the latter half of the nineteenth century and the early years of the twentieth century, neither increased rewards nor more severe punishments appreciably improved the Navy's desertion problem. Desertions remained high, as did the Navy's need for cells.

Boston Naval Prison

The building that became the Boston prison was built in 1857, a three-story granite structure with an attic that served as a storehouse (see photo 5). The conversion to a prison was done at minimal expense. Captain of the Yard E. O. Matthews described the conversion to Commo. W. P. Claren a few months after the prison opened: "When the prison was fitted out, it was supplied, I believe with a view to economy, having no means of heating the water that is required for bathing and other purposes." "Ventilation of prison and walls is bad—the circulation of air being interrupted by the high partition walls separating the cells which rise up to within a few inches of the floor above. . . . The lighting in the cells in very insufficient."[18]

A letter from the commander of the Post Marines, Capt. H. L. Cochrane, USMC, to Matthews in March 1889 provides more evidence of the hasty conversion. Cochrane suggests the guards were more uncomfortable in their quarters than the prisoners in their cells: "If the term 'repairs' will comprehend a much needed alteration I would respectfully recommend that the angular bulkhead which now makes proper lighting and ventilating of the quarters provided for the guard impracticable, and renders the custodians more uncomfortable than the prisoners, be made straight . . . [so as] to provide both light and air for the pocket in which the men are now quartered, and offset the heat of the galley which in summer is oppressive.[19]

The original forty-two cells quickly proved to be woefully short of the needed capacity. Cochrane recommended an upgrade and expansion of the overloaded prison instead of continued temporary repairs: "A vastly better plan, however, in view of the eminently successful operation of the prison, and the fact that it is now filled to its utmost capacity, would be to add the remaining sixty two (62) feet of that floor to the prison which would permit the construction of a messroom and bagroom, which I understand was originally contemplated, make the illumination and ventilation complete, and permit the addition of about twenty new cells which could be made with iron grating fronts . . . for the better observation of inmates, who might need it."[20] This was the start of twenty years of expansions and modifications that would end only with the opening of Portsmouth prison in 1908.

An 1895 incident at the prison illustrates the increasing complexity of naval discipline. A medical officer refused to approve, as required by Navy regulations, a diet of bread and water as part of a punishment for an AWOL offense. The officer in charge of the Marine detachment at the yard, Maj. Robert L. Meade, referred the matter to the commandant of the Boston Navy Yard, Commo. J. N. Miller, who requested clarification from Secretary of the Navy H. L. Herbert. Meade maintained the senior medical officer at the yard had inappropriately obstructed a sentence allowed by Article 30 of the Articles of War. The senior medical officer, surgeon Frank Rodger, had initially objected to four days on bread and water and then again objected when the sentence was shortened to three days. Meade suspected Rodger objected to a punishment of bread and water in general. The secretary of the Navy advised the commodore to get a statement from the senior medical officer. In his statement, Rodger wrote, "The opinions referred to are professional in intent, and in no way intended to be regarded in any other light."[21] Although Rodger's statement is inconclusive and the archives provide no final resolution of the matter, the example does illustrate how far the system of naval discipline had strayed from the absolute authority that commanding officers had exercised a few years earlier.[22]

The authority of commands to impose the maximum bread and water punishment allowed, which required full rations every fifth day, was further eroded by General Order 470 of 22 March 1897. The order discouraged "the imposition by summery courts, except in extreme cases, of the maximum deprivation of full rations allowed by the regulations where the sentence of solitary confinement, in irons, on bread and water is imposed."[23] This order was issued because the Navy Department had noticed the maximum sentence allowance of a full ration every fifth day was being routinely imposed. According to Capt. S. C. Lemly, "Courts were counseled to restrict . . . this form of punishment to a shorter interval."[24] Senior Navy Department officials continued to believe that the punishments being administered in the fleet were more severe than deserved.

The improvements made to the Boston prison over its first ten years of operation included humanitarian considerations found lacking in the northeast prisons inspected by Lt. Col. J. L. Broome, USMC, in 1872. In 1898 the sixty-two cells at the Boston prison were "lighted by electricity, heated by steam, and [were] well ventilated." With a touch of humor, and showing a familiarity with Boston's inclement weather, Lemly stated that the cells were constructed to admit "an abundance of light and as much real sunshine as can be reasonably expected in Boston." A typical weekly menu showed a lot of variety and an abundance of food with an emphasis on beans, which were served frequently because "the prison is located within the shadow of Bunker Hill monument." Upon completion of their sentences in this favorable environment, prisoners were sent on their way with a gift of twenty to twenty-five dollars.[25] At Boston prison, flogging was a distant memory.

The Boston prison acquired a reputation as a soft prison. After one of his visits to the prison Lemly said he was "was chaffed by the newspapers" because the prisoners "were altogether too well fed for men without active employment."[26] He was probably referring to an article in the *Boston Sunday Daily Globe* of 1 January 1893 titled "They Have an Easy Time, Inmates at the Naval Prison at Charlestown." Physically the prison did resemble in any way the imposing northeast prison structures Broome had observed in 1872 or the daunting Portsmouth "castle" that would be built fifteen years later. The article stated, "The prison is a mere shell when compared with civilian institutions. . . . The general public is not aware that there is a prison in the Charleston Navy Yard. . . . The prison is situated in the northern end of the provisions and clothing building." The article described a comfortable imprisonment that included good food, plenty of ventilation, an exercise program, clean clothing and bedding, satisfactory visiting, mail delivery, bathing privileges, few discipline problems, and a gift of twenty dollars on the completion of a sentence. The *Globe* concluded, "Those confined there are at present as happy a lot as imprisoned men can well be."[27] Not surprisingly, during the five years since its establishment in 1888 there had not been a single escape. Then again, prisoners did try to sneak into the prison. During the winter months, deserters, who came to be known as "winter birds," often surrendered to naval authorities "in order to find food and shelter, preferring a sentence of six months imprisonment to a struggle for existence in civil life."[28]

The Navy's efforts to be more selective with its recruits were not always successful. Maurice J. Flynn, a coal heaver on the *Concord* who ended up at the Boston prison in April 1891, was one who slipped through the recruiting filter. Described by the *Boston Daily Globe* as "a powerful young man . . . fond of strong drink," Flynn was the type of "old Navy" sailor for which flogging was a well-suited discipline. However, in this case he was fortunate to be subjected to the "new Navy" discipline that sentenced him to six months at the Boston prison for smuggling whiskey on board the *Concord* while at anchor in the Brooklyn Navy Yard. In its colorful description of Flynn's offense, the *Globe* reported that he had gone ashore without permission, "painted the city of churches [Brooklyn] a fiery red," and later been caught attempting to smuggle a small boatload of bottled whiskey on board the *Concord*. He was "placed in irons and lodged in the ship prison below decks" while his case was forwarded to the Navy Department for review. Secretary of the Navy Benjamin J. Tracey ordered the general court-martial that tried and sentenced Flynn to Boston prison.[29]

Forty years earlier, Flynn would have been flogged within days and immediately restored to duty. Twenty years earlier he might have been confined on board the *Concord* for ten days and denied shore liberty for six months to a year. Instead, in 1891, he was transported under guard from Brooklyn to Boston to serve his sentence. Naval discipline had become much more complex and consuming of resources. Worse yet, confinement conditions at Boston prison were not particularly onerous when compared with twelve lashes with the cat or shipboard confinement in double irons.

The Boston prison was always overloaded. In March 1898 the prison had sixty-six prisoners confined in sixty-one cells, with another twenty-five prisoners about to arrive from the Brooklyn Navy Yard.[30] In March 1901 the yard chief engineer reported "a plan of enlargement has been found which will give 150 cells in place of the 61 now available."[31] A 15 April 1901 letter from Secretary of the Navy John D.

Long to the commandant of the Boston Navy Yard, Rear Adm. William T. Sampson, described the Navy's embarrassment over a backlog of prisoners waiting for cells to become available at Boston and the urgent need for expansion: "The Department's somewhat embarrassed by the number of general courts-martial prisoners awaiting, at the various stations where the facilities for their confinement are not sufficient and suitable, transportation to the prison at the Navy yard under your command, which it is understood is full to its utmost capacity unless some further temporary arrangement can be made pending its enlargement, now in progress."[32]

Sampson advised the secretary of the Navy on 27 May 1901 that a more ambitious plan was needed to accommodate prisoners during the renovation of the prison. Sampson recommended thirty-eight deserving prisoners be released, leaving eighty at the prison.[33] The chief engineer stated on 30 November 1901 that "the 90 cells should be ready for occupancy about the time stated, April 15, 1902 . . . the work should be completed by June 15, and ready for confining of prisoners by July 1, 1902. At which time the capacity of the prison would be 150 cells."[34] The number of cells at the Boston prison increased over 500 percent during the first fifteen years of operation.

Overcrowding led to the reassignment of naval prison ship *Southery* from Norfolk to Boston in April 1902 so that prisoners could be confined on the *Southery* concurrent with the latest repair and enlargement of the prison.[35] In addition to confining prisoners on the *Southery,* a liberal policy of sentence reductions released fifty-five prisoners for having good conduct records while imprisoned. At the turn of the century, the Boston prison was in a constant state of upgrade and expansion, and large numbers of prisoners were frequently released early to free up cells for prisoners waiting to serve their sentences.

With time, overcrowding and sharing cells at the prison contributed to quarrels, which occasionally led to extended sentences for those involved. In late October 1907, a disagreement between two cellmates resulted in an attempted murder: After a quarrel had apparently subsided, SA Merle M. Clark removed a pipe from his bed, blindsided George Whitney, and beat him over the head with it. It was reported that Clark "intended to kill Whitney, and expressed regret that he was unsuccessful."[36] He was charged with assault with a dangerous weapon and undoubtedly had his prison sentence extended. This case was typical of many young seamen sentenced to a naval prison for a relatively minor military offense who, while in prison, committed a more serious offense that extended their sentences.

Escapes became more prevalent with time. In August 1908 Frank Kelly and Albert S. Marsh, both twenty-year-old sailors, escaped for the second time. They had been caught after their first escape and three years were added to their original sentences of four years for desertion.[37] The following spring five prisoners escaped by sawing through the bars in the washroom window, sliding down a rope to the Navy yard, and scaling a wall. Following an inquiry into the escape, prison commanding officer Capt. Charles C. Carpenter, USMC, was relieved "on the ground that he was not sufficiently strict in prison discipline."[38] Capt. Charles S. Hatch, USMC, was detached from duty at the newly commissioned Portsmouth Naval Prison to relieve Carpenter. Hatch assumed command of the prison on 27 April 1909, just two weeks after the commissioning at Portsmouth on 11 April 1909.[39] Another escape occurred the following year when prisoner Edward J. Fitzgerald overpowered a Marine guard. Armed with the guard's revolver and dressed in his uniform, Fitzgerald surprised the sentry at the main gate who opened the gate under duress.[40] Originally a comfortable place to spend confinement and seek relief from the cold weather in the early 1890s, within fifteen years, the Boston prison had become an overcrowded prison from which inmates were eager to escape.

After the Portsmouth prison opened, Boston prisoners were frequently transferred there for reasons of better security or to relieve overcrowded conditions elsewhere. Even then, the Boston guards had difficulties making successful prisoner transfers. During a transfer of five prisoners in July 1912, prisoner C. Dennison escaped by jumping from the train carrying the prisoners as it left Boston's North Station.[41] All escape attempts ceased a few years later when the Boston prison was closed because of the naval prison reorganization of 1914; all its prisoners were moved to Portsmouth. The other original naval prison at Mare Island would enjoy a longer run than the Boston prison.

MARE ISLAND NAVAL PRISON

As early as 1865 the commanding officer of the Marine barracks at Mare Island Navy Yard was overseeing the escorting of naval prisoners between Mare Island and the California state prison at San Quentin. On 4 January 1866, Lt. Col. M. K. Hintzings, USMC, advised the shipyard commandant, Capt. David McDougal, that Pvt. John Cullen, USMC, had been delivered under guard to the state prison at San Quentin, California, on 9 December 1865.[42] Cullen was received back at Mare Island eight months later.[43] On 4 September 1866, Capt. W. T. Craven, USN, advised Secretary of the Navy Gideon Welles by letter that OS William Rodwell, who had been confined at the California state prison, had been recently received at the yard and "taken up general service for the North Pacific Squadron."[44] Shortly after the end of the Civil War, the commandant of the Mare Island Navy Yard routinely supported the North Pacific fleet by assigning local Marines to escort prisoners to and from the San Quentin prison.

In 1867 naval prisoners were being confined at the Marine barracks jail, as evidenced by the commandant's 23 August 1867 letter to Welles reporting an escape: "Four of the prisoners serving sentences of a General Court Martial at this Navy Yard . . . were taken sick with fever . . . [from] jail to hospital . . . last night. Patrick Heffrom . . . though sick with fever made his escape. . . . Reward has been offered for his apprehension."[45]

Two weeks later, on 9 September 1867, the commandant wrote Welles that the escapee had been captured in Alabama: "Brig Genl O. Shepherd Commander Post Mobile, Ala says he has Heffrom. . . . [I advised] hold him until he can be sent over by public conveyance. . . . [I am unable to receive him] at this time owing to prevalence of yellow fever."[46] It is to Patrick Heffrom's credit that, though sick, he was able to escape and make his way across the continent in two weeks. It is to the discredit of the Marine guards that one of the earliest reports of prisoner confinement at the Marine barracks was the reporting of an escape.

The scale of prison operations at the Marine barracks increased in 1868, and the commandant began submitting quarterly reports of punishment to the secretary of the Navy.[47] A cumbersome and inefficient system of prison administration followed, which required the yard commandant to communicate and receive approvals from the secretary of the Navy for each prisoner processed at the yard. For example, a 4 April 1870 letter from the commandant, Capt. John Gordsborough, to Secretary of the Navy George M. Robeson acknowledged receipt of the secretary's letter about sentences of four men (OS John Clark, SM Martin Bjorith, SM Frank Thompson, and Pvt. Patrick Mackey) and reported, "The necessary directions have been given to the Commanding Officer of the Marine Barracks at this place."[48] Inordinate time delays and confusion about sentences were the rule when communicating with the Navy Department by mail from Mare Island.

On 13 July 1868, the *San Francisco Bulletin* reported, "We learn that orders had been received per last steamer for a prison and other buildings to be built at the marine barracks."[49] The April 1872 *Scribner's Monthly* had an article about the Mare Island Navy Yard that described the Marine barracks and noted, "There is a fine prison in the rear."[50] That fine prison was subject to continual expansion over the next thirty years.

Unlike the Boston prison, where expansion was accomplished by incrementally adding cells within the confines of an existing large stone building, the Mare Island prison grew by adding wings and floors to the original structure. The first floor with sixteen cells was completed in the early 1870s.[51] The second floor with another sixteen cells was added during the early 1890s. The early 1900s addition included a tower and two-story wing, again doubling the size of the prison. In a 28 September 1906 JAG report, Capt. S. W. B. Diehl described the cells in the original prison as "built of brick, closed with solid metal doors with a very small opening for ventilation—veritable dungeons, so pronounced and scarcely in keeping with present-day ideas of punishment for military offenses."[52] He recommended that "the antiquated and unhealthy cells be replaced with modern, open, steel cells."[53] Diehl also recommended the addition of another wing as the "the number of prisoners has averaged more than 50 percent greater than designed for."[54] The prison was consistently overloaded and in need of expansion from its inception in the early 1870s through the early 1900s. (See the Mare Island prison structure, photo 6.)

In 1871, as a result of increased prisoner activity at the prison, the Navy Department required monthly reports of prisoners confined.[55] The prison's support to the Asiatic Fleet continued to grow; in August 1872 the commandant, Capt. E. J. Parrott, wrote Secretary of the Navy George M. Robeson asking for directions concerning five courts-martialed prisoners received from the Asiatic Station. The prisoners had been court-martialed on the *Colorado* and transported to the shipyard on the *Benica*, to be confined in any prison of the secretary of the Navy's choosing before being dishonorably discharged. The procedure at the time was to send the prisoners to Mare Island and have the yard commandant sort out with the Navy Department where the prisoners were to be confined. A summary of the prisoners received follows:[56]

NAME	TRIAL DATE	SENTENCE
SM Ed. Dunlop	2 Feb 1871	Confinement with hard labor for 5 yrs and loss of some pay
OS Jos. Starkweather	2 Feb 1871	Solitary confinement until 1 Mar 1873 and loss of some pay
LM Orannus Vianello	2 Feb 1871	Solitary confinement until 1 Mar 1873 and loss of some pay
LM James Conner	7 Sept 1871	Solitary confinement until 15 Sept 1873, w/o irons in cell and double irons when not in cell, loss of some pay
LM George Roberts	7 Sept 1871	Solitary confinement until 15 Sept 1873, w/o irons in cell and double irons when not in cell, loss of some pay

Note that the commandant's letter requesting directions from the secretary was eighteen months after the trial date of the first three prisoners and over one year after the trial date of the other two prisoners. Justice was not swift for some sailors of the Asiatic Fleet in 1871. The offenses are not described in the correspondence, but they must have been aggravated to merit confinement sentences of five years in one case and two years in the other cases. Confinement sentences of several years required prison cells ashore, which were in short supply. During this timeframe the Navy Department began to investigate the possibility of building a naval prison.

On 7 September 1872, the commandant of the yard, Capt. T. H. Selfridge, reported to Robeson that he had recently received thirteen more prisoners, including three Marines from USS *Pensacola* and one seaman from USS *Saranac*. The commandant advised the secretary that the prisoners were confined at the Marine barracks awaiting "your orders . . . for disposition."[57] At the time, the prison only had sixteen cells and overcrowding had become a problem.[58] Frequently the solution for overcrowding was to release prisoners with good conduct records during confinement. In this case, after an exchange of letters addressing overcrowding, Selfridge wrote Robeson on 28 December 1872 he had "mitigated sentences for eight prisoners and approved the others [the new prisoners] for confinement at this yard." Continuing the micromanaging of prisoner sentences at the secretary's level, Selfridge asked if the prisoners confined at the yard prison were to be "kept at hard labor in the day time or confined in cells[.]"[59]

In April 1873 the prison received six prisoners specifically sentenced to confinement at the Mare Island prison from Rear Adm. Pennock, U.S. Naval Forces North Pacific. Court-martial boards were now routinely sentencing prisoners to the Mare

Island prison for terms much longer than previous shipboard terms for the same offenses. Consider the following sentences for the six prisoners:[60]

- Francis Gallagher, Private Marine, AWOL, double irons six months at Mare Island Marine Barracks and loss of some pay
- Frederick Johnson, Ordinary Seaman, refusal to obey orders, reduction to next inferior rating, 4 months hard labor at Mare Island Marine Barracks
- John Sullivan, landsman, drunk, obscene language to officer, resisting arrest, six months hard labor at Mare Island Marine Barracks, and loss of some pay
- John Williams, Ordinary Seaman, Willful & persistent disobedience of orders, hard labor at Mare Island Marine Barracks or other prison per secretary of the Navy for 3 years with *18 lb ball & chain attached to left leg* [emphasis mine]
- Thomas Perry, landsman, attempting to desert, reduction to next inferior rank, 4 months at Mare Island Marine Barracks

The convenience of a prison ashore apparently encouraged longer and less imaginative confinement sentences, notwithstanding the "18 lb ball & chain attached to left leg" punishment. In the above cases, commanding officers were opting to get rid of serious troublemakers for a long time—if not forever—instead of assigning innovative punishments that would allow them to, perhaps, continue as productive members of the ship's crew.

Late in 1873 Robeson responded negatively to a request from Commo. John Rodgers to enlarge the prison: "the Naval Prison . . . cannot now be enlarged . . . [however] the Department is willing to relieve it [of overcrowding] by remitting a portion of the sentences of prisoners who may be recommended to clemency."[61] This time six prisoners were released on good conduct.[62] About this time prisoner sentences began to be confirmed by telegram instead of time-consuming letter exchanges.[63]

The case of Pvt. Joseph Brennan, USMC, highlighted the confusion caused by a lack of basic rules governing administration of prisoner sentences when thousands of miles of transoceanic transport were involved. Brennan had been court-martialed at Valparaiso, Chile, on 15 February 1873 and sentenced to one-year confinement with loss of all pay except fifty dollars. The sentence was approved by Rear Adm. Charles Steadman, commodore South Pacific Fleet, on 25 February 1873. Brennan was transported in double irons on board a ship to Mare Island, arriving 28 June 1873, to serve his sentence. Brennan wrote Robeson on 4 March 1874, more than one year after his trial, from the Mare Island Marine barracks seeking clarification of his sentence, which he thought he had already fulfilled: "For four months after this [approval of sentence on 25 February 1873] I was confined in double irons on board ship and was transferred to the prison at Marine Barracks, Mare Island to serve the remainder of my sentence, June 28, 1873. I therefore humbly submit that I have served out my term of one year imprisonment, but if my sentence counts only from the date of my transfer to the prison at these Barracks, I would respectfully ask that you be pleased to remit the unexpired portion of my confinement."[64] The endorsement of the commanding officer of the prison noted that Brennan was received at his post on 28 June 1873 with a general court-martial sentence requiring him to be confined "for one year in such Penitentiary as the Honorable Secretary of the Navy may designate."[65] Brennan maintained that the time he had spent in double irons on board ship should count toward his sentence.

Commandant Rodgers' endorsement of Brennan's letter asked, "What rule governs the commencement of Naval imprisonment under the law?" Quoting an 18 December 1872 letter from the Navy Department—"the term of confinement in each case is to be computed from the date of the sentence"—Rodgers asked if that meant the date the sentence was approved by commander of the fleet or the date it was approved by the secretary of the Navy. Clearly sympathizing with Brennan, Rodgers added, "The rules of the Civil Law where prisoners can be delivered to sentence in a day, scarcely apply in humanity or equity, to Naval prisoners thousands of miles away and separated by oceans from the reviewing power." Rodgers recommended that "sentences begin from the date of approval of the sentence by the officer ordering the Court."[66] Robeson remitted Brennan's sentence; subsequent correspondence involving follow-on prisoners indicates that Rodgers' recommendation was approved.[67] In 1873, twenty-three years after flogging was abolished, the Navy was still sorting out the basic rules for confinement sentences.

The case of SM Charles E. Stauton, received at Mare Island from the Asiatic Fleet in June 1874, after having been court-martialed at Yokohama, Japan, illustrates another significant naval discipline problem of the time. Staunton deserted from USS *Hartford* in Shanghai; six weeks later he shipped on USS *Yantie* in Hong Kong as LM Charles E. Reilly, where his true identity was uncovered. Lacking an effective personnel administration system, the Navy had little control over fraudulent enlistments. Seamen routinely deserted an unpleasant situation on one ship to sign on with another ship some distance away with hopes of a better deal.[68] In this case, Stauton's better deal was short lived.

In July 1876 the prison was once again filled to capacity. Commandant Rodgers wrote Robeson, "There are sixteen cells in the Naval Prison at this Yard, fifteen of which are in good condition. There are now confined in this prison including those recently received from the USS *Saco*, fifteen (15) General Court Martial prisoners."[69] Rodgers recommended the release of the following six prisoners on the basis of good conduct to vacate cells.

LM = Landsman, SM = Seaman, LP = loss of pay, DD = dishonorable discharge

- Harry Teveston, LM, embezzlement & desertion, 4 years confinement, LP, DD, 9 months served
- Cornelius Klods, LM, desertion, 5 yrs confinement, LP, DD, 6 months served
- Charles Davis, LM, desertion, confined until 10/9/1877, LP, DD, 5 months served

- Wm Stanley, SM, disobedience of orders & desertion, 1 yr confinement, LP, DD, 5 months served
- John Brown, Marine, *sodomy and scandalous conduct, 10 years confinement* [emphasis mine], LP, DD, 5 months served
- Louis Bantay, LM, desertion, 1 year confinement, LP, DD, 4 months served

Two important observations can be made from the above list. First, for lack of cells prisoners were being released after serving only a fraction of their sentences. Second, the case of John Brown shows how seriously morality crimes were viewed relative to other offenses. Brown's sentence is twice as severe as that of Teveston, who was an embezzler and deserter. While the sentences for some offenses, such as desertion, drunkenness, and smuggling liquor, became progressively less severe, this was not the case for morality crimes. These crimes, which continued to reap harsh sentences, would become the source of much controversy during Osborne's years at Portsmouth.

The overcrowded Mare Island prison was constantly modified and expanded in an attempt to keep up with the increasing prisoner workload. On 22 December 1890, the *San Francisco Bulletin* reported plans to add a second story to the original prison: "The telegraph announced this morning . . . An additional story will be put on the prison in the rear of the marine barracks at the yard. At present the room is not large enough for those being sent there for confinement."[70] In 1892 Secretary of the Navy Tracy reported completion of the project: "The capacity of the prison at Mare Island has been doubled, as well as other essential improvements made."[71] By 1900 the capacity of Mare Island prison was still "insufficient to accommodate the number of prisoners sent to it" due to "the large naval force maintained in the Far East."

▪▪▪▪▪▪▪▪▪▪▪▪▪

The JAG annual reports for 1904 to 1908 paint a bleak picture for the Mare Island and Boston prisons. The reports consistently cited overcrowded conditions that necessitated the early release of prisoners. In 1904 Capt. S. W. B. Diehl wrote:

> The naval prisons at Boston, Portsmouth (the prison ship *Southery*) [emphasis mine], and Mare Island, are at present inadequate for the proper accommodation of the prisoners necessarily sent to them for incarceration. Owing to the excess in the number of persons sentenced by general court-martial to confinement over the capacity of the prisons, it has become necessary, in order to relieve congestion, to release offenders before the expiration of their terms of confinement, by the exercise of special clemency to the most deserving. Releases in case of the *Southery* average about 25 monthly. The effect upon discipline of such enforced action is questionable.[72]

Four years later, in 1908, the overcrowded conditions persisted and the early release of prisoners continued. The prisons were so overloaded that, at Boston, the "winterbirds" were turned away or had their sentences remitted. Capt. E. H. Campbell wrote: "The capacity of these prisons has been greatly overtaxed during the year, and it has been necessary to discharge many prisoners whose periods of confinement were less than one-third expired, in order to make room for other men sentenced to confinement. For a short time during the winter, when it was suspected that deserters were surrendering in the hope of receiving a few months confinement to tide them over the cold weather, the confinement in some cases was entirely remitted."[73]

In 1907 about 50 percent of the convictions for naval offenses were for desertion. Many of those deserters were released after serving only a small portion of their sentence and some without serving any time at all. Many considered naval discipline a sham for the lack of adequate confinement facilities.

In 1908 the JAG estimated "prison accommodations are less than one-half those required."[74] Moreover, Capt. E. H. Campbell, USN, believed the early release of prisoners for lack of capacity was making a travesty of naval discipline. "The release of prisoners after serving such small proportions of the sentences adjudged can not but have a detrimental effect upon the maintenance of naval discipline throughout the service . . . and it should not be permitted to continue . . . the deterrent effect of punishment is lost. Such conditions would not be permitted to continue in any state penal institution, and they should not be permitted to exist in the Navy."[75]

The table below shows the capacities at each prison and prison ship in 1904 and 1908.[76] The prison ships *Southery* at Portsmouth and *Nipsic* at Puget Sound were positioned to absorb the overflow of prisoners from Boston and Mare Island, respectively. The opening of the new Portsmouth prison was being eagerly anticipated to provide much needed relief.

	1904	1908
Boston Navy Yard	150	150
Portsmouth Navy Yard	Under construction	140
Prison ship *Southery*	150	300
Mare Island Navy Yard	52	52
Prison ship *Nipsic*		125
	352	767

Naval criminals in state prisons are not shown; in 1908 there were only fourteen such prisoners at the Wethersfield, Connecticut, prison and seventeen prisoners at the San Quentin, California, prison.[77] Confinement of these hard-core offenders was not the problem; the many sailors convicted of naval offenses, most notably desertion, were causing the Navy to take unusual measures to meet its prison needs.

Cavite Naval Prison

The treaty ending the Spanish-American War, signed on 10 December 1898, ceded Puerto Rico, Guam, and the Philippines to the United States, creating an opportunity to build a prison at Cavite in the Philippines to service the Asiatic Fleet. An

18 June 1900 letter from the commander in chief, U.S. Naval Forces on Asiatic Station, Adm. Thomas L. Meade, to the secretary of the Navy, John D. Long, described the crude and minimal Philippine prison that included three small buildings and an inconveniently located water closet: "The Naval Prison at this station . . . consisting of three buildings situated on the east parapet of Fort San Felipe. Their inside dimensions are as follows: number One 52 ½′ by 21′ by 13′ (average height) (old prison); number Two 47′ by 25′ by 12 ½′ (new prison) and number Three, solitary confinement cells 8 ½′ by 5 ⅔′ by 10′ (average height). These cells are dark and have no ventilation except through the door. Building Number One was built before, but has been repaired since 1898; the other two are of recent construction. . . . The water closet is outside, down by the sea wall, and distant about 140 yards."[78] Meade recommended that "the maximum number of prisoners allowed in each building be as follows: in Number One, 19, in Number Two, 20; in Number Three, 4."[79] At the maximum recommended capacities, buildings number one and two would be crowded at about sixty square feet per prisoner. The solitary confinement cells in building number three allowed only forty-eight square feet per prisoner. Progressive reform had obviously not reached the Philippine Islands, especially Cavite prison, at the turn of the century.

Improvements recommended by the admiral included the installation of urinals, portable closet stools, and better ventilation. Because of the arduous confinement conditions and severe climate, the admiral recommended no prisoner under sentence for a longer term of confinement than six months be sent to Cavite prison. Finally, the admiral recommended that "this prison be continued as a Naval prison" to service the Asiatic fleet. Cavite prison continued to be a small, but important piece of the naval prison system.[80]

PRISON SHIPS

Prison ships were also significant in the expanding Navy's turn-of-the-century struggle to find enough prison cells to accommodate its growing prisoner population. The *Southery* was one of the most valuable of the prison ships, moving frequently up and down the East Coast to wherever the Navy's need for cells was greatest.

Originally built in England as a steamer in 1889, the *Southery* (see photo 7) was purchased by the U.S. Navy in 1898 and converted to a collier at the Boston Navy Yard. The next year she was converted to a prison ship at the Norfolk Navy Yard and then moved back to Boston in June 1901, while the prison was being enlarged. On 7 April 1902, *Southery* was relocated to Charleston, South Carolina, to assume duties as a prison ship.[81] After a year in Charleston, the ship was sent to Portsmouth in July 1903 to be placed in commission "as a receiving ship, for prisoners, at that yard."[82]

When the *Southery* reached Portsmouth, the Navy yard commandant, reluctant to fly his flag from the mast of a prison ship, wrote the secretary of the Navy, "I beg leave to request the privilege of flying my flag from flagstaff on office building, instead of on board the *Southery*, a prison ship."[83] The commandant may not have flown his flag from the *Southery*, but the ship remained a valuable asset at the yard until 1922 and played an important role in the progressive reform experiment at the prison during World War I.

In 1908 the around-the-world cruise of sixteen first-line battleships, directed by President Theodore Roosevelt to generate international goodwill and a show of naval strength, also generated an excess of naval prisoners. In December 1907 the fleet "steamed south from Hampton Roads [for the West Coast] on the first leg of its 46,000-mile, 14-month voyage."[84] In mid-1908 it was anticipated that the Great White Fleet's imminent departure from the West Coast would generate a need for additional cells to accommodate those sailors who would opt for desertion over sailing for the Orient. The JAG advised the secretary of the Navy of the need to once again empty Mare Island cells to make room for an anticipated glut of prisoners from the Atlantic Fleet.

> It is anticipated that a large number of the absentees from the Atlantic Fleet, of which there are 600 now, will be apprehended or surrender after the Fleet sails for the Orient. Owing to the present congested state of the prison at Mare Island, in order to meet the demand that will be made for the accommodation of these men, I respectfully recommend that all the men now serving sentence at that place whose terms of confinement expire after January 1, 1909, be transferred by Government conveyance to the prison ship *Nipsic* at Puget Sound; this would occasion a transfer of about 70 men.[85]

Unable to stem the high desertion rate, the Navy was forced to plan for it. USS *Tennessee* and *Washington* were assigned the task to transfer the seventy prisoners from Mare Island to the *Nipsic* at Puget Sound.[86] Two weeks later, the secretary of the Navy directed the Portsmouth commandant to also "prepare the *Topeka* for service as a prison ship, and place her in service at the earliest possible moment."[87] The new but incomplete Portsmouth Naval Prison was rushed into service in April 1908 to further accommodate the anticipated glut of prisoners.

In 1908 the JAG estimated that the capacity of the naval prison system was about half what was needed. In 1907 Mare Island, with a capacity of 52 prisoners, had an average of 105 prisoners confined. On 1 July 1907, with a capacity of 150 prisoners, Boston had 260 prisoners. The capacity of *Southery* had been doubled without modifications to the ship. *Topeka* with a capacity of 200 prisoners was converted to a prison ship and stationed at Portsmouth to augment *Southery* until the new prison came on line. In 1906 *Nipsic* was fitted out as a prison ship but not put in service for lack of a crew and Marine guards. The ship was later commissioned at Puget Sound, where it shared crews and guards with the receiving ship *Philadelphia*. The Navy was scrambling, making maximum use of prison ships to create enough cells to accommodate its rising prison population.

In 1908 as construction of Portsmouth prison was nearing completion, excess prisoners were being crowded on board prison ships or being released early to make room for the next prisoners. Conditions at the naval prisons were not harsh, and conditions on prison ships were described as comfortable. An expanding Navy was producing increasing numbers of offenders, and the overburdened confinement facilities did not provide an environment sufficient to deter potential offenders. The Navy had a need for a large, modern, intimidating prison to serve as the centerpiece of its naval prison system. Portsmouth prison would fill that need.

6

The Navy Finally Gets a Real Prison
(1908–14)

Viewed from the harbor and river, the completed structure will have the
appearance of an enormous castle, its score or more of castellated turrets
and huge gray walls lending to that structure . . . the largest structure
of its kind in the United States.

—*Boston Daily Globe*, 27 November 1904, "Naval Prison at Portsmouth"

The Navy's longtime dream of having a real prison of its own finally came
to fruition on 11 April 1908 when Portsmouth Naval Prison was commissioned and quickly assumed the preeminent position among naval prisons.
The state prison at Concord, New Hampshire, assumed a similar position of prom-
inence among the three state prisons that confined naval prisoners. Portsmouth
prison, with its adjunct at Concord, soon became the hub of the naval prison system.

In the early 1890s naval authorities began to think seriously about a more permanent solution to the Navy's prisoner confinement needs. A prison on Seavey's Island
at the Portsmouth Navy Yard appeared to be the answer. In October 1891 Secretary
of the Navy Benjamin F. Tracy proposed that a prison be built at Portsmouth Navy
Yard: "A regular prison should be built on Seavey Island, a part of the Portsmouth,
N. H. Navy-yard. There is room not only for the building, but for a proper yard for
exercise as well as for workshops. There is also an inexhaustible supply of granite, to
utilize which would give employment to the prisoners. It is estimated that a suitable
structure can be built for $75,000."[1] Tracy's proposal to build a "regular" prison at
Portsmouth speaks to the temporary nature of the Boston and Mare Island prisons.

Reporting on an inspection of the naval prison at the Boston Navy Yard by the
chief of the Bureau of Yards and Docks, 21 January 1893, the *New York Times* quoted
Commo. N. H. Farquhar as saying, "The present prison [at Boston] is inadequate for
the accommodation of Navy criminals, as it is the only one on the east coast. It is too
small, and it is situated that the convicts are obliged to spend their terms of imprisonment in idleness. It is proposed to enlarge the building or rearrange the interior."[2]
The article further noted, "Commodore Farquhar is in favor of erecting a prison
on Seavey Island near the Portsmouth Navy Yard, where the prisoners would have

an opportunity of working while they are serving their time."[3] Twenty years after Commo. C. R. P. Rodgers had inspected Lewes prison and Lt. Col. J. L. Broome had inspected five northeast prisons with aspirations of gaining congressional approval for a naval prison, the Navy had made little progress toward that goal.

Any discussion about the building of a new naval prison on Seavey's Island was put on hold in the late 1890s when the Navy operated a prison camp on the eventual site of the Portsmouth prison to confine Spanish prisoners from the Spanish–American War. The Navy's positive experience with this prison camp contributed to the ultimate decision to build the Portsmouth Naval Prison on the same site.

CAMP LONG

The haste with which Camp Long was assembled in mid-1898 was nothing short of miraculous. Spanish admiral Cervera's fleet was annihilated on 3 July 1898 at the Battle of Santiago and two weeks later there were 1,610 Spanish prisoners from that battle confined on Seavey's Island at the Portsmouth Navy Yard.

The U.S. Navy forces at the Battle of Santiago were under the direct command of Rear Adm. Winfield Scott Schley who, in 1886 as the chief of the Bureau of Equipment and Recruiting, had led the charge for more consistent and humane shipboard punishment of seamen. As a result of the battle, Schley became involved in an ugly controversy with his boss, Rear Adm. William T. Sampson, who accused him of "procrastination in locating and blockading Cervera."[4] Secretary of the Navy John D. Long, after whom the camp on Seavey's Island was named, advanced Sampson's position only to have President Theodore Roosevelt put an end to the matter when he decided there was "no excuse whatever from either side for any further agitation on this unhappy controversy"[5]

In prior wars, naval prisoners had been turned over to military authorities for confinement. In this case, Navy and Marine Corps authorities decided to confine the Spanish prisoners at a Navy yard with a Marine Corps guard force. Camp Long consisted of eleven barracks buildings, a mess hall, cook house, wash house, and various other buildings (see photo 8, depicting the Camp Long prisoner stockade). The camp was in the process of being closed when Captain Lemly addressed the Proceedings of the Annual Congress of the National Prison Association of the United States in October 1898. That address, quoted earlier in conjunction with the origins of the naval prison system, also reported on the operation of Camp Long in considerable detail. According to Lemly, the site was a most pleasant and favorable one for a prison: "The camp was beautifully located upon elevated ground, with southern exposure, commanding a fine view of the harbor and open to prevailing winds of the summer direct from the water. The site is an exceedingly good one in every respect; in a healthful locality and in a situation generally cool and comfortable in the summer."[6] Had the camp been established and operated during the winter months, the prevailing summer winds might have been cold and snowy, and the report might have been less positive.

Camp Long played to rave reviews, both with U.S. naval authorities and the Spanish prisoners. The camp was clean, medical care was excellent, and the food was of high quality. Discipline was excellent and the prisoners, especially the officers, were treated with dignity and respect. A few quotes from Lemly's address will highlight that Camp Long was a most unusual POW camp, where prisoners gained weight, officers were granted parole and were served wine in their mess, and local citizens brought presents to hospitalized prisoners:

> The average increase in weight in the two months of imprisonment was probably between ten and fifteen pounds. . . . The Spanish physicians and priests were put on parole, so far as the island was concerned. . . . Later this parole was extended to all officers. . . . The commissioned officers had a separate house with servants from the prisoners to wait on them. They had better fare than the rest and claret was served to them. . . . They never broke their parole. . . . Many delicacies were sent [to the sick in the hospital], by kind hearted persons, and flowers were from time to time given to each by ladies going through the wards, while cigarettes and tobacco were distributed by men.[7]

As a final testament to the unusual conditions existing at Camp Long, Lemly noted, "The strongest evidence perhaps of the excellent manner in which this temporary prison was administered is afforded by the fact that when our men-of-war passed in and out of the harbor of Portsmouth they were invariably cheered by their fallen enemy."[8] He also noted that Admiral Cervera visited the camp on 15 August 1898 and was favorably impressed. Cervera received a cordial reception from his men and from the people of the city of Portsmouth.

The Spanish prisoners and Admiral Cervera became tourist attractions during the summer of 1898. According to local Portsmouth historian Dennis Robinson,

> Locals and tourists observed the prisoners from boats in the Piscataqua River and one newspaper even issued a souvenir booklet. Though technically a prisoner, captured Spanish Admiral Pascual Cervera y Topete was allowed to roam the region as he negotiated the release of his officers and men, traveling back and forth from New Hampshire to Annapolis. . . . The public immediately took to the distinguished bearded man in his white suit and cane. They treated him like a superstar. When the admiral visited the Wentworth Hotel in August he was so mobbed by admiring ladies, the paper said, that no one could get within 50 feet of him.[9]

A crowd of admirers, mostly young boys, can be seen following Cervera in a photograph of him walking the streets of Portsmouth—looking very distinguished with his cane, bowler, and bow tie.[10] The Spanish prisoners and their leader were well received by the local residents.

The Navy's positive experience with Camp Long was in sharp contrast to the difficulties being experienced at the Boston and Mare Island prisons where marginal conditions existed because the facilities could not be expanded fast enough to keep up with demands. The success of Camp Long reinforced the earlier conjecture that the Navy's much-needed new prison should be constructed on Seavey's Island at the Portsmouth Navy Yard.

PORTSMOUTH PRISON PRE-COMMISSIONING

The Navy resumed its push for a new prison after the Spanish-American War. On 3 October 1902, a *Portsmouth Herald* headline stated, "Coming to Portsmouth, Naval Prison Likely to Be Removed from Boston, Believed Change Will Be Made in the Near Future, Secretary Moody of the Opinion that Prison Should Be Located Here."[11] According to Secretary of the Navy William H. Moody, "A growing and busy yard like Boston yard was no place for a prison. . . . A much better place for it would be the Portsmouth yard."[12]

Portsmouth Navy Yard was considered a more attractive site for a prison because it was on a quiet, out-of-the-way island as compared with Boston Navy Yard, which was in the heart of a bustling urban area. Ten years after the opening of the prison, Portsmouth would also be a growing and busy yard during World War I. Osborne would find it difficult to implement his progressive prison reform experiment, which relied heavily on prisoner work parties performing tasks throughout the yard, in a bustling wartime industrial environment. Conflicts between prisoners and shipyard employees would prove to be inevitable. Moody's words rang true, "A growing and busy yard . . . was no place for a prison."

On 17 October 1902, the *New York Times* confirmed the Navy's plans to have Portsmouth replace Boston as the primary East Coast naval prison. The newspaper quoted Captain Lemly as saying, "Work on the Boston Prison has stopped and preparations are making to relocate it on Seavey Island, Me., a part of the Portsmouth Navy Yard."[13] As noted earlier, the prison ship *Southery* was moored at a pier near the present site of the Portsmouth prison in 1903 to relieve the overflow of general courts-martial prisoners at Boston. By October 1903 the U.S. Congress had approved the site for the new prison and the Bureau of Yards and Docks was actively soliciting bids for construction. Though officials in Washington were convinced Portsmouth Navy Yard was the best location for the prison, local residents were less sure.

On 18 October 1903, local objections to the prison were expressed in the *Boston Daily Globe* article "Portsmouth Protest. Citizens in that Town Don't Want the Naval Prison There." The article explained, "Capt. Goodrich, commandant of the Portsmouth, NH Navy yard has transmitted to Washington a protest against having the naval prison at that yard." The letter noted that local residents and naval officers questioned the suitability of the Navy yard as a site for a prison and suggested that the land selected for the prison was better suited for the construction of a hospital. The late protest fell on deaf ears. Plans were in place and preparations were under way to build the prison. The hospital recommended as a substitute for the prison was eventually built just a short walk from the main gate of the prison.[14]

When the prison was under construction, observers were in awe of its enormity and unique features. The 27 November 1904 *Boston Daily Globe* reported, "Viewed from the harbor and river, the completed structure will have the appearance of an enormous castle, its score or more of castellated turrets and huge gray walls lending to that structure . . . the largest structure of its kind in the United States."[15] Unlike the Boston prison, where local residents might not even be aware that a prison existed at the yard, the Portsmouth prison would dominate the harbor and proclaim its presence to the most casual observer. During World War II another wing with even more castlelike turrets was added to the prison, enhancing its size and commanding appearance. More than a century after its opening in 1908, the "Castle" remains an imposing structure looking out over the Portsmouth harbor (photo 2 shows the prison, circa 1910, shortly after its commissioning; compare with photo 9, which shows World War II enhancements).

On 22 July 1905, "the biggest explosion and the greatest engineering feat of the 20th century [to that time]" occurred a short distance from the prison construction site. To improve the access to Portsmouth Harbor, fifty tons of dynamite were exploded "to lift an estimated 70,000 tons of rock" and remove the last remnants of Henderson Point. Preparations had started on 29 May 1901: the first granite block was laid for a thirty-five-foot cofferdam to hold back the Piscataqua River, enabling removal of 500,000 tons of rock over four years before the final event that was witnessed by 35,000 people. Pictures taken immediately before and after the historic explosion on 22 July 1905 show the prison impressively in the background looking much as shown in photo 2. The exterior of the prison was completed and the Castle prominently overlooked the harbor in the summer of 1905, almost three years before its commissioning. Completion of the prison interior, however, had slowed for lack of funds.[16]

In his 1906 annual report to Secretary of the Navy Charles J. Bonaparte, the JAG, Capt. S. W. B. Diehl, summarized the status of construction of the new Portsmouth prison. That summary included a plea for the funding needed to complete the authorized work and a recommendation that additional wings be authorized to achieve the Navy Department's goal of consolidating all East Coast naval prisoners in one location:

> The progress of completion of this prison is slow, due to failure in appropriating the necessary funds. The construction of the present wing was commenced on March 11, 1904. . . . On June 30, 1906, all work appropriated for on the prison wing was completed, leaving 25 percent of the authorized work unfinished. . . . The original policy of the Department in deciding upon this prison intended that it should eventually do away with other prisons on the east coast. Its design and location contemplate the possibility of enlarging its capacity by the addition of wings, equal in number of cells to the present one. The increase in personnel of the service and its needs have far outstripped the progress of construction of this prison, and preparations and estimates for a second wing in the immediate future can not, it is believed, be much longer

delayed without detriment to the interests of the service. Moreover, it would appear to be a wise economy to have one prison of adequate capacity for military offenders assigned to confinement of the east coast than several widely separated as at present. More than 82 percent of all naval prisoners are consigned to prisons on the east coast.[17]

Despite its impressive size, the original design of Portsmouth prison was predicted to fall far short of the Navy's growing need for cells. Before it had even opened, plans were under way to greatly expand the prison.

PORTSMOUTH PRISON EARLY YEARS

With the Navy desperate for cells, the new prison at Portsmouth was rushed into service in an incomplete state. The prison received its first prisoners on 11 April 1908, and by 1 July, 151 prisoners had been processed. Initially the commanding officer, Col. Allan C. Kelton, USMC, had more complaints about Marine guards than prisoners. In his first annual report (14 July 1908) to the secretary of the Navy he wrote, "Owing to the urgent demand for Marines, ten [of an initial assignment of forty-two Marine guards] of my command were transferred for duty in Panama and just following this serious reduction, three privates of this command became involved in some alleged rascality and they are now held in confinement awaiting action, while two of the total have been discharged and one deserted, and one sergeant transferred to Boston because of his uselessness." With the Marine detachment seriously under-staffed owing to transfers, rascality, desertion, and uselessness, he added, "I am obliged to keep a large number [of prisoners] in their cells all day and this is unfortunate as I am anxious to accomplish much grading and clearing this summer."[18] The commanding officer had planned to employ prisoner labor to continue the construction of the incomplete prison.

The JAG's 1908 annual report noted that the unfinished prison was opened prematurely because of an urgent need for cells: "The one wing now built is in an incomplete state, as it was intended to contain 320 cells, and but 160 have been installed, funds running out after this number were completed. . . . Owing to the very urgent necessity for additional prison facilities during the past winter, the department authorized the occupation of this prison in spite of the unfavorable conditions."[19] Portsmouth prison, commissioned with 160 cells, quickly expanded to the designed capacity of 320 cells. Plans were immediately developed for expansion to accommodate 1,200 prisoners. However, the JAG noted, "These added facilities will improve conditions, but the situation will be far from satisfactory. There should be accommodations for 2,000 prisoners, and it is recommended that Congress be requested to appropriate for a further extension of the prison at Portsmouth, NH."[20]

The physical surroundings and the environment at the new Portsmouth prison were harsher than those at the Boston prison forty-five miles to the south. The Boston prisoners wore the uniform of the day, but Portsmouth prisoners wore distinctive prison garb as Capt. A. S. Williams, USMC, had recommended in his U.S. Naval

Institute *Proceedings* article (1904). Robert J. Verge's *A History of the U.S. Naval Prison at Portsmouth, New Hampshire* (1946) confirms the wearing of distinctive prison clothing: "The prisoners wore uniforms with huge yellow numbers painted across the backs of their coats, the front of their shirts, and on the knees of their trousers. The repeaters wore red-legged pants with a red band around the bottom of their coats giving rise to their nickname, 'red legs.' The prisoners wore their hair close cropped in conformance with the prison policy of the day."[21]

Unlike the inactivity and "police duties" assigned at Boston, Portsmouth prisoners, from the time the prison was commissioned, worked in the prison shops and were assigned duties throughout the Navy yard. Duties at the prison included assignments in the garden, bakery, laundry, carpenter shop, shoe shop, stable, and blacksmith shop. Verge wrote, "The work was long and hard and entertainment scarce."[22] The environment at the new prison was much more intimidating and threatening than that at the Boston prison. Perhaps the Navy, at last, had a facility able to deter potential offenders.

Naïve young sailors proved difficult to threaten, and the high desertion rates continued. Desertion during peacetime was often the result of a young sailor's ignorance or misunderstanding of naval regulations, as opposed to attempts to flee from hardships and rigors of naval service. The "new" prison still had to deal with the "old" problem of young, immature sailors deserting without considering the consequences. The several case studies that follow tell the stories of a few of the young sailors sentenced to Portsmouth prison for desertion during the early years of the prison.

About six months after the commissioning of the prison, a young love-struck sailor was sentenced to Portsmouth for desertion. The 20 November 1908 *New York Times* reported, "Secretary [of the Navy] Metcalf today approved the sentence in the case of Charles J. Hartlove, musician first class, (alias C. J. Magness) who left the service to marry the daughter of the late Senator P. Gorman of Maryland . . . [he was sentenced to] one year at the naval prison, Portsmouth, NH, at the end of which he is to be dishonorably discharged."[23] What was the sailor's reason for deserting? Curiously, Hartlove's name was an appropriate match for the crime of heart he had committed. Hartlove's counsel pled that Hartlove "was in a state of mind that might be called delirium of anticipation of his honeymoon."[24] Delirious or not, Hartlove, and many other young sailors, ended up serving time at Portsmouth for precipitous or frivolous actions that translated to military offenses. Not to be overlooked is that Hartlove had enlisted under an alias, suggesting that the Navy was still grappling with the problem of fraudulent enlistments.

Another deserter with an appropriate name for a prisoner, Charles Crook, found some unexpected leniency when his sentence of two years six months at Portsmouth prison was reduced to nine months. However, the circumstances that sentenced him to Portsmouth in the first place were anything but lenient. Crook had deserted after being denied leave to attend to his brother and sister after his father had murdered his mother in Dayton, Ohio. Court-martialed and sentenced to Portsmouth, he was serving his sentence when his family petitioned the Navy for his release because of the father's pending execution in Columbus, Ohio. Showing that the Navy judicial system was not totally lacking in sympathy, Crook, who had been a model prisoner on the *Southery*, was released after serving only nine months of this sentence in January 1909.[25]

SM Arthur V. Monahan was another naïve young man who, because of unfortunate circumstances, found himself at Portsmouth prison serving time for desertion. Seaman Monahan's request for clemency, dated 28 September 1913, describes how he failed to return from leave in New York City, where he was attending his destitute, psychotic, and distraught wife, who had just given birth to his son. He had no money for transportation back to his ship in Boston. After conscientiously reporting his situation to local naval authorities, he found work to raise some money for transportation but was picked up and charged with desertion before he could return to his ship.

Unaware of the seriousness of the charge against him and understanding that he would get off with a light sentence if he pled guilty, he did so as advised by his Navy counsel. After his guilty plea, Monahan understood that he was sentenced to two and one half years at Portsmouth prison, but when he arrived at Portsmouth he learned that the sentence was actually five years.[26] The archival records do not explain this discrepancy in sentencing. Perhaps Monahan misunderstood his sentence. Perhaps he committed some offense during confinement that doubled his sentence. Though sentences were severe, the prison system, as previously noted, was not without mercy. Monahan's request for clemency was favorably endorsed and he departed Portsmouth prison a few months later. Seaman Monahan and many of his Portsmouth inmates were inexperienced and naïve young men who had run afoul of a rather harsh military justice system. Not all were as fortunate as Monahan.

Sentences at Portsmouth often had less successful outcomes than those of Hartlove, Crook, and Monahan; occasionally the outcomes were a matter or life or death. The latter was the case in late January 1910. Three prisoners fled from a work party in the Navy yard and attempted to escape from the island in a stolen boat. They had only gotten a few hundred feet into the Piscataqua River when the guards caught up with them and demanded their surrender. When the demand was disregarded the guards opened fire, killing one and wounding the other two prisoners. The prisoners, unfortunately, had been on the receiving end of a recent order encouraging guards to fire early at prisoners attempting to escape. The 29 January 1910 *Boston Daily Globe* reported, "Owing to recent escapes . . . guards in charge of prisoners have been cautioned to fire at any prisoner attempting to run. Failure to do this and allow prisoners to escape meant for the guard to serve the sentence that was being imposed on the prisoner."[27] Tragically, these prisoners "were serving short terms for minor offenses."[28] If too many sailors found their way to Portsmouth prison for frivolous reasons, there were also too many who compounded their problems, once there, with actions that added to their sentences or, as in this extreme case, took a young sailor's life.

Shortly after opening, the prison was frequently a subject of curiosity in the local press. The 25 January 1909 *Portsmouth Herald* reported how a crew of naval prisoners rescued a shipyard workman from suffocation. Keep in mind that January is typically a bitter cold month at the yard and working outside under the best of conditions can be an unpleasant challenge. Cold temperatures, however, were the least of concerns for Timothy Kiley, a watchman at the yard's coal pile that day.

Kiley had been on top of a pile of coal taking the temperature of the coal "when the pile began to slide toward one of the chutes and Kiley went with it."[29] The paper vividly described Kiley's adventure: "He shot down the tube to the bottom of the pocket and enough coal came after to completely bury his body. When near the bottom, his body stuck and there he remained hard and fast, slowly smothering in the close quarters and no way of freeing himself. Nothing but death faced him, as he was unable to make any cry that could be heard and he made up his mind that he must die."[30]

Fortunately "one of the crew [of prisoners] got a glimpse of Kiley's leg hanging from the chute . . . [and] hurried to his assistance and after much hard work released the man in an exhausted condition from the death trap."[31] Understandably, the article closed with the observation that Kiley "was unable to go to work for a day or so after."[32] Timothy Kiley must have been especially pleased that the Navy had decided to open a prison at his shipyard.

By 1916 many prisoners were actively and productively employed at the prison and the Navy yard. JAG Capt. Ridley McLean noted, "At Portsmouth N.H . . . the prisoners are employed as much as possible in the open air . . . care of buildings and prison surroundings, running a large garden, . . . clearing snow, getting out rock, and harvesting ice. About 1,800 tons of ice were cut last winter for use at the Navy yard . . . machine shop, blacksmith shop, carpenter shop, electrical shop, in the laundry, and in repairing shoes, and printing."[33] Cutting 1,800 tons of ice could keep many prisoners productively employed for a long time.

About the same time, tests revealed that a high percentage of prisoners lacked a basic education. Surveys indicated that only 40 percent of incoming prisoners had achieved an education level of sixth grade. A grammar school and basic trade-school training classes were organized in 1916 under the supervision of the chaplain.[34] A few years later, Osborne and his primary assistant, Austin MacCormick, significantly expanded the scope and content of the education program. Later in his career, Austin MacCormick became one of the world's foremost authorities on prison education.

Portsmouth prison was a much more imposing structure, with a harsher and more demanding confinement environment, than existed at the makeshift prisons at Boston and Mare Island. The Navy finally had a threatening prison environment to deter potential offenders. Portsmouth prisoners, unlike those at Boston, wore distinctive prison garb and were required to work in prison shops and at other shipyard worksites. A high percentage of the prisoners were young, uneducated, and misguided sailors who had deserted for frivolous reasons. Too frequently they compounded their problems with inappropriate behavior while serving their sentences. Portsmouth prison was no sooner commissioned than plans were under way to double its capacity. The prison was poised to quickly assume the dominant position among naval prisons.

7

The Naval Prison System Matures
(1914–17)

It will be seen that the establishment of the detention system and the consequent ability to segregate offenders of the different classes [suggests that] the whole subject of the treatment of prisoners in the Navy has, in general, been developed along modern prison reform.

—Acting Secretary of the Navy Beckman Winthrop, 1913

With the expansion of Portsmouth prison, the Navy was finally able to establish an effective prison system. A massive reorganization in 1914 left only two naval prisons, Portsmouth on the East Coast and Mare Island on the West Coast. The purpose of the reorganization was to consolidate and standardize prison operations to achieve more uniform treatment of prisoners, to reduce costs, and to be able to separate prisoners according to the seriousness of their offenses.

The Navy, questioning the wisdom of filling much-needed prison cells with young naïve sailors convicted of minor military offenses, sought another solution to its problem. The solution introduced a new concept in naval discipline, a system of disciplinary barracks to rehabilitate lesser offenders with high potential for restoration. A three-tier prison system resulted that achieved the desired separation of prisoners while providing relief to the overcrowded naval prisons and prison ships. Criminals were sentenced to state prisons, those men guilty of military offenses with little potential for restoration were sentenced to naval prisons and prison ships, and those convicted of minor military offenses with high restoration potential were sentenced to disciplinary barracks for rehabilitation.

The naval prisoner population on 1 January 1908, immediately before Portsmouth prison opened and before any disciplinary barracks were established, was 696 (the distribution of prisoners is shown below in parentheses).[1]

USS *Southery*, Portsmouth, New Hampshire (303)

Boston Naval Prison (228)

USS *Hancock*, New York Navy Yard (1)

> Mare Island Naval Prison (114)
>
> USS *Nipsic*, Puget Sound Navy Yard (10) (held on *Philadelphia* until *Nipsic* was ready)
>
> Cavite Naval Prison (20)
>
> Connecticut State Prison at Wethersfield (14)
>
> California State Prison at San Quentin (6)

The *Southery* was overloaded with prisoners in anticipation of the opening of the new prison. The prison ship *Nipsic* had been positioned at Puget Sound to provide relief for Mare Island. Only a few naval prisoners were at the two state prisons and none at New Hampshire state prison.

Portsmouth opened for business on 11 April 1908, and within one year the naval prison system was overloaded; as discussed in chapter 5, the imminent deployment of the Great White Fleet had generated increased numbers of naval prisoners. The 14 March 1909 *Boston Daily Globe* reported that the sudden increase in naval prisoners resulted from a high number of discipline problems on the ships participating in the world-circling tour: "The result of the many court-martials which are said to have taken place on the ships that participated in the world circling tour are beginning to be felt at this Navy yard [Portsmouth] where the naval prisoner ships *Southery* and *Topeka* are stationed."[2] The *Globe* reported that more than one hundred prisoners had recently arrived at Portsmouth, including thirty prisoners from ships at Hampton Roads, twenty-four prisoners from Norfolk ships, and thirty prisoners from Philadelphia ships. In addition, another two hundred or three hundred men were believed to be under sentence or awaiting court martial. The *Globe* noted that the recently opened Portsmouth prison "had its full quota of men and both the prison ships *Southery* and *Topeka* have about all the men they can handle."

The naval prisoner population explosion continued, nearly doubling from 696 prisoners in 1908 to 1,669 prisoners in 1912. The prisoners were distributed throughout the newly created three-tier naval discipline system, which now included disciplinary barracks, as follows:[3]

> Portsmouth Naval Prison, Portsmouth Navy Yard, New Hampshire (578)
>   Including the prison ship USS *Southery*
>
> Boston Naval Prison, Boston Navy Yard, Massachusetts (131)
>
> Cob Dock (New York) Naval Prison, New York Navy Yard, New York (42)
>
> Norfolk Naval Prison, Norfolk Navy Yard, Virginia (16)
>
> Mare Island Naval Prison, Mare Island Navy Yard, California (192)
>
> Cavite Naval Prison, Philippine Islands (58)
>
> U.S. Naval Disciplinary Barracks, Port Royal, South Carolina (312)
>
> U.S. Naval Disciplinary Barracks, Puget Sound Navy Yard, Bremerton, Washington (99)

USS *Nipsic*, Puget Sound Navy Yard, Bremerton, Washington (45)

USS *Philadelphia*, Puget Sound Navy Yard, Bremerton, Washington (6)
  In the process of replacing USS *Nipsic*

Connecticut State Prison, Wethersfield, Connecticut (25)

New Hampshire State Prison, Concord, New Hampshire (59)

California State Prison, San Quentin, California (28)

Other ships, probation, etc. (108)

The table highlights two important changes to the naval prison system. First, the newly introduced disciplinary barracks at Port Royal, South Carolina, and Puget Sound, Washington, had begun to provide much needed relief to the overcrowded prisons. Second, the center of gravity of the naval prison system had shifted decidedly in the direction of Portsmouth. The new Portsmouth prison and *Southery*, moored at a nearby pier, had more prisoners than all the other naval prisons and prison ships combined. Likewise, the state prison at Concord, New Hampshire, had more naval prisoners than the total number of prisoners at the other two state prisons. Concord had become the state prison of choice for naval prisoners, and Portsmouth held the same distinction among naval prisons.

Immediately prior to the opening of the Boston and Mare Island prisons in 1888 the JAG was accounting for fewer than one hundred courts-martial prisoners annually among all of the numerous facilities. Twenty-five years later, Portsmouth prison alone was processing more than five hundred prisoners annually, with expectations of doubling that number in the near future. Naval prisons had become a huge, expensive operation consuming massive resources. The Navy Department, struggling with how best to manage those resources, had decided that a system of naval disciplinary barracks might be the solution.

NAVAL DISCIPLINARY BARRACKS

Secretary of the Navy Josephus Daniels must be credited with many naval prison reforms during his tenure between 5 March 1913 and 6 March 1921. Daniels' predecessor, George von L. Meyer, also deserves credit for making an important contribution to naval discipline. The naval disciplinary barracks were established near the end of Meyer's tenure, giving deserving prisoners better confinement conditions and increased opportunities for rehabilitation. The change was in total consonance with the progressive prison reforms gaining favor in the civilian sector.

The 17 August 1911 *Christian Science Monitor* reported about a naval detention camp at Port Royal, South Carolina, established to rehabilitate young sailors guilty of military offenses. Reflecting a growing sentiment for prison reform nationwide, the newspaper stated, "The punitive idea wanes. The reformative and education principle waxes." The article described important changes to naval discipline that would result in less harsh punishments and better separation of first offenders from seasoned criminals. "Secretary Meyer and Assistant Secretary Winthrop are determined to put an end to harsh and fast methods of dealing with offenders against naval discipline. . . . They do not believe that the desertion of a raw recruit deserves anything like the severe punishment hitherto awarded. . . . They refuse to huddle first offenders with seasoned criminals. . . . Offending seamen are to be disciplined but also trusted."[4] Confinement conditions at the disciplinary barracks were much less harsh than those at the naval prisons and prison ships. Instead of merely serving time for punishment, the emphasis at the disciplinary barracks was on receiving shipboard training and acquiring skills that would be helpful when the sailor returned to the fleet.

In August 1912 the *Portsmouth Herald* attributed the early success of the barracks at Port Royal to a well-known local Marine Corps officer, Maj. Charles Hatch. According to the *Herald*, Hatch was "exceptionally well known here [Portsmouth] having been stationed here first as a second lieutenant at Camp Long during the Spanish war, and then as second in command at the [Portsmouth] naval prison. . . . He is not only in command of the U. S. detention camp at Port Royal but as one of the originators of the idea . . . has been officially commended several times by Secretary Von Meyer of the Navy and by the leading naval officers."[5] According to the *Herald*, "The great increase in the number of prisoners at the naval prison here [Portsmouth] and Boston aroused the naval authorities to the fact that there was something radically wrong with the system which made so many prisoners."[6] The disciplinary barracks system had gotten off to a good start under Hatch.

Disciplinary barracks were intended for (1) deserters who surrendered, (2) prisoners under the age of twenty-one previously sentenced to confinement at hard labor in naval prisons, and (3) older prisoners who had exhibited exemplary behavior while serving sentences at naval prisons. Military offenders serving sentences at naval prisons now had a better chance of restoration through advancement to the disciplinary barracks, where they would no longer associate with criminals.[7] Sailors assigned to the disciplinary barracks were called detentioners instead of prisoners. They wore naval uniforms instead of prison garb and performed daily drills and tasks rather than hard labor.[8] Detentioners fared far better than their nineteenth-century predecessors who were flogged, confined in double irons, or deprived of shore liberty for months on end. The Navy had changed with the times.

THE CHANGING NAVAL PRISONER

The naval discipline and prison system that evolved during the early twentieth century paralleled the progressive societal changes of the times. That evolution was heavily influenced by the changing attributes of American sailors who bore little resemblance to their counterparts in the "old Navy."

At mid-nineteenth century, the crews of American ships were dominated by foreigners, hooligans, and ruffians who were frequently whipped for crimes of debauchery and aggressive behavior. The review of midcentury punishment reports (chapter 2) show the following most frequent offenses: Drunkenness, Disobedience, Fighting,

Insolence & Insubordination & Disrespect, Neglect of Duty, Desertion & AWOL, and Smuggling Liquor. The sampling of postflogging shipboard punishments of the 1870s and 1880s (reviewed in chapter 3) reveal American crews with less violent habits, committing fewer aggressive crimes. Instead, they were more likely to fall astray of naval regulations, especially desertion and AWOL. Early twentieth-century sailors reflected the Navy's increased emphasis on recruitment of a higher-quality young American sailor. Innocent, and often unaware of the rigors of the sailor's life, he was even more likely to have difficulties adjusting to rules and regulations.

Prisoner interviews were initiated at Portsmouth prison in 1911 to determine "the physical and mental effect of confinement on each prisoner." The interviews also obtained prisoner profiles "by means of a Binet test for intelligence levels."[9] These tests showed that the typical sailor at Portsmouth prison during its early years was far removed from "Poor Jack" of the mid-nineteenth century who required corporal punishment to keep him in line. In 1911 the prison commander, Maj. Henry Leonard described the typical Portsmouth prisoner as an immature adolescent with questionable habits. "From inspecting and questioning every prisoner when he is discharged . . . the vast majority bear the marks of early adolescence: e.g., all began using tobacco (invariably cigarettes) at an average age of 16.1 years; sixty-four percent began taking intoxicating beverages at an average age of 18.1 years. These figures suggest that the men in question were not fit, by reason of undisciplined youth and previous irregularity of life, to seriously consider a term of enlistment."[10] The teenage activities used to illustrate undisciplined teenage years—smoking by age sixteen and drinking by age eighteen—are hardly considered to induce criminal behavior by today's standards. The tests confirmed suspicions that many of the young men did not know what they were getting into when they joined the Navy. Once in the Navy, they were not equipped with the self-discipline needed to survive in an environment centered on strict compliance to rules and regulations.

Convinced that many of the prisoners were not hardened criminals, Major Leonard thought rehabilitation had its merits: "One or two years of all work and no play certainly induced thoughtfulness and brings realization of the seriousness of life that was never suggested in their previous careless way of living. . . . Thus a few of these men before or at the expiration of their sentences would make excellent men for the service and were much more valuable than the untutored recruit."[11] Leonard was not a progressive reformer by any stretch of the imagination; he was a hardened veteran of the Boxer Rebellion, during which he had been wounded and lost an arm on the march to Peking.[12] His background would stand in sharp contrast to that of Thomas Mott Osborne, a privileged civilian and short-term naval reservist who never saw any combat except for the political battles that he seemed to precipitate ad nauseam.

Major Leonard's enthusiasm for restoration produced few results. The Navy was channeling restorations through the disciplinary barracks at that time; direct restorations at naval prisons remained low. There was another factor that contributed to the low number of restorations: rehabilitation did not enjoy a high priority because the Navy and the Marine Corps did not have a shortage of manpower. In 1914, pursuant to the possible rehabilitation of three Marines at Portsmouth prison, the JAG explained that recruitment was good and the need for restorations was low: "It has been noted that the Commandant of the Marine Corps has not viewed with favor restoration of duty of men convicted by general court-martial on account of the fact that the personnel of the Marine Corps is recruited to full strength and at present there is no difficulty in obtaining recruits."[13] The need for manpower would change dramatically a few years later with the start of World War I, and Osborne would readily accommodate that need.

Although the typical naval prisoner had changed, there was one aspect of naval discipline that had not. One of the leading offenses in 1850, desertion in its many forms, increased in popularity later in the century and remained popular well into the twentieth century. A high percentage of the Portsmouth prisoners before World War I were deserters (figure 6). In 1912 three-quarters of Portsmouth's prisoners were committed for desertion (66 percent) or desertion combined with another charge (11 percent). It can be concluded that the Navy's various efforts to bring desertion under control had been largely unsuccessful. Although desertion was by far the most prevalent offense, other leading reasons for confinement at Portsmouth are shown in table 4. (Table 4 accounts for the difference between the total and deserters bars in figure 6.) Drunkenness was not one of the leading offenses attributed to prisoners at Portsmouth; the 1848 punishment data showed that 28 percent of those offenses were related to drunkenness. Among the total population of naval prisoners in 1912 (1,699), only one sailor served a sentence for drunkenness and only forty-six (3 percent) were incarcerated for multiple offenses including drunkenness.[14] The abolishment of the daily spirits ration in 1862 and improved screening of recruits had contributed significantly to reduced drunkenness. Also, officers were now apparently more tolerant of drunkenness ashore unless it also involved more serious offenses.

Recorded sex crimes and morality offenses were rare in 1848; however, an appreciable number of sentences for scandalous conduct and sodomy were served at Portsmouth (table 4). Most of these offenders would end up at Concord. For example, the fifty-eight naval prisoners committed to Concord in 1912 served sentences for offenses involving scandalous conduct (16 percent), sodomy (12 percent), or some combination of offenses including scandalous conduct (35 percent). Morality offenses, or at least the reporting and prosecution of such offenses, had increased significantly by 1912.

The Navy's classifying of sex offenders as criminals and requiring that all criminals be imprisoned separately from other offenders often resulted in young sailors guilty of morality offenses being confined with hardened criminals. Because the state prison at Concord was reserved for "those convicted [of] offenses involving moral turpitude or violation of general laws of the country,"[15] young sailors were often incarcerated with the dregs of society. The practice of confining sexual offenders with hardened criminals would become a contentious issue during Osborne's tenure. Osborne, who was much more sympathetic to such offenders than were naval regulations and naval authorities, resisted transferring these prisoners to Concord.

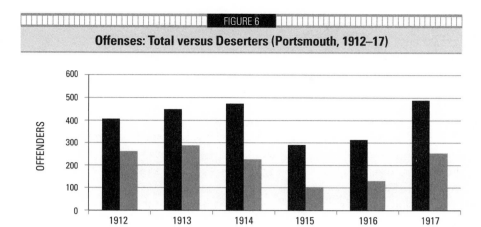

FIGURE 6

Offenses: Total versus Deserters (Portsmouth, 1912–17)

■ *Total*   ■ *Deserters*

Source: Commanding Officer Portsmouth Naval Prison, *Annual Reports for the Fiscal Years Ending 30 June 1912–1917,* NARA Waltham, RG 181, Portsmouth General Collection.

Table 4   Leading Offenses other than Desertion (Portsmouth, 1912–17)

Offense	1912	1913	1914	1915	1916	1917
AWOL	10	4	7	10	29	113
Fraudulent Enlistment	64	76	77	18	10	0
Theft	17	6	17	19	22	33
Assault	3	5	10	18	16	11
Scandalous Conduct	2	11	27	34	17	17
Sodomy	0	1	5	7	2	7

Source: Commanding Officer Portsmouth Naval Prison, *Annual Reports for the Fiscal Years Ending 30 June 1912–1917,* NARA Waltham, RG 181, Portsmouth General Collection.

Fraudulent enlistments plagued the Navy well into the twentieth century (see table 4). The remarkable drop in fraudulent enlistments with the advent of World War I suggests there may have been less scrutiny of enlistments as the need for enlisted men increased. Similarly, some thought that Osborne's remarkable increase in restorations at Portsmouth prison during the war was more the result of reduced scrutiny than improved methods of rehabilitation. The dramatic increase in AWOL convictions in 1917 also reflected the dynamics of a war environment; once in the military, many apparently decided it was not the place to be during a war.

In summary, "Poor Jack" was long gone by 1915 and the typical naval prisoner was an inexperienced young sailor without the self-discipline to adjust to the naval service. Desertion in its various forms remained high, drunkenness was no longer the problem it once had been, and morality offenses were more prevalent and dealt with more severely. The changes in the naval discipline system, especially the newly created detention system, reflected the Navy's determined efforts to adjust to the new naval prisoner.

Acting Secretary of the Navy Beckman Winthrop's 7 January 1913 report to the Senate stressed the Navy's recent changes: "It will be seen that the establishment of the detention system and the consequent ability to segregate offenders of the different classes [suggests that] the whole subject of the treatment of prisoners in the Navy has, in general, been developed along modern prison reform."[16] With the disciplinary barracks assuming a large number of the prisoners previously committed to naval prisons, the secretary of the Navy also reported, "The naval prisons and prison ships, which, prior to the inauguration of the detention system, were inadequate and constantly overcrowded, are now ample."[17] The naval prison system finally appeared to be under control thanks to the new mega-prison at Portsmouth and the successful implementation of the disciplinary barracks system. The naval prison system, although effective, had grown like Topsy. It was spread out, expensive, and ripe for consolidation. The new secretary of the Navy, Josephus Daniels, would lead that consolidation.

NAVAL PRISON REORGANIZATION OF 1914

Daniels, who assumed office on 5 March 1913 with a strong commitment to naval reform, decided to include naval prisons in his reform agenda. After a tour of Portsmouth prison in the summer of 1913 he noted, "The most archaic prison practice prevailed" and expressed his belief that "we ought to mend, not break prisoners."[18] With impressions of Portsmouth prison fresh in mind, he revised the naval prison system in 1914 to treat military offenses less seriously, reduce the number of prisoners in confinement for military offenses, and reduce prison costs. The result was a consolidation of naval prisons and detention centers that positioned Portsmouth prison to play an even more important role within the community of naval prisons.

One of the first steps toward consolidation was the short notice closing of Boston prison on 25 April 1914 and the transfer of all 150 prisoners to Portsmouth. The commanding officer of the Boston prison was Capt. H. South, USMC. He is the same officer who would later reverse the reforms Lt. Cdr. Thomas Mott Osborne, USN, had installed at Portsmouth prison. At the time some people thought that the prisoners were moved to free up the Boston Marine guard contingent for duty in Mexico, as World War I was heating up.[19] Instead, the prisoner transfers were the first stage of Daniels' grand plan.

The naval prisoner population was 1,271 in June 1914 (distribution shown in table 5). This lineup bears a close resemblance to that of 1912, with the notable exception that the Boston prison is gone. The disciplinary barracks continued to house slightly more than four hundred detentioners just as they did in 1912. Portsmouth and *Southery*, which assumed even larger roles, now had more than twice as many prisoners as the rest of the naval prisons and prison ships combined. The Navy, though initially pleased with the disciplinary barracks, decided within a few years that "the expense of the detention system was out of all proportion to its results." Studies had shown "the percentage of those reclaimed after a period of detention is approximately [only] 33⅓."[20] The Navy found a more cost-effective way to achieve the same goal. The disciplinary barracks were replaced with disciplinary ships co-located at naval prison sites, where costs and resources could be shared.

Daniels' consolidation of naval prisons in 1914 made the shift to disciplinary ships and cut the number of Navy prison facilities in half, from the eight (table 5) to four (table 6). More important, the number of prison sites was reduced to just two, with *Southery* moored at Portsmouth and *Philadelphia* moored at Mare Island. *Philadelphia* was towed from Puget Sound Naval Shipyard in Bremerton, Washington, to Mare Island Naval Shipyard and docked near the Mare Island Naval Prison. *Southery* was already moored adjacent to Portsmouth Naval Prison. The Port Royal detention facility was turned over to the Marine Corps for a recruit depot that eventually became Parris Island. The closing of the disciplinary barracks at Port

Table 5	Geographic Distribution of Naval Prisoners before 1914 Prisoner Consolidation		
Location		*Number*	*Status*
State Prisons		152	Criminal Offense
Naval Prison, Portsmouth, NH		304	Military Offense
Naval Prison, USS *Southery* at Portsmouth, NH		196	Military Offense
Naval Prison, Norfolk, VA		13	Military Offense
Naval Prison, Cavite, Philippines		22	Military Offense
Naval Prison, Mare Island, CA		126	Military Offense
Naval Prison, USS *Philadelphia* at Puget Sound, WA		43	Military Offense
Disciplinary Barracks, Port Royal, SC		290	Retraining for service
Disciplinary Barracks, Puget Sound, WA		125	Retraining for service
	TOTAL	1,271	

Source: Judge Advocate General letter, 12 August 1914, NARA Waltham, RG 181, Portsmouth General Collection.

Table 6	Geographic Distribution of Naval Prisoners after 1914 Prisoner Consolidation		
	Portsmouth	*USS Southery*	*Mare Island*	*USS Philadelphia*
Normal Capacity	330	300	124	150
Maximum Capacity	500	400	210	170
Estimated Prisoners	385	130		
Estimated Detentioners			226	90

Source: Judge Advocate General letter, 12 August 1914, NARA Waltham, RG 181, Portsmouth General Collection.

Royal and Puget Sound, and the transfer of detentioner responsibilities to *Southery* and *Philadelphia*, resulted in considerable savings of personnel and funds. The consolidation reduced the total requirements for Marine Corps guards at the prisons from 21 officers and 836 enlisted men to 8 officers and 500 enlisted men and reduced operating costs accordingly.[21]

The consolidation left Portsmouth the much larger of the two naval prison sites. Thus, Daniels could most effectively implement his hopes for prison reform by focusing his efforts at Portsmouth. A few years later, when the East Coast became the staging area for the European theater of World War I operations, the number of inmates at Portsmouth increased dramatically and Portsmouth assumed even more importance within the naval prison system. There could have been no doubt in Daniels' mind that prison reform would have the greatest impact if implemented at Portsmouth Naval Prison.

GENERAL ORDER 110

In 1915 the Navy supplemented the reorganization with what the JAG described as "probably the most radical disciplinary measure that has ever been placed in operation in the Navy."[22] General Order 110 continued the Navy's move toward more humanitarian treatment of prisoners; it introduced a probation system that allowed some offenders to continue in service at reduced pay. Instead of being sent to a detention ship, military offenders with a high probability of successful restoration were permitted to remain on their ships at reduced pay and earn restoration with good behavior.

General Order 110 also targeted offenders with little or no potential for restoration for immediate discharge from the service. Offenders "guilty of certain offenses which demonstrate unfitness for the service, but which are not of a nature to render imprisonment essential for the maintenance of discipline were summarily [dishonorably] discharged instead of being imprisoned."[23] The immediate effect of the order was to rid the Navy of large numbers of chronic liberty offenders while giving deserving sailors the opportunity to avoid the stigma of imprisonment and to earn restoration.[24]

The effect on the naval prison system was dramatic. During FY 1915, 3,080 men were discharged from the Navy as the result of summary courts-martial. This was 1,278 more prisoners than the average number discharged the previous three years. The number of naval prisoners and detentioners was reduced from 1,835 on 1 April 1915 to 740 on 1 October 1915. Suddenly the naval prison system had excess capacity and was overstaffed. In his annual report for FY 1916, the JAG, Capt. Ridley McLean, summarized the positive contribution that General Order 110 and the new probation system had made to reducing the population of naval prisoners while improving discipline and reducing costs: "The system of probation . . . has been established on a permanent basis after fully demonstrating its merit . . . a reduction of more than 66 percent has been effected in the number of men imprisoned under previous systems, the number of naval prisons has correspondingly been reduced, discipline has been improved, as is almost unanimously testified to by commanding officers, and at the same time a saving [has been realized] . . . of more than $850,000 each year."[25] McLean went on to highlight the recent changes to the naval prison system: "Since April 1914, the following penal institutions have been closed: Naval prison, Navy yard, Boston, Mass.; U.S.S. *Philadelphia*, and U.S.S. *Topeka*, which have been totally abandoned as prison ships and returned to other duty in the Navy; and the disciplinary barracks at Port Royal, S.C., and Puget Sound, Wash." McLean closed his report, "I point with pride to the above enumerated results accomplished by this reform."[26] It appeared the Navy had finally gained control of its prisoner confinement needs with the caveat that the new probation system would continue to perform as expected. With World War I on the horizon, that would not remain the case for long.

On the Eve of World War I

On the eve of World War I, the Navy had made significant progress and achieved considerable success with is naval prison system as the result of the 1914 reorganization and General Order 110. Unfortunately, World War I and the need to treat military offenses more seriously during wartime would reverse much of that success.

When war was declared on 6 April 1917, the new probation system had enjoyed a two-year success rate of about 40 percent, meaning 40 percent of those in the system achieved full restoration within one year. The positive affect of General Order 110 and the Navy's new probation system on the eve of World War I is apparent in table 7.[27] The number of detentioners processed annually dropped precipitously with General Order 110 and the implementation of the probation system in 1915. During the same period, the number of prisoners sentenced to naval prisons remained relatively stable. Table 8 shows the Navy's total number of personnel versus confined prisoners on 30 June during the years 1914–17.[28] This table also shows the success of the probation system with the drop in detentioners confined on 30 June in 1916 and 1917. The Navy's goal of ridding the Navy of military offenders judged to be unfit for naval service and maximizing restoration opportunities for the deserving appeared to be working well.

The probation system remained in effect during the war with far less application because minor offenses during peacetime, especially the various forms of desertion, became major offenses during wartime. The JAG, Capt. W. C. Watts, confirmed the reduced application of General Order 110 during the war in his annual report for FY 1917: "The outbreak of the war found this system [General Order 110] in operation as previously, and during the first nine months of the fiscal year a large number of men were placed on probation in accordance with this provision, both as regards discharge and loss of pay. Thereafter, in view of the greater seriousness attaching to all offenses in time of war, comparatively few sentences of general courts-martial have been remitted in accordance with General Order 110. . . . Furthermore, the schedule of punishments published therein is obviously inapplicable to war conditions."[29] The

Table 7	Naval Prisoners Confined during Fiscal Year (1914–17)			
	1914	*1915*	*1916*	*1917*
Detention	1,534	644	367	252
Naval prisons	1,409	1,445	1,351	1,418
State prisons	251	208	167	133

Source: Annual Reports of the Judge Advocate General for the Fiscal Years 1914–17. Navy Department Library.

Table 8	Naval Personnel versus Naval Prisoners Confined on 30 June (1914–17)			
	1914	*1915*	*1916*	*1917*
Average Personnel in the Naval Service during the Fiscal Year	57,568	60,198	62,539	95,548
Confined on 30 June				
Detention	390	210	53	30
Naval prisons	746	547	464	501
State prisons	151	109	167	133

Source: Annual Reports of the Judge Advocate General for the Fiscal Year 1917. Navy Department Library, 122, 130.

reduced applicability of General Order 110 and the probation system contributed to a sudden increase in prisoners at Portsmouth prison. The detention system was winding down and being phased out with the success of the probation system. The last vestige of the detention system was abandoned in April 1917 when it was discontinued on *Southery.* According to the JAG, Capt. W. C. Watts:

> The detention system on board U.S.S. *Southery* at Portsmouth, N.H. was continued until April 25, 1917, when on account of several objections, it was abandoned. . . . No sufficient reason was apparent why the class of younger men previously placed in detention should have special opportunities for rehabilitation which were denied to regular naval prisoners. . . . [I]t was evident that certain offenders by reason of conviction comparatively near to Portsmouth were thus gaining the benefit of the detention system there, while others in exactly similar conditions elsewhere would be committed to a naval prison.[30]

The naval prisoners at Portsmouth were not long denied opportunities for rehabilitation. Four months later Osborne arrived on the scene and began opening the prison gates to prisoners en masse.

On 1 March 1917, there were 4,625 officers and 72,000 enlisted men in the Navy and Marine Corps. The United States entered World War I on 6 April 1917, and a few months later those figures had approximately tripled. On 1 July 1917, there were 12,500 officers and 203,000 enlisted men.[31] Shortly after the war started, important changes were made to the naval prison system in anticipation of an increased wartime prison population. A temporary building was erected at Parris Island, South Carolina, to accommodate 200 prisoners. At Portsmouth prison, expansion was once again the order of the day as the number of prisoners increased from 561 on 1 July 1917 to 843 on 1 September 1917. At the start of World War I, all naval prisoners stateside were at Portsmouth, Mare Island, and Parris Island. The JAG thought this concentration was important because "the fewer the places where prisoners are concentrated, the more uniform is the treatment that is possible to accord them."[32] The naval prison system had been reduced to a few sites of which Portsmouth was definitely the largest. At this point Thomas Mott Osborne arrived to take charge of operations at Portsmouth prison.

Osborne could not have stepped into a better environment in which to practice his progressive prison management theories. With the detention system shut down and the probation system having lost much of its applicability, the restoration pipeline would flow directly from the naval prisons during the war. Many prisoners convicted of desertion and AWOL, instead of serving sentences in the detention system or being placed in a probation status, were sent to Portsmouth prison. It was wartime and the Navy needed men. Osborne was determined to restore as many prisoners as possible to meet that need. In the process he would validate his theories on prison management. Better yet, with strong support from Daniels and FDR, he alone could control and maximize the restoration process at Portsmouth prison.

8

Secretary of the Navy
Josephus Daniels
(1912–20)

No Secretary of the Navy was the subject of more controversy or received
more personal abuse than Daniels during his term of service.

—E. David Cronon, 1963, *The Cabinet Diaries of Josephus Daniels, 1913–1921*

The policy of the Navy is to make, not break, prisoners. . . . Old time
methods of punishment have passed away, never to return.

—Secretary of the Navy Josephus Daniels, 1913

T hus far, the progress of the naval prison system and Portsmouth prison up to
the eve of World War I has been addressed. This chapter and the next focus
on two of the three personalities that will dominate the remainder of this
volume: Secretary of the Navy Josephus Daniels and Thomas Mott Osborne. Their
relationships with a third personality, Assistant Secretary of the Navy Franklin Delano
Roosevelt, will be woven into their narratives. The story of the Portsmouth experiment in progressive prison reform revolves around these three men.

The civilian leadership of the U.S. Navy took a strong turn toward liberalism in
1912 when the Democratic Party regained power for the first time in sixteen years.
President Woodrow Wilson appointed Josephus Daniels (see photo10) to be secretary
of the Navy. Daniels chose another rising liberal, Franklin Delano Roosevelt, to be
his assistant secretary of the Navy. Daniels, longtime editor of the *Raleigh News and
Observer* and active supporter of liberal reform and the Populist movement within
the Democratic Party, had been a close friend and supporter of another noted liberal reformer, William Jennings Bryan, who became Wilson's secretary of state. The
administration was top heavy with progressive reformers. President Wilson and some
of his cabinet, including Bryan, Daniels, and FDR, are depicted in photo 11.

Daniels' son considered his father and Bryan to be "the kind of radical Democrats whom even [the incumbent Democratic president] Grover Cleveland had
helped keep out of town in the revolutionary election of 1896."[1] William McKinley's

election in 1896 started sixteen years of Republican rule during his presidency (1896–1900), then continued by Theodore Roosevelt (1900–1908), and finally William Howard Taft (1908–12). Daniels' efforts as a Democratic national committeeman for those unsuccessful Democratic campaigns were finally rewarded with Wilson's election in 1912. Wilson's cabinet, headed by men such as Bryan and Daniels, was poised to advance the interests of the poor, the oppressed, and the unfortunate, including naval prisoners.

Daniels' acceptance letter to Wilson noted his eagerness to share the president's "ambitions to make easier the path for those who toil and have been forgotten by those in power."[2] Daniels did not have a long association with FDR before asking him to be his assistant. They first met at the Democratic convention in Baltimore in July 1912 where FDR and Osborne were working in support of Wilson's nomination. FDR would be Daniels' link to Osborne; the two of them had served together in New York state politics. Daniels convinced Wilson to approve his choice of FDR as assistant secretary of the Navy because "he [too] was one of our kind of liberals."[3] On Inauguration Day, 4 March 1913, Daniels offered FDR the job, which he accepted without hesitation. With the liberals in charge, the U.S. Navy was about to experience a tumultuous eight years of reform—and a world war.

Liberalism was one of the few attributes Daniels and FDR had in common at the start of their tenure. FDR considered himself a disciple of Mahan in naval strategy, much like his cousin Teddy. Daniels, on the other hand, had given little thought to naval matters prior to his appointment as secretary of the Navy. Daniels, who was fifty years old, and FDR, the handsome thirty-year-old aristocrat, "moved in an entirely different social world" and "represented two utterly different Americas."[4] FDR reportedly told a presidential secretary, "When I first knew him [Daniels], he was the funniest looking hillbilly I had ever seen."[5] Daniels' biographer, Joseph L. Morrison, wrote, "FDR thought Daniels too slow for words, and the young man's impatience—it often bordered on insubordination—would have cost the head of any admiral who had dared venture into such turbulent waters."[6] FDR's exuberance often resulted in spontaneous and independent actions, which frequently involved considerable self-promotion—all patiently tolerated by Daniels. In time Daniels' patience was rewarded with growing respect from his assistant, who later referred to his boss as the "man who taught me a lot that I needed to know."[7]

Progressive prison reform was only one of many liberal initiatives Daniels introduced as secretary of the Navy, but it was Osborne's singular passion—his life's work, his crusade. Successful introduction of progressive prison reform in the Navy depended on these two individuals. Daniels had the power to make prison reform a high Navy priority. Osborne had the knowledge and practical experience to make it happen. Together they formed quite a team.

Many naval officers considered Daniels to be a poor choice for secretary of the Navy because of inexperience in naval matters. Historian E. David Cronon noted Daniels' lack of naval experience and his other shortcomings for the job, especially his lack of appreciation for naval traditions: "Critics charged that he lacked an elementary comprehension of the role and requirements of a modern Navy, that he played favorites in appointments, and that he had no respect for Naval custom or discipline."[8] Osborne shared Daniels' lack of respect for naval customs and traditions. The consequence for both was contentious relations with the many naval officers who revered their service.

Daniels, an outspoken liberal and progressive prohibitionist, did not appear to be a good fit for the Navy with its long history of conservative leadership and an affinity for alcoholic beverages. Daniels challenged the conservative admirals with numerous liberal initiatives, including General Order 99 of 1 July 1914 that eliminated the popular officer wine mess on board U.S. naval vessels, and in Navy yards and Navy stations.[9] Daniels gave two reasons for his order—efficiency and democracy. He believed "temperance is the only sure method to efficiency." Noting that the sailors' daily ration of grog had been eliminated long ago, he declared: "What is good enough for an officer is good enough for an enlisted man."[10] The *Christian Science Monitor* applauded the order: "For it is agreed by observers in Washington that never before has the capital had within it so many public men hostile to the liquor business, who feel disposed to see its privileges curtailed before this administration closes."[11] The *Christian Science Monitor* reporting could not have been more accurate. Daniels' order was a precursor to the elimination of everyone's wine mess: the passing of the Volstead Act on 29 October 1919, better known as National Prohibition Act, which established the start of prohibition on 17 January 1920.

To the disappointment of his critics, Daniels' tenure, from 1913 to 1921, was longer than any of his predecessors except Gideon Welles, secretary of the Navy during the Lincoln administration. In addition to eliminating the wine mess, Daniels' reforms included a revision of traditional naval terminology that attempted to substitute "left" and "right" for "port" and "starboard," the introduction of enlisted men to the U.S. Naval Academy, and a penchant for sending bureaucratic Washingtonian admirals back to sea.[12] Daniels considered the lack of democracy to be "the most serious defect in the Navy" and he especially resented "the chasm that separated the officers from the enlisted men."[13] This belief prompted him to push initiatives to quarter enlisted men with officers and promote opportunities for them to attend the Naval Academy at Annapolis. Daniels delighted in these and other gains for enlisted men during his administration. His empathy for enlisted men was further displayed in his determination to reform the naval prison system.

The enlisted men were much more appreciative of Daniels' initiatives than were the officers. Strong differences of opinion about his management of the Navy caused frequent public disagreements between Daniels and senior naval officers. Daniels did not hesitate to call officers on the carpet and criticize them publicly when he judged their performance to be less than he expected. His public comments expressing disgust with the findings of an August 1913 court-martial board, just five months after he had assumed office, were typical of his outspoken criticism of officers. The case involved graft operations valued at upwards of $7,000 on the battleships *Louisiana* and *New Hampshire*. PM T. J. Arms, three stewards, and eight civilians were indicted, but only one person was found guilty, steward W. T. Dickey. He was sentenced to Portsmouth prison. Paymaster Arms was found guilty of culpable negligence and reduced in rank. But he was not found guilty of any other charges, some of which involved his complicity in the operation. Daniels expressed extreme disgust with the findings and his displeasure with the officers of the court. He entered the following comment for the record: "In spite of the fact that the sentence is totally inadequate, six members of the court, three of them officers of the Pay Corps [implying protection of a fellow officer], apparently regarded even this light sentence as too severe and recommended [for] the accused [Paymaster Arms] . . . clemency. [Those] officers have placed themselves on record as in favor of condoning an offense which any one having the real interests of the service at heart must regard as calling for severe punishment."[14] Daniels' comment appeared not only in the record, but in the pages of the *New York Times.* His suspicion and criticism of naval officers did not develop gradually with his time in office; from the time he assumed his new responsibilities he was determined to challenge the privileges and performances of senior officers.

One Daniels admirer wrote, "He entered the department with a profound suspicion that whatever an Admiral told him was wrong. . . . In nine cases out of ten his formula was correct: the Navy was packed at the top with dead wood, and with politics all the way through."[15] Daniels apparently assumed office with a chip on his shoulder and an intention to provoke the status quo of the Navy Department.

One of the major bones of contention between flag officers and the secretary was the perceived unpreparedness of the Navy for war under Daniels' leadership. In May 1916 an open dispute developed between Daniels and Rear Adm. Bradley A. Fiske, aide of Operations, who had submitted a report to the secretary highlighting the Navy's unpreparedness for war. When the Senate learned of the report and requested to see it, Daniels claimed he had not seen the report until long after it was delivered, claiming it had been filed without his knowledge.

Fiske advised the Senate in writing that he had personally delivered the report to the secretary and that several officers had witnessed the delivery. The admiral was essentially telling the Senate that the secretary was a liar. Few punches were pulled during these disputes between Daniels and his flag officers.[16] According to George T. Davis, "There developed an animosity which became an open scandal and finally led to the latter's [Fiske's] resignation. . . . The criticism of naval affairs became in part a personal attack on Mr. Daniels. His efforts to foster a dry, 'pure,' and democratic Navy, which would educate boys like a university at sea, brought ridicule in the press."[17]

Fiske was especially outspoken in his postwar criticism of Daniels; he claimed the management of the Navy had been committed to "unworthy hands." Expecting the secretary of the Navy to be "a man of the highest order of ability, knowledge and foresight," he found Daniels to fall "far below this standard." Also citing the need for the secretary to be "a man of the highest character," he again thought that Daniels fell short because he "made many statements about important naval matters within his cognizance that were absolutely false."[18] Another critic, Cdr. A. D. Turnbull, near the end of Daniels' tenure wrote, "Mr. Daniels, after seven years of office, will leave the Navy a battered hulk, which it will take several years of careful repairing to make seaworthy."[19] Yet another critic, historian Tracy Barrett Kittredge, who served as a naval reserve officer on Sims' staff, thought that Daniels "ruled as a despot, ruthlessly crushing opposition, by czaristic and underhanded methods." Kittredge also believed "he regarded the Navy primarily as a source of political capital for himself and his party."[20] Clearly, Daniels was held in low esteem by some naval officers.

The most serious of the disputes involved post–World War I accusations by Vice Adm. William S. Sims and other senior ranking naval officers who stated that, under Daniels' leadership, the Navy Department had been guilty of failure "to immediately send its full force of destroyers and anti-submarine craft [to Europe]."[21] Sims claimed this delay "prolonged the war four months and occasioned the staggering loss to the Allies of 2,500,000 tons of shipping, 500,000 lives and $1,500,000,000."[22] Numerous cartoon caricatures of Daniels appeared in newspapers late in, and immediately after, the war. Photo 12 is one such example; here Sims is shooting Daniels' war record full of holes. Not all were in favor of Sims. One cartoon shows Daniels roasting a bewildered and sweating Sims on a spit over an open fire. Their dispute was very heated and very public. Portsmouth prison and Thomas Mott Osborne would become one of several contentious issues between Daniels and Sims.

Critics accused Daniels of delaying the Navy's preparations for, and involvement in, World War I for political reasons. They argued that because President Woodrow Wilson ran for reelection in 1916 on the slogan "He kept us out of war," Daniels had avoided the decisions needed to mobilize the Navy so as not to undermine the president's campaign. Naval historian E. B. Potter falls into this school of thought: "Despite protests from administrative officers and from the Chief of Naval Operations, Secretary Daniels resisted all pressure to prepare for war. He refused to allow the Navy to build suitable antisubmarine vessels, to equip and man the ships they had in commission, or to put the ships themselves in top condition. President Wilson was running for re-election on the slogan 'He kept us out of war.' The Secretary regarded effective preparations as politically inexpedient."[23]

Others, at the onset of World War I, accused Daniels of being a pacifist and thus unable to lead the needed preparations for war.[24] Teddy Roosevelt placed the blame on President Wilson for appointing pacifists to his cabinet. He wrote, "To have appointed Daniels and [Secretary of War Newton] Baker originally was evil enough; to have kept them on during a great war was a criminal thing."[25] Some thought Daniels might be a pacifist, but there was no doubt about Daniels' good friend, Secretary of State William Jennings Bryan. Bryan resigned in protest over President Wilson's strong note to Germany on the *Lusitania* sinking "averring that it would bring war."[26] Pacifist, political hack, incompetent, and inexperienced in naval matters were just a few of the criticisms raised by Daniels' detractors.

Daniels responded to Sims' criticisms with attacks of his own. He claimed Sims "was aggrieved because he had not been given 'carte blanche' during the war; that many of Sims' recommendations were unsound; and that the naval officers in the

department and Sims' superior, Admiral Mayo, had disagreed with him." In his statement before the Senate Naval Affairs Committee in February 1920, Daniels accused
Sims of disloyalty. He said Sims "did not measure up to expectations in certain
particular ways," citing six examples that primarily accused Sims of being "unduly
pro-British during the war." Considerable tension existed within the Navy Department. Relationships were strained and each side was quick to publicly criticize the
other. With the Navy embroiled in controversy and contentiousness, it is not surprising that some of that pressure would vent at Portsmouth prison.[27]

The acrimonious disagreements between Daniels and senior naval officers eventually included the management of Portsmouth Naval Prison. Osborne enjoyed the
encouragement and backing of the secretary of the Navy on many important matters
of prison reform, but he had to interact daily with many naval officers who did not
see eye-to-eye with Daniels on not only prison reform but also his overall management of the Navy. Thus, Osborne's close personal relationship with Daniels was a
blessing and a curse. Osborne could expect to gain Daniels' support for prison reform
whenever needed; however, that support often brought resentment and animosity
from contemporaries and fellow officers who did not share his views or passion for
prison reform.

Daniels' compassion for prisoners was shown a few days before Christmas in
1915 when he granted early release to twenty-five Portsmouth prisoners. The confinement history of one of those released is a sad commentary on how young sailors
compounded their problems after arrival at Portsmouth. According to the *Boston
Daily Globe*, "Included in the group was William Raugh of Philadelphia who had
been confined in the Naval Prison on Seavey Island since it was opened. His original
sentence was for two years, but infractions of prison rules brought it up to seven years
and nine months."[28] The *Globe* did not provide any details about Raugh's offenses.
Whatever the transgressions, this "plank owner" at Portsmouth prison had nearly
quadrupled his sentence with misbehavior at the prison.

In February 1917 Daniels directed the commandant of the Portsmouth Navy
Yard, Capt. Harry Lee, to implement changes to improve treatment of prisoners at
the naval prison and the disciplinary ship *Southery*.[29] These changes were directed
one month after Osborne's inspection of the prison and six months before his arrival
at Portsmouth to assume command of the prison. After his inspection, Osborne
reported to Daniels, "The place is a perfect mass of useless iron and steel . . . conducted upon a system so bad that it is hard to see how it could well be worse."[30] The
report motivated Daniels to immediately improve conditions at the prison.

The major changes directed by Daniels included suspension of the requirements
for prisoners to maintain silence during meals and march in lockstep. Other changes
directed at prisoner self-respect included eliminating censorship stamps on prisoners'
mail, making identifying numbers on prisoners' clothing small and inconsequen-
tial, and conducting fewer searches of prisoners. In a 20 February 1917 letter Daniels stressed his intention to improve prisoner self-respect by removing many of the
degrading conditions of confinement:

> From the foregoing it will be apparent that the Department is desirous
> of emphasizing the importance of giving such consideration to the
> personal feelings of self-respect of the prisoners as may be consistent
> with the strict discipline of the Department . . . every effort should be
> directed toward minimizing the degrading influences wherever possi-
> ble and such personal annoyances to prisoners. . . . It is needless to add
> that the Department expects great care to prevent insulting or unduly
> harsh or over-bearing conduct on the part of sentries or other prison
> authorities toward prisoners.[31]

In his response to Daniels' directive, Lee stated that he had implemented many of the directed initiatives and several others as well. Lights had been installed in individual cells, a writing board and stool had been provided in each cell, and movies were being shown on Sunday evenings. Progressive reform was creeping into Portsmouth prison.

The above changes were directed by Daniels early in 1917. At that time, he had one more important change planned for Portsmouth prison. Daniels had already contacted Thomas Mott Osborne and set in motion a series of events that would culminate in Osborne's assignment as warden at the prison six months later. The same Navy yard authorities who thought that Sunday night movies represented the cutting edge of prison reform in early 1917 would, a year later, find themselves involved with far more aggressive prison reform when Osborne literally opened prison cells and turned prison management over to the prisoners.

In June 1917 Daniels revised the "Manual for the Government of United States Naval Prisons and Detention Systems," thereby extending changes specifically directed at Portsmouth earlier that year to all naval prisons and detention facilities. Six pages of major revisions included, "No form of lock-step will be used in naval prisons except the usual military marching and formation. . . . Prisoners will not be required to keep silence at meals except when necessary to preserve discipline. . . . Prisoners heads will not be shaved, but the hair will be worn short and of the regulation military cut." The revisions stressed that prisoners were to be divided into two general classes, "criminals" and "naval prisoners." Criminals included "those guilty of moral turpitude . . . punishable [as] if the offender were a civilian." Naval prisoners were defined as "offenders convicted of strictly military offenses." The revisions described a detailed classification system for naval prisoners that would enable them to earn privileges, up to and including probation, depending upon their behavior in prison. Criminals were to be physically separated from naval prisoners and were not to be included in the classification system.[32]

Productive employment of prison labor to the mutual benefit of the Navy and the prisoners was another goal of Daniels. As early as December 1914, Daniels expressed interest in utilizing prisoners at Portsmouth for "coaling, chipping, and scaling ships . . . painting as does not require expert labor, rough repair labor."[33] By 1917 prisoner work parties were a firmly established source of shipyard labor. During the war, prison labor was frequently employed to off-load ships, maintain the shipyard grounds, and perform other labor-intensive jobs. Interaction between prisoner work parties and shipyard employees and residents was an invitation to conflicts and mis-understandings that would plague Osborne. Despite this, prison labor was a valuable shipyard resource during the war, which would be sorely missed after the war when shipyard budgets were sharply reduced.

Daniels' remarks to the assembled prisoners at Portsmouth on 18 November 1917, a few months after Osborne had assumed command of the prison, revealed his strong commitment to progressive prison reform and the changes needed to provide much-improved opportunities for young sailors to redress their errors in judgment and gain restoration to the Navy and society. Expounding on the need for discipline in the home, the Navy, and life in general, he preached, "You were not brought here for punishment, but to come face to face with yourselves; to look into your hearts and minds and reflect upon what you have done. No one looks down upon you, no one regards you as having committed an offense that must forever bar you from society. Here you have the opportunity to strengthen your character and your purpose that you may go forth from here into life through this discipline stronger and better men."[34]

Daniels would "open the door—the door of opportunity, of hope; the door for rehabilitation, for service." Daniels' fondest wish was that many of the young inmates at Portsmouth prison would walk through the door of opportunity about to be thrown open under the leadership of Thomas Mott Osborne. And many did.

Daniels' vision and the reforms he put in place immediately prior to Osborne's arrival were the essence of progressive prison reform: indeterminate sentences, humane treatment of prisoners, the earning of privileges based on behavior, and productive employment of prison labor. Osborne not only shared Daniels' vision of prison reform, he had a passion for it. Handpicked to implement reform at Portsmouth, Osborne seized the opportunity, extended the boundaries of Daniels' vision, and quickly advanced his own, more aggressive reform agenda.

9

Osborne prior to Portsmouth
(1859–1917)

Not only did the blood of reformers leap in his veins, but from early youth he was exposed to the inspiration of famous progressives associated with his family. . . . Born of liberals, raised in liberalism, with tradition and inclination urging him on, he might be deemed preordained for the course he was to follow.

—Rudolph W. Chamberlain, 1935, *There Is No Truce: A Life of Thomas Mott Osborne*

Osborne's reputation as one of the most ambitious progressive prison reformers of his era was well established before his assignment to Portsmouth prison. Daniels could not have chosen a more qualified, more dedicated man for the job; Osborne had a commanding presence (photo 13). His personal crusade for prison reform stemmed from early exposure to the philosophies of some of the most noted reformers of his day. Osborne, born on 23 September 1859, had concern for social issues that can be traced back to his childhood in Auburn, New York, where his family had long been closely associated with reform movements and politics. The list of his family's relatives and friends reads as a Who's Who of nineteenth-century human rights activists.

Among the family's early activists were abolitionists Lucretia Coffin Mott and William Lloyd Garrison and suffragette Martha Coffin.[1] Martha Coffin was Thomas Mott Osborne's grandmother and sister to Lucretia Coffin Mott. Osborne was related to William Lloyd Garrison through marriage of his aunt to Garrison's second son. Antislavery activist James Russell Lowell was an uncle of Osborne's wife, Agnes Devens. Osborne's biographer, Rudolph W. Chamberlain, notes that Osborne's parents occasionally hosted meetings in their home in Auburn attended by Elizabeth Cady Stanton, Susan B. Anthony, the Motts, the Garrisons, and others.[2] Osborne's passion for prison reform was a natural consequence of his early exposure to such notable reformers. Chamberlain wrote, "Not only did the blood of reformers leap in his veins, but from early youth he was exposed to the inspiration of famous progressives associated with his family. . . . Born of liberals, raised in liberalism, with tradition and inclination urging him on, he might be deemed preordained for the course he was to follow."[3] Osborne's stay at Portsmouth would be but one of many stops in

Osborne's lifelong journey of reform that began with his early exposure to the liberal thoughts and actions of his immediate family.

Osborne's close ties to his grandmother Martha Coffin Wright exposed him to a unique social environment during his formative years. Martha, sister to staunch abolitionist and devoted women's rights leader Lucretia Coffin Mott, was an activist for the same causes. Osborne's mother, Eliza, and Martha "remained physically close, as well as emotionally close, throughout Martha's life."[4] According to Martha's biographers, Sherry H. Penney and James D. Livingston, "Her [Osborne's mother's] home, like Martha's, was frequently visited by Elizabeth Cady Stanton, Susan B. Anthony, Harriet Tubman, and other reformers."[5] His grandmother's active involvement in antislavery and women's rights movements, and her frequent hosting of the leaders of those movements in her Auburn home, spilled over into the Osborne household and exposed young Osborne to progressive issues on a regular basis.

At the time of his birth his grandmother was a well-established resident of Auburn. She and her husband, David Wright, had lived there since 1839. The Wrights relocated from Philadelphia to Auburn so that he could practice law in the county seat with rail access to the state capital at Albany. Martha and Lucretia had been committed abolitionists since 1833 as the result of their involvement with William Lloyd Garrison and the American Anti-Slavery Society.

In 1848 the sisters joined forces with Elizabeth Cady Stanton to organize the historic Women's Rights Convention in nearby Seneca Falls, New York. Following Seneca Falls, Martha continued to be a champion for women's rights, a path that merged with that of Susan B. Anthony who became a lifelong friend. In 1858, 1859, and 1860 the Women's Rights Convention was coordinated with the Anti-Slavery Society Convention in New York City. Martha Coffin Wright was heavily involved in both movements. Soon after the coordinated convention of 1860, Martha's Auburn neighbor, William Henry Seward, was passed over at the Chicago Republican convention in favor of Abraham Lincoln. Seward had been governor of New York and would become Lincoln's secretary of state. Thomas Mott Osborne was born into this hotbed of political activity and social unrest.[6]

In January 1860, just a few months after Osborne's birth, Susan B. Anthony, Elizabeth Cady Stanton, Frederick Douglass, and Lucretia Mott took shelter in his grandmother's house to escape mob violence that had broken out in response to antislavery demonstrations the group had organized in several locations near Auburn. With the women's rights movement put on hold during the Civil War, Osborne's family and friends shifted their allegiance to the abolitionists. As a result of his grandmother's active involvement, Auburn became a hub for the Underground Railroad. Osborne's mother wrote in her memoir, "A branch of the underground railway came through Auburn, and our house was one of the stations."[7] As a consequence of the Osborne family's strong antislavery sentiments, Harriet Tubman, a close personal friend of Martha Coffin Wright, established a home in Auburn as a haven for freed blacks.[8] Osborne's early years were filled with a family environment ripe with sentiments and active support for Negro rights.

During the late 1860s the women's rights movement was resurrected and once again joined forces with blacks under the banner of the American Equal Rights Association (AERA). The merger goal was to aid women in their efforts to obtaining equal rights, along with blacks, under the Fifteenth Amendment. However, controversy reigned and the women's movement split in 1869, with Stanton and Anthony heading up the aggressive National Women Suffrage Association (NWSA) and Lucy Stone forming the more conservative American Woman Suffrage Association (AWSA). After trying unsuccessfully for five years to reconcile the differences between the two organizations, Osborne's grandmother was elected president of NWSA in 1874 with hopes for unifying the women's movement. Those hopes were short lived; Martha Coffin Wright died on 4 January 1875 of complications from "typhoid pneumonia." At the time Osborne was an impressionable sixteen-year-old whose pubescent years had been packed with social controversy and close association with some of the more important social activists of the era.

Shortly after his grandmother's death, Osborne left Auburn to continue his education at Adams Academy in Quincy, Massachusetts. This experience was followed by his acceptance to Harvard University. Prior to entering Adams Academy, he attended public primary schools and the first two years of high school in Auburn. According to Rudolph W. Chamberlain, as a result of his relocation to Massachusetts, "he was thrown into the very citadel of liberalism."[9] During his stay in the Boston area, he spent many Sundays with the William Lloyd Garrisons. During his prep school and college years in Massachusetts Osborne continued to be heavily influenced by liberal and progressive thinkers through associations with his mother's side of his family. He graduated from Harvard in 1884.

As a result of exposure to women's rights and abolition movement leaders, Osborne gained firsthand knowledge of the aggressive measures needed to advance social causes. This early training would serve him well in his later years when equally aggressive measures were needed to advance his prison reform agenda. Auburn, the geographical epicenter for the advancement of the rights of blacks and women, would also become the epicenter for the advancement of prisoners' rights. It was only natural that Osborne would carry on the family tradition and assume a leadership role for that cause.

If his mother's side of the family provided Osborne his commitment to social causes and prison reform, his father's genes and inclination toward politics equipped him to advance those causes. His father, David Munson Osborne, was mayor of Auburn (1879–80) after having served as a city alderman from 1871 to 1874. Thomas Mott Osborne, unsuccessful candidate for lieutenant governor of New York in 1894 and governor in 1910, became mayor of Auburn in 1902. Thomas Mott Osborne's son, Charles P. Osborne, also served as mayor of Auburn from 1928 to 1931 and again from 1937 to 1939. Another son, Lithgow Osborne, was the vice president and editorial writer of the Auburn *Citizen-Advertiser* in the 1920s. He served as commissioner of conservation for the state of New York in the 1930s, served in various State Department assignments, and, during World War II, was assigned ambassador to Norway by President Roosevelt, continuing the longtime Roosevelt-Osborne connection. The Osborne family's political background would lead Thomas Mott Osborne to powerful and influential friends who would serve him well in his quest for prison reform.

As a leader of the state's Democratic party Osborne became involved with an organization of liberal Democrats to combat the long-standing influence of the Tammany Hall political machine.[10] His campaign against Tammany Hall included an unsuccessful bid for governor in 1910. Historian Geoffrey C. Ward wrote, "His 1910 bid for the governorship failed, broken largely on the stony shoals of his own excessive rhetoric (he had refused even to parlay with Tammany, whose ranks he said were filled with 'dogs' and 'curs')."[11] It would not be the last time Osborne created problems for himself by refusing to compromise his principles or hold his tongue.

During the fight with Tammany Hall, Osborne became a good friend of FDR, who shared many of Osborne's views about the need for social and political reforms. The two first met in 1904 on board the *Prinzessin Victoria Luisa* while FDR, a Harvard senior at the time, was cruising the Caribbean with his mother. Historian Thomas Fleming wrote, "They quickly discovered they were both members of Alpha Delta Phi, Harvard's 'Fly Club,' and the older man [Osborne] had been immediately attracted to the handsome, gregarious young Democrat with the right sentiments and the famous Republican name."[12] In 1909 Osborne "announced the formation of the Democratic League of the State of New York to provide the voters with progressive candidates opposed to Tammany Hall."[13] FDR was one of those progressive candidates.

FDR was elected to the state senate in 1910. According to Ward, the new state senator dined the evening after the inauguration, 3 January 1911, with the new governor, John Alden Dix, and "Franklin's reformist patron, Thomas Mott Osborne."[14] Such was Osborne's status with the state's leading Democrats. FDR joined with Osborne to help break the dominance of Tammany Hall and was reelected to the state senate in 1912 after he and Osborne had worked hard to deliver upstate New York to Woodrow Wilson in the presidential campaign; he later resigned his position as state senator in 1913 to become the assistant secretary of the Navy. FDR was responsible for recommending to Secretary of the Navy Daniels that his good friend, Thomas Mott Osborne, become the warden at Portsmouth Naval Prison.

Ward suggests FDR's career as a politician was advanced in 1912 when Osborne withdrew from politics and his longtime supporter, Albany newspaperman Louis Howe, assumed the leadership of FDR's campaign for reelection to the New York state senate. According to Ward, FDR was not the first "charismatic New York reformer whose career Howe attempted to shape." Ward, who believed "the magnetic former mayor of Auburn" had a "great future in politics," promoted Osborne from 1906 until he withdrew from politics to begin his career in prison reform in 1912. In addition to being magnetic and charismatic, Osborne was described by Ward as "handsome, eloquent, and high-minded (he would become the best-known prison reformer of his day), but he was also vain, bombastic, and gratuitously insulting." These personal attributes, well established by 1912, would heavily influence

Osborne's career in prison reform. After directing FDR's successful bid for reelection in 1912, Howe "remained at his [FDR's] side until his own death in 1936."[15]

After stepping down as mayor of Auburn in 1905, Osborne served in various assignments in the New York state government, including Public Services commissioner and Forest, Fish and Game commissioner, before being appointed chair of the New York State Commission on Prison Reform in 1913. The latter job launched Osborne on a career of prison reform. As a prison reformer, Osborne is most remembered for his innovative concepts of prisoner self-government. He first implemented these concepts at Sing Sing Prison in 1913; *Within Prison Walls* (1914) is an account of his experience at Sing Sing. His subsequent works on prison reform include *Society and Prisons* (1916) and *Prisons and Common Sense* (1924). These works and his biography, *There Is No Truce* by Rudolph W. Chamberlain, sing the praises of the Mutual Welfare League, his blueprint for prisoner self-government.

Osborne often used disguises to anonymously gain insight into the living conditions of his employees or prisoners. His frequent use of impersonations can be traced to his lifelong love of the theater and the arts. One historian thought "everything about him was theater."[16] He had been a member of the Hasty Pudding Club and directed the orchestra and glee club at Harvard. Later in life he wrote drama, organized and funded theatrical performances in Auburn, conducted Auburn's amateur orchestra, and on one occasion directed the Syracuse Symphony Orchestra. As a prison warden he encouraged prisoners to form theater groups to perform musicals and plays; at Portsmouth prison these performances were frequently presented to civilian audiences in local theaters.

There are many examples of Osborne going incognito to gain workplace insight that, he believed, he could not have experienced otherwise. In 1907, when assigned to the New York Public Services Commission, he posed as a workman and "rode the freights to gather his information first hand."[17] Later he disguised himself as a hobo and rode the rails to experience potential strike conditions.[18] He disguised himself as a prisoner at Sing Sing Prison in 1913 to better appreciate prison conditions before taking the job as warden; he did the same at Portsmouth prison in 1917. Finally, during his tenure at Portsmouth he did a stint as a disguised sailor on board the battleship *North Dakota* to gain a better appreciation of a sailor's life at sea (Osborne is disguised as Seaman Brown in photo 14). Osborne took delight in these opportunities to mingle with employees, prisoners, and sailors to gather firsthand information that would allow him to perform his job better. His ability to sincerely and passionately relate to prisoner living conditions motivated him to aggressively implement progressive reform at both Sing Sing and Portsmouth prisons. According to David J. Rothman, "Some Progressives went to live in slums; Osborne went to live in prisons."[19]

Ward suggests the possibility that Osborne's disguises had more sinister motives—raising the possibility that they may have been used to facilitate homosexual encounters. He wrote:

PHOTO 1. Portsmouth Naval Shipyard (circa 1970). Portsmouth Naval Prison is the imposing white structure in the upper right corner.

Courtesy of Milne Special Collections, University of New Hampshire Library, Durham, NH

PHOTO 2. Portsmouth prison circa 1910

Courtesy of Milne Special Collections, University of New Hampshire Library, Durham, NH

Flogging on a Man-of-War.

"Again, and again, and again; and at every blow, higher and higher rose the long, purple bars on the prisoner's back; but he merely bowed over his head and still."—Page 273.

Entered according to Act of Congress, A. D. 4MCCCLV, by Henry Howe, in the clerk's office of the District Court of the United States for the Southern District of Ohio

PHOTO 4. Flogging on a man-of-war

Courtesy of Library of Congress,
LOT 4425C, LC-USZ62-46517

PHOTO 3. Thomas Mott Osborne
demonstrating prisoner head cage
restraint.

Author's personal collection

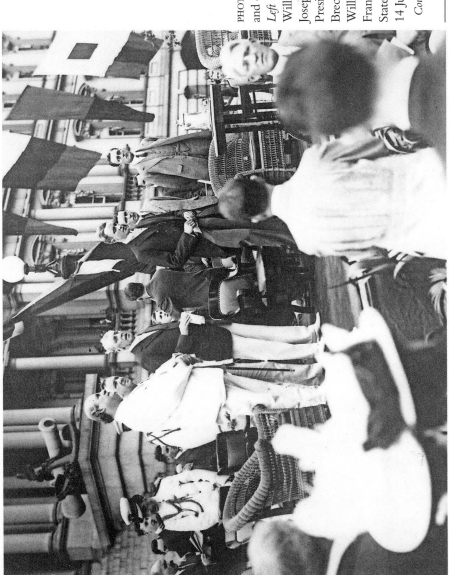

PHOTO 11. President Wilson and cabinet members. *Left to right,* William J. Bryan, Josephus Daniels, President Wilson, Breckenridge Long, William Phillips, Franklin D. Roosevelt. State Department, 14 June 1914.

Courtesy of Library of Congress, LC-USZ62-10466

PHOTO 12. Admiral Sims shooting Daniels' war record full of holes. Note that the admiral's name is misspelled.

Courtesy of Library of Congress, LOT 5382 (G)
Illustration by Roland Kirby, titled "Something the Navy Never Did"

PHOTO 13. Thomas Mott
Osborne

Author's personal collection

PHOTO 14. Osborne disguised as
Seaman Brown on board USS
North Dakota. Note the dedication to Jonathan Daniels, the
son of Josephus Daniels.

Courtesy of Milne Special Collections,
University of New Hampshire Library,
Durham, NH

PHOTO 15. Additional wooden buildings to house Portsmouth prisoners. Note prison
tower in lower left corner.

Courtesy of Milne Special Collections, University of New Hampshire Library, Durham, NH

PHOTO 16. Long line of prisoners in double file with Marine guards

Courtesy of Milne Special Collections, University of New Hampshire Library, Durham, NH

PHOTO 17. Prisoner work party pulling cask.

Courtesy of Milne Special Collections, University of New Hampshire Library, Durham, NH

PHOTO 18. Christening of USS *O-1*, 9 July 1918. Admiral Boush is shown to the right of the sponsor with flowers.

Courtesy of Milne Special Collections, University of New Hampshire Library, Durham, NH

PHOTO 19. Rear Adm. William S. Sims and Assistant Secretary of the Navy Franklin D. Roosevelt. Note that Sims is a rear admiral here and an admiral in photo 12. He was promoted from rear admiral at the start of the war to vice admiral in December 1918 and then to admiral in March 1919.

Author's personal collection

PHOTO 20. Edwin Denby and Josephus Daniels

Author's personal collection

In 1913, Osborne began disappearing from his home at night to haunt workingmen's bars and hobo jungles, elaborately costumed and made up, according to his own terse diary, variously as a minister, doctor, "Dude, Old Gent, Mexican, Italian, Colored Gent." He was often accompanied on these nocturnal masquerades—for which he never offered any coherent explanation—by a handsome, muscular young man whom he had found in a reform school and employed ostensibly as a handyman. Wide-spread whispering about his midnight rambles had helped torpedo his political career in New York state and lent credence to later rumors that his friendships with good-looking young convicts were more complicated than they first seemed . . . others charged that he had forced homosexual advances on the men under his charge.[20]

Ward admits, "It is impossible to know how much truth, if any, there was in the more violent attacks on his character."[21] Osborne's life was a whirlwind of whispers and accusations interrupted by strong voices of support from the powerful and well respected.

Obviously troubled by Osborne's costume antics, his biographer and admirer, Rudolph W. Chamberlain, thought it important to dispel any notion that Osborne might be a transvestite. He wrote: "In view of the slanders [rumors and accusations of homosexuality] that were to be spread later, it is worth recording that Osborne exhibited not the slightest trace of transvestism, that strange urge which drives some persons to dress in the costume of the opposite sex. Not once did he put on a female disguise. To him that would have been an unnatural act."[22]

Chamberlain's insistence that Osborne was not a transvestite, without the same aggressive denial of the possibility of his homosexuality, raises even more questions about his sexuality. These suspicions and innuendoes are all part of the riddle that was Osborne. Undoubtedly, the cloud of suspicion of homosexuality hovered over much of Osborne's actions and accomplishments. However, as this book affirms, he always successfully defended himself against any such attacks.

Osborne was inclined to run institutions autocratically while treating the responsible bureaucracy with utter disregard, if not contempt; an inclination that contributed to his problems at Sing Sing and Portsmouth. (See chapters 11 and 12 for more about his avoidance of the chain of command at Portsmouth.) This same trait was very much evident during his time as warden of Sing Sing; Rebecca M. McLennan wrote, "Osborne ran the institution [Sing Sing] . . . in a manner that severely disrupted the routines and violated the rules . . . [his] general disregard for the procedures of bureaucracy was evident from the very first day . . . [he] avoided con-sultation with authorities whenever possible . . . [he] ignored the orders of his bureau-cratic superior."[23] His penchant to independently run his own show encouraged controversy in the ranks, invited criticism from superiors, and fueled the emotions of both critics and supporters. Osborne's presence ensured that authority would be challenged and the status quo toppled—not a good recipe for success as commanding officer of a naval prison.

Always a champion of prisoners' rights and a defender of their causes, Osborne frequently involved himself with capital punishment issues at Sing Sing Prison. On several occasions he challenged authorities, up to and including the governor, on behalf of prisoners awaiting execution.[24] These challenges were often not well received by local politicians and other authorities. He eventually ran afoul of influential politicians who resented his democratic reforms as well as his repeated attacks on capital punishment.[25] The controversy turned to a personal vendetta to have Osborne discredited and removed from office. The attack against his liberal reforms began in spectacular fashion when one prisoner accused twenty-one others of sodomy. All initially denied the charge but subsequently confessed, supposedly fearing transfer to a more oppressive prison if they were eventually convicted of the charge. Osborne assigned the confessors duty digging sewers for punishment and thought the matter finished. Rumors surfaced, and Osborne was questioned about rampant immorality at his prison by state authorities. Carefully selecting his words to protect the punished prisoners, he was ultimately accused of perjury. The follow-on investigation turned into a witch hunt that resulted in a number of charges. According to Rudolph W. Chamberlain, "On December 28 [1915], the Grand Jury of Westchester County brought two indictments against Osborne—one for perjury, and one for neglect of duty. Of the six accounts contained in the letter of indictment, the first five charged willful and unlawful violation of prison rules, together with a general breakdown of discipline and morale. The sixth and last count alleged that Warden Osborne 'did commit various unlawful and unnatural acts with inmates of Sing Sing Prison, over whom he had supervision and control.'"[26]

Penal historian Frank Tannenbaum believed Osborne's critics were hopeful that they could pressure some of the twenty-one prisoners involved in the case to provide testimony against Osborne that would lead to his dismissal.[27] That did not happen. Over the next six months, Osborne mounted a counterattack against the charges with the help of an outpouring of public support, the hiring of the best defense lawyers available, and a personal expenditure of $75,000.[28] Public support included a mass meeting of thirty-five hundred people at Carnegie Hall at which Charles W. Eliot, president of Harvard, spoke on Osborne's behalf.[29] The morals charge was dismissed as without foundation and the other charges were reduced to three counts dealing with the general mismanagement of the prison. Ultimately the entire case was dropped and Osborne was vindicated.

Osborne made a triumphant return to Sing Sing Prison on 16 July 1916 and resigned his position as warden three months later. Osborne's career at Sing Sing came to a close after vindictive personal attacks, attempts to discredit his reforms, and political turmoil. This closure would bear a remarkable resemblance to his final days at Portsmouth prison, which would also involve an investigation into his unpopular democratic prison practices and accusations of immoral and scandalous practices among prisoners. Also at Portsmouth, his friends, especially FDR, rushed to his defense.

On 25 October 1916, Osborne published a scathing letter to New York governor Whitman, whom he considered to be the source of his troubles: "Thanks to you, sir, the name I inherited from my honored father . . . has been linked in people's hearts to the vilest of crimes. . . . I have had to fight . . . against a powerful and remorseless political organization. . . . I do desire to influence the future, so far as I may, to the end that no man so weak as yourself—so shifty, so selfish, so false, so cruel, may be trusted with public power."[30] Osborne, never content to let well enough alone, always sought to have the last word. He was not a compromising or accommodating individual. He was relentless in the prosecution of the truth, as he saw it. He was an accomplished writer, brilliant organizer, and skilled debater; these traits, so troublesome for his critics at Sing Sing Prison, would also prove to be a problem for his critics at Portsmouth prison.

Within one month after leaving Sing Sing in October 1916, Osborne was tasked by Daniels to investigate Portsmouth prison. After directing the 1914 prison reorganization, which improved the living conditions of naval prisoners, Daniels wanted to do even more. And Osborne was just the man to take things to the next level. Some thought that Daniels' goal was to eliminate all naval prisons. In an article titled "Move to Abolish all Naval Prisons," the 22 November 1916 *Boston Daily Globe* reported, "The visit of Ex-Warden Thomas Mott Osborne of Sing Sing . . . it is said, [will] result in the abolishing of all naval prisons and the use of detention ships [instead]. . . . It is known that Sec. Daniels is opposed to prisons and it is thought that the investigation by Mr. Osborne is a part of his plan to eliminate them."[31] The *Globe* article was overly ambitious in reporting the possible elimination of all naval prisons; however, it does confirm Daniels' solid reputation for prison reform.

When Osborne walked away from Sing Sing Prison in the fall of 1916, the Great War was under way in Europe. The United States entered the war in the spring of 1917, about the time FDR and Daniels were seriously considering him for the job at Portsmouth prison. With their assistance, Osborne was commissioned a lieutenant commander and given orders to assume command of the prison, which he did on 10 August 1917. At age fifty-eight, the new warden was much older, far more experienced in prison matters, and much better connected politically than any of his predecessors. The new warden brought strong beliefs about social justice and the need for prison reform to his new job, and he was not at all hesitant about voicing those beliefs. In addition, he had friends in high places, whom he would not hesitate to call upon when needed to achieve his goals. All of this combined to make his tour at Portsmouth prison every bit as controversial as his years leading up to that assignment.

10

Reform Comes to Portsmouth

[Portsmouth prisoners] needed to be repaired instead of being thrown upon the scrap heap.

—Thomas Mott Osborne, 1917

Osborne's success with progressive reform at Portsmouth, highlighted in the introduction, will be examined in more detail here and in the following chapters. There is no question that the restoration numbers and the many prisoner testimonies to salvaged lives are impressive. This chapter examines the methods Osborne employed to achieve those successes, most notably the Mutual Welfare League, as well as some of Osborne's personal traits and beliefs that led to the adversarial relationships that undermined his cause, which include a disrespect of naval custom and protocol, especially the chain of command, a perceived arrogance regarding the proper handling of prisoners, and an insistence on not segregating prisoners according to the seriousness of their offenses.

First let us examine the setting that Osborne found at Portsmouth Navy Yard when he arrived in August 1917. Osborne's priority was clearly prison reform; but the number one priority of his immediate superior in the chain of command, shipyard commandant Rear Adm. Clifford J. Boush, and his contemporaries at the yard was wartime industrial mobilization. Conflicting priorities were more often the rule than the exception.

Portsmouth Navy Yard (1917–20)

On 6 April 1917, four months before Osborne's arrival at the shipyard, the United States entered World War I. During the period that Osborne was the commanding officer of Portsmouth Naval Prison, the shipyard was heavily involved with the mobilization of industrial resources to meet wartime production schedules. At the same time, the shipyard managers were also converting the yard's infrastructure for a new mission of national importance—the building of submarines. The wartime industrial activity at the yard was at an all-time high when Osborne arrived to start his own personal war against prisoner maltreatment.

During the Osborne years at Portsmouth, the primary mission of the shipyard transitioned from surface ship construction to submarine construction. The shipyard was devoted to wooden sailing ship construction for most of the nineteenth century and, during the latter nineteenth and early twentieth centuries, to steel-hulled, steam-propelled vessels. Shortly before Osborne's arrival at the yard, the U.S. Navy made a serious commitment to develop the yard as its premier submarine design and construction yard.

The Navy's commitment stemmed from its dissatisfaction with the submarine acquisition process that existed prior to, and during, World War I. Private submarine builders, Electric Boat and Lake Torpedo companies, designed and built submarines with little input sought or accepted from the Navy. Navy officials felt they were paying too much money for inferior and ill-designed submarines. In addition, many thought that the motivation of private shipbuilders during those years had more to do with profiteering than providing the fleet with the ships and submarines it needed.[1] The Navy decided to develop Portsmouth Navy Yard as a builder of submarines so it could wrest control of submarine design and construction from private shipbuilders. Portsmouth Navy Yard was picked to be the future for American submarine design and construction.[2] Just a few weeks after Osborne assumed command of the prison, the yard commissioned the first submarine it ever built, the L-8, on 30 August 1917. The L-8 was the first step of the Navy's strategy to develop Portsmouth Navy Yard into a first-class submarine designing and building yard.

Capt. Andrew I. McKee, planning officer at Portsmouth Navy Yard during World War II, wrote in a 1945 article for *Historical Transactions 1893–1943*, a fiftieth-anniversary special publication by the Society of Naval Architects and Marine Engineers, explaining how the Navy wrested control of submarine design from the private yards:[3]

> As the first step in familiarizing its personnel with submarines and their designs, an order was placed in June 1914 for the building of the L-8, to the design of the Lake Torpedo Company, at the Navy Yard Portsmouth, N.H. Two years later, the O-1, of the Holland type, was ordered built at Portsmouth to the design of the Electric Boat Company. Late in 1916, the Navy Department decided that Portsmouth had acquired enough experience in its work on these two ships to be trusted with the development of the working plans for a third design, the preliminary design of which had been prepared by the Navy Department, and [the Navy Department] placed an order for one submarine, the S-3, at Portsmouth. At the same time, orders were placed for the S-1 with Electric Boat and the S-2 with the Lake Torpedo Company.[4]

In effect, the Navy had set up a design competition between the two well-established private submarine building shipyards and the newcomer, the Portsmouth Navy Yard. The newcomer had the obvious advantage of having gained considerable experience with the designs of its competitors. Portsmouth built its first submarine, the

L–8, to a Lake Torpedo Company design and its second submarine, O–1, to an Electric Boat design.

As a result of that competition, Portsmouth's design and workmanship were judged superior to the others and the yard quickly became the nation's preeminent submarine designing and building shipyard. The submarines commissioned after the L–8 (30 Aug 1917), all critical to the development of the yard as a leader in the construction of submarines, were the O–1 (5 Nov 1918), S–3 (30 Jan 1919), S–4 (19 Nov 1919), S–5 (17 May 1920), S–6 (17 May 1920), S–7 (1 Jul 1920), and S–8 (1 Oct 1920). The commissioning dates indicate that most submarines were either delivered or were under construction during Osborne's time at Portsmouth prison. The yard's workload was heavy; its commitment to the Navy's long-term strategic plan was critical to the success of that plan. Osborne's commitment to prison reform frequently conflicted with the shipyard's industrial commitments and national defense priorities.

In addition to the construction of submarines, the shipyard overhauled and repaired 122 surface ships during the 19 months of direct U.S. involvement in World War I (6 April 1917–11 November 1918). Many of those months required three-shift operations; also during that period, 51 buildings were erected on the shipyard to support the expanding workload and workforce. The shipyard saw a fourfold increase in civilian employment from 1,450 in 1916 to 5,550 in 1918. Osborne's tenure at Portsmouth Prison (10 August 1917–17 March 1920) coincided with this period of heavy wartime industrial workload and infrastructure development.[5]

As commandant of a shipyard with a challenging wartime workload, Rear Adm. Boush had a full plate of day-to-day industrial responsibilities. It was Osborne's misfortune that Boush was his immediate superior in the chain of command. Supposedly Osborne would have to work with, and through, Boush to achieve his goals at the prison. Conflicting priorities often resulted in strained relations that distracted both men from the accomplishment of their goals. It is not surprising that priorities often clashed or that Osborne would bypass the chain of command to gain the backing of his good friends, Daniels and FDR.

OSBORNE ARRIVES

With the encouragement of FDR, Daniels asked Osborne to make a study of conditions in naval prisons during the fall of 1916.[6] The study was primarily centered on an investigation into conditions at Portsmouth prison. Addressing the Twentieth Century Club in Boston on 3 December 1916, Osborne provided the highlights of the report he had submitted to Daniels. He told Daniels that Portsmouth prison was absurdly managed, the prisoner uniforms were degrading, and the treatment of the men was the most severe anywhere.[7] As usual, he pulled no punches when prisoner treatment was concerned.

In January 1917, with the full support of Daniels and FDR, and as he had done previously at Auburn prison, Osborne had himself committed to Portsmouth prison to evaluate living conditions first hand. Austin MacCormick, who would later become Osborne's primary assistant at Portsmouth, and Osborne's secretary, Harry Bolansky, joined him in the adventure. There was nothing secretive about the trio's being committed to the prison. The *New York Times* covered the story the next day: "Ex-Warden and Bowdoin Professor [MacCormick] Start Investigation of Conditions at Portsmouth."[8] The *Boston Daily Globe* had similar front page coverage the same day: "Thomas Mott Osborne Will Break Stone at Portsmouth."[9] Two days later, the *Globe* reported, "Osborne May Be Put on Ice Cutting Crew."[10] And two days after that it was "Osborne in a Role of a Coalheaver."[11] These articles, which reinforced Osborne's reputation as a unique spokesman for prison reform, provided very visible evidence that he was also willing to "walk the walk."

Timely and extensive press coverage of Osborne's prison episodes was extraordinary throughout his career. At times the coverage seemed a carefully scripted soap opera designed to capture the public's imagination and enhance his reputation. Articles in the *New York Times* and *Boston Daily Globe* often appeared to be duplicate copies of the same press release, suggesting the story may have originated at Osborne's desk. His passion for the theater and his flare for the dramatic carried over into his workplace. It would not have been out of character for him to write his own version of events and give it wide distribution. The headlines of most of the articles about him in the New York and Boston press identify him by last name only—his notoriety as a prison reformer was such that readers immediately recognized his name and were aware of his past exploits. It is doubtful that any other lieutenant commander in the U.S. Navy ever enjoyed the headlines and instant name recognition that Osborne did.

Press coverage continued after his release from Portsmouth prison. On 30 January 1917, the *New York Times* and *Boston Daily Globe* reported, again almost verbatim, follow-up stories about Osborne's pseudoconfinement. Apparently he had initially refused to part with his wife's two gold wedding rings that hung around his neck on a leather string until he was threatened with solitary confinement on bread and water. It was also reported that he peeled potatoes, scrubbed decks, ate prison fare, and was treated as any ordinary prisoner.[12] One could almost hear the announcer saying, "Stay tuned for the next thrilling adventure of Tom Osborne."

Another adventure received wide press coverage in July 1919 when he spent some time on the battleship USS *North Dakota*, supposedly disguised as Seaman Brown, to gain an appreciation for a sailor's life at sea. Photo 14 shows Osborne disguised as Seaman Brown. According to David J. Rothman, Osborne "may have been the first prison reformer to practice anonymous participant–observation."[13] Osborne's stint as Seaman Brown was hardly as anonymous as Rothman suggests. On 11 July 1919, the *Christian Science Monitor* reported, "Mr Daniels said his [Osborne's] presence on the ship was known to all the officers and men."[14]

As the result of his confinement in January 1917, Osborne concluded that the government was making a bad investment in Portsmouth prison. It was his opinion that hundreds of sailors, most guilty of minor offenses, were being lodged and fed at considerable expense, only to be turned loose with bad conduct discharges at the expiration of their terms.[15]

Osborne thought that the prison was "a degrading influence and was breeding criminals."[16] Daniels, impressed with Osborne's report, offered him the assignment as warden at Portsmouth prison and directed him to implement the recommendations from his study. Osborne was commissioned a lieutenant commander in the U.S. Navy Reserve. He assumed command of the prison on 10 August 1917. When interviewed in Auburn immediately before reporting to Portsmouth, he said he wanted to "save good sailors for the Navy" and that the men "needed to be repaired instead of being thrown upon the scrap heap."[17] Osborne planned to bring the same dedication and commitment to prison reform to Portsmouth that he had brought to Sing Sing— with hopes for a better outcome.

It is rare for someone with absolutely no naval experience or training to enter the Navy as a lieutenant commander, the fourth commissioned officer rank after ensign, lieutenant junior grade, and lieutenant. It would take political approval to do so, and Osborne was well connected politically. To place things in perspective, Osborne would be relieved two and a half years later by an officer three ranks above him, Commo. A.V. Wadhams, USN. It appears that the rank of lieutenant commander was selected for Osborne to give him the minimal prestige and authority needed to function as a prison commander. If Osborne had been commissioned at a higher rank, senior naval officers, who had devoted a career to achieving such rank, would have been disturbed, to say the least. As a sixty-year-old lieutenant commander, he was older than the commandant at the Navy yard and nearly twice as old as other officers of the same rank. In addition to the huge age difference, he shared almost nothing in way of background and experience with his peers at the yard; he was an anomaly among his fellow officers at the yard, if not an accident waiting to happen. Critics of Lieutenant Commander Osborne's lack of naval experience might also point out that he had as much naval experience as Secretary of the Navy Daniels— namely none. Both would bring fresh insights into the management to the Navy, but both would also suffer the consequences of that inexperience.

In his biography of Osborne, *There Is No Truce*, Chamberlain draws a connection between the wearing of the uniform of a lieutenant commander and Osborne's love of the theater and his passion for donning disguises: "When he took part in costume plays or operettas, he was enchanted by his magnificent appearance. He never failed to derive and exhibit a naïve pleasure in donning the uniform of lieutenant commander in the Naval Reserve, a rank he attained during the World War through appointment as head of the naval prison at Portsmouth, New Hampshire."[18] There is something a little disturbing about the suggestion that Osborne's time at Portsmouth as a naval officer was another costumed role on one of the many stages that made up his life.

Osborne arrived at Portsmouth with a strong personal commitment to the humanitarian treatment of prisoners. His views about prisoners, simply stated in his *Prisons and Common Sense* (1924), were well formed by 1917:[19]

1. Prisoners are human beings; for the most part remarkably like the rest of us.

2. They can be clubbed into submission—with occasional outbursts; but they cannot be reformed by that process.

3. Neither can they be reformed by bribery in the shape of privileges: special favors or tolerant treatment.

4. They will not respond to sentimentality; they do not like gush.

5. They appreciate a "square deal"—when they can get one.

6. There are not many of them mental defectives; on the contrary, the majority are embarrassingly clever. All these facts must be taken into consideration if we want prisons which will protect society.

These guiding principles can be seen in many of the reforms Osborne implemented at the naval prison. Pretentiousness played a role in some aspects of Osborne's life, but it played no role when it came to his attitude concerning prisoners. His commitment and dedication to their cause was sincere and beyond reproach.

When he was the warden at Sing Sing Prison, Osborne wrote an article, "The Prison of the Future," for a handbook on prison reform presenting his beliefs about the changes needed in prison systems. He argued that the key to the future of prisons was the indeterminate sentence for every crime, with opportunities for prisoners to progress through decreasing confinement restrictions based on prisoner behavior as evaluated by his peers. According to Osborne, "The most deterrent effect would be gained by an indeterminate sentence for every crime, the prison being reformative, remedial and educational. Of what use is it to punish a man for a few years if at the end of that time he returns to society a worthless or dangerous misfit?"[20] Osborne arrived at Portsmouth with this concept of restoration firmly rooted in his past. He set out to make it the basic precept for the future of Portsmouth prison.

Lieutenant Commander Osborne held a meeting of the prisoners the first night he was on the job to tell them the secretary of the Navy had ordered him to turn the prison "from a scrap-heap to a repair-shop."[21] To help get Osborne off to a good start, FDR paid a social visit to the prison a few weeks after Osborne assumed command.[22] Osborne's personal diary entry for 2 September 1917 humorously details the visit. Osborne had left the prison with FDR at 10:30 a.m. to catch the 11:00 a.m. train [in Portsmouth]. Cryptic notes indicate "motor stalled," "Rage [does not indicate whose rage]," and finally, "We made the train."

Apparently trains were not held for the assistant secretary of the Navy in 1917. As the result of FDR's visit, it was obvious from the outset to all concerned that Osborne had friends in high places. Daniels' visit on 19 November 1917, two months later, to investigate crowded conditions at the prison, confirmed that impression.[23]

Daniels addressed the assembled prisoners during his visit. Assuming the role of understanding father and compassionate counselor, he invoked frequent references to home, mothers, immature and rash acts, the need for discipline, and opportunities for second chances. He closed with "Old-time methods of punishment have passed away. It is with you to say what you will do with your lives.[24] With visits from the assistant secretary and the secretary of the Navy during the first three months after his arrival, there could be little doubt that change was in the air. Something important was about to happen at Portsmouth prison.

In his annual report for FY 1918, Daniels enthusiastically endorsed the new Osborne administration at Portsmouth prison and made very positive comments about conditions he had observed during his visit:

> Good prison government has resulted in great moral benefit to men undergoing punishment. As relates to the Portsmouth prison, under the direction of that able and humane commandant, Commander Thomas Mott Osborne, where by far the greater number of the men are confined, this result is believed to be due in a large measure to the system of modified self-government known as the Welfare League. . . . Mr. Osborne has given signal proof that good discipline and humane administration must get together. . . . I recently visited the Portsmouth prison, upon the dedication of the Y.M.C.A. building there, and observed the new and better spirit in the men who had been sent to prison.

Things had gotten off to a good start at Portsmouth prison.

Osborne relieved Capt. Lowry B. Stephenson, USMC, who had command of the prison for only one month and who had relieved Lieutenant Colonel Lee in July 1917. Rear Adm. Clifford J. Boush relieved Captain Howard as commandant of the yard ten days after FDR's visit to the prison. Osborne's start at Portsmouth could not have been better orchestrated. He received a strong show of support from the highest level of the Navy Department, and he had a new boss with no previous experience or prejudice about the running of a naval prison. The latter was important because a new commandant would probably be less resistant to the changes Osborne had in mind than an experienced commandant with established opinions about prison operations.

A cryptic entry in Osborne's appointment calendar for 12 September 1917, referring to the Navy yard change-of-command ceremony, speaks volumes about his general perception of naval officers and naval tradition: "Ab 10 Com. Office 'with Indians'—(absurd) New Comd. Admiral Boush (?) etc. back to work."[25] A naval officer's interpretation of the notes would suggest that Osborne had little or no use for the time-honored change-of-command tradition and ceremony, nor had he even taken enough interest in his new boss to learn how to spell his name. He apparently considered the whole ceremony to be foolish and absurd and he could not wait to get back to his real work. His initial impression of the shipyard management team, and possibly their impression of him, was not favorable. And his attitude left a lot to be desired.

With the war heating up, and the U.S. Navy rapidly increasing in numbers, it was inevitable that more sailors would find themselves serving sentences at Portsmouth. A few weeks before Osborne's arrival, and in response to the shipyard's expressed concerns about the increasing number of prisoners, the Navy Department advised the shipyard, "This office is carefully watching the number of prisoners at Portsmouth and will endeavor to avoid overcrowding that prison."[26] Despite that assurance, six weeks later the medical officer at the prison "urgently recommended that no more prisoners be transferred to the U.S. Naval prison on account of the present overcrowded condition."[27]

Osborne had inherited a rapidly growing and overcrowded prison that had strained prison logistics and infrastructure. He immediately processed urgent requisitions to obtain additional cots, pillows, and blankets. These were followed with requests for Navy yard services to address inadequate water pressure, fire protection, telephone service, and mail delivery. These requests were the first of many made of the shipyard. It would not be long before shipyard managers had the impression that Osborne's demands for support far exceeded his appreciation for that support.

Faced with increasing numbers of prisoners, Osborne immediately submitted a proposal to double up prisoners in cells and to use other prison buildings for prisoner confinement. Use of the administration building and the chapel, under extreme conditions, could significantly increase prison capacity.[28] In September 1917, Osborne advised the Navy Department of current prison capacities under various conditions:

Table 9	Portsmouth Prison Capacities in 1917 under Various Conditions		
	Favorable	Under Pressure	Extreme Pressure
Use of cell blocks [normal]	470	842	1,116
Use of administration bldg. [move Marines]	222	300	765
Use of USS *Southery* [for prisoners]	380	400	500
TOTAL	1,072	1,542	2,381

Source: Commanding Officer Portsmouth Naval Prison letter, 26 September 1917, NARA Waltham, RG 181, Portsmouth General Collection.

At that time, the *Southery* had "been placed in commission for prisoner purposes."[29] Within two months, the Marine guards were moved from the prison administration building to the old naval hospital to make room for three hundred more prisoners. Moving the Marines served two purposes: more space was made available for prisoners and, equally as important to Osborne, they were relocated at some distance from the prison. This was the first of many attempts by Osborne to reduce or eliminate the Marine guards' control of the prisoners.

At the time of the consolidation of prisons in 1914, the maximum capacity of Portsmouth prison was advertised to be five hundred prisoners. Early in the war, that maximum was exceeded by more than 100 percent. Osborne's crusade to improve prisoners' living conditions would be hard pressed to keep up with basic prisoner needs as facilities were being stretched to the limit and dozens of new prisoners arrived daily. Despite new buildings being critically needed to house the exploding prison population, Osborne considered establishing a Mutual Welfare League at the prison equally as important as erecting new buildings. The buildings took some time to plan and construct; the League was put in place immediately.

THE MUTUAL WELFARE LEAGUE

The Mutual Welfare League Osborne installed at Portsmouth prison was based on his belief that prisoners were capable of making good choices and exercising self-discipline for the good of the group in an environment that rewarded such behavior. The concept assumed that prisoners were capable of individual responsibility and accountability. By complying with the League's rules and expectations, prisoners could earn privileges that made prison confinement much more tolerable. According to biographer Rudolph W. Chamberlain, Osborne's methods stemmed directly from his philosophical beliefs about the goodness of man: "To begin with, he stood squarely on the fundamental principle of Romanticism: the inherent goodness of human nature. . . . Man is born good. He becomes evil through environment and associations. The inevitable corollary is that regeneration is possible only through an appeal to latent decency. In this struggle of the individual to regain self-respect and a sense of social responsibility, society is obligated to help by providing wholesome and inspiring conditions."[30] This romantic philosophy led Osborne to the Mutual Welfare League and a commitment to humane treatment of prisoners. Osborne strongly believed in society's obligation to provide a wholesome and inspiring environment for prisoners to demonstrate self- respect and social responsibility. The theory and ideology were good. As it turned out, the practical implementation of the concepts left much to be desired.

According to David Rothman, Osborne's Mutual Welfare League was "the design that best exemplified Progressive ambitions . . . an attempt to introduce the startling concept of inmate self-government into the penitentiary."[31] Osborne had initially implemented the Mutual Welfare League as warden of Sing Sing Prison. Introduction of this ambitious concept of progressive reform at Portsmouth, although eminently successful in terms of rehabilitated prisoners, brought much criticism and a host of problems.

The Mutual Welfare League relied on personally tailored programs for prisoners that depended on each individual's needs. According to Osborne, "Any system that does not allow for individual difference will be a failure. That is the tragic failure of the old prison system, that it treated every man alike except those who were able to pull strings of some kind or get favors. It treated every man alike and had a theoretical man, for whom the system was intended, who never existed."[32] Individual attention and the tailoring of prisoner privileges to match an individual's behavior and performance were the hallmarks of progressive prison reform.

Osborne reiterated the need for prison reforms tailored to the individual in an interview in *The Survey* (1919): "The trouble is that in our desire to index people accurately we leave out the unknown x, his quality that gives each man his individuality. Our prison methods are prepared for men in the mass, and we endeavor to enforce them without remembering that the mass is made up of individuals."[33] Osborne's vision combined the need for individual treatment with individual responsibility so as to give the prisoner the opportunity to demonstrate his capacity for rehabilitation and release.

Osborne first conceived of the Mutual Welfare League when he was chair of the New York State Commission on Prison Reform in 1913. He credits the origin of the League to a conversation he had with a fellow prisoner named Jack Murphy, whom he met when voluntarily consigned to Auburn prison for a week in October 1913. During a discussion about the possibility of gaining the warden's permission to spend a few hours on Sunday afternoon in the prison yard, Murphy suggested the privilege be granted to those prisoners in good standing, as evidenced by their membership in a good conduct league. In *Within Prison Walls*, Osborne's diary account of the week he spent as a prisoner at Auburn, he wrote, "Jack Murphy's Good Conduct League will give me plenty of food for thought. I believe he has struck the path for which I have been groping."[34] Osborne believed "that Murphy had hit on the practical way to make prisoners feel responsibility." Reflecting back on his career in *Prisons and Common Sense*, Osborne wrote "This [his conversation with Jack Murphy] was the beginning of the Mutual Welfare League."[35]

According to Frank Tannenbaum, Osborne's Mutual Welfare League at Sing Sing applied all the trappings of democracy to prison needs, including a general election of delegates from the prison population that became the government of the prison. The delegates, in turn, assigned an executive board in direct charge of the activities of the prison and a sergeant-at-arms who was responsible for discipline and order.[36] Issues were addressed through committees appointed by the executive board. Examples of issues included everything from spoons in the gravy bowls to the distribution of mail and requests for a doctor's attention.[37]

Success or failure of the system depended upon the effectiveness of the court, usually five judges, appointed by the executive board. Court cases included a wide range of charges, including fighting, assault, refusal to work, spitting in the chapel, shooting craps, and insolence to the foremen.[38] Trials were held in the prison chapel with "two or three hundred men present during the court sessions."[39] Appeals could be made to the warden's courts comprising the warden and a couple of his officials; the system effectively removed the warden from being the direct source of discipline for the prison. His role changed from an inflictor of punishment to a public defender. Sentencing involved the suspension of rights that could result in everything from reduced yard privileges to the denial of all privileges.

The Mutual Welfare League Osborne championed at Sing Sing became the Naval Welfare League at Portsmouth prison. The Naval Welfare League was a close facsimile to the Mutual Welfare League with minor changes to accommodate its new environment. According to Osborne, it was "the application here [at Portsmouth] of the idea that was developed at Auburn prison, with such changes as were necessary to apply it to a naval prison."[40] Osborne initially organized, and advertised, the league at Portsmouth prison as the Naval Welfare League, but in time it was frequently referred to as the Mutual Welfare League. The two names were essentially interchangeable during Osborne's time at Portsmouth; both will be interchangeable in this volume as well.

Osborne described the Naval Welfare League in a letter to the JAG in January 1918: The purpose of the League was "to encourage in the men confined in naval prison a stronger sense of their personal share of responsibility for good conduct and the maintenance of good order"[41] by giving them "a large share of responsibility for the prison management."[42] The privileges that a prisoner could earn through good behavior included:

1. Ordinary conversation with other prisoners
2. Smoking after meals
3. Attendance at school
4. Freedom of the cell block (winter) or out of doors recreation (summer) on Sunday afternoons and after working hours on weekdays
5. Attendance at moving pictures and such other entertainments as may be approved by the prison authorities
6. Attendance at concerts by the prison band
7. Additional letter writing
8. Self-government in the manner and to the extent shown in the bylaws hereto annexed

The League was composed of a twenty-one-member board of delegates chosen by popular vote of the League members (all prisoners in good standing) every three months. From the board of delegates, a permanent five-member executive committee and a rotating five-member judiciary committee were chosen to act as the governing authorities. The judiciary committee was responsible to "examine all cases of disorder, misconduct, breaking of rules, or breaches of discipline reported to them by the sergeant of arms" and to report their findings and recommendations to the commanding officer. Osborne quickly made it a goal to extend the power of the judiciary committee by having League members replace the Marine Corps prison guards.

Osborne arrived at Portsmouth convinced of the merits of the Mutual Welfare League, and he took every opportunity to preach its virtues. In a January 1918 letter to the JAG he wrote, "There can not be the slightest question, in the mind of any unprejudiced person who examines the matter that the League system works. While we must wait to learn of the conduct of the men restored to the service before we can fully determine the success of the system ("The proof of the pudding is in the eating"), yet, just as you can determine a circle from the smallest segment of the arc, so we can tell the general effect of the League from its effect on individual members."[43]

To make his point about the positive effects on individual members, Osborne included a number of letters from inmates attesting to the value of the League. Using personal testimony from inmates to reinforce an argument became one of Osborne's most popular tactics while at Portsmouth prison. His argument that "the proof of the pudding is in the eating" eventually came up short in the eyes of some fleet commanders who were concerned about the restoration of marginal performers to the fleet. One could say the fleet commanders did not swallow the pudding Osborne was trying to feed them.

In conjunction with the Naval Welfare League, Osborne also started a prison newspaper, written and published by inmates. *The Naval Welfare News*, later *The Mutual Welfare News,* was a well-written, attractive newspaper that grew to an average of eight pages in length. It routinely reported on events at the prison, highlighted the accomplishments of the Naval Welfare League, featured short stories and poems written by prisoners, and published letters from "graduates" who had made good on the outside. The first page of the first issue of *The Naval Welfare News*, issued less than a month after Osborne's arrival, contained a journalistic tribute to Osborne that illustrated the immediate positive affect he had on the prisoners:

O   is for old orders that he banished.

S   is sentence, shorter every day.

B   is beastly treatment that he has banished.

O   means only that he wore grey.

R   is restoration that we long for.

N   stands for NAVY, true and brave.

E   ase them all together, they spell OSBORNE—A MAN that sticks up for the men in grey.[44]

Osborne was the prisoners' champion from his very first days at Portsmouth. He would remain such until his very last hours as their leader. However, the zeal with which he served as their champion contributed to his undoing. *The Mutual Welfare News* routinely chronicled Osborne's achievements. It also gave Osborne a mechanism to keep his message of individual responsibility and accountability in front of the prisoners.

The Mutual Welfare News was but one of a wide range of educational, recreational, and cultural programs for the prisoners. The prison library was another. A wartime evaluation of the library by William Adams Slade, a representative of the Library War Service of the American Literary Association, stated: "The record sheets in the prison library . . . included, among others, books for use in teaching reading, writing, spelling, arithmetic, French, Spanish, shorthand, bookkeeping, elementary science, chemistry, physics, geology, biology, astronomy, mechanical drawing, machine shop practice, operation of marine and gas engines, Naval architecture, telegraphy, telephony, wireless electricity, navigation, seamanship, history, biography, and music. . . . [T]he prisoners who are the better educated or the greater in professional or technical skill, serve as instructors."[45] Austin MacCormick, who later became one of the nation's foremost experts in prison education, began his career with Osborne at the Portsmouth prison. MacCormick was one of those who donned disguises and voluntarily confined themselves with Osborne in January 1917. The influence of Osborne and MacCormick can be found in the quality of the library and other innovative educational and training programs implemented at the prison.

Increased participation in the many training, educational, and cultural activities could be earned by being a member in good standing of the League. Neither rewards nor punishments were administered en masse to a community of prisoners; both were individually given according to an individual's behavior and capacity for assuming individual accountability and responsibility. Frank Tannenbaum noted the difference in individual accountability under the old and new systems: "Under the old system the entire population was suppressed in an attempt to prevent the individual from breaking the rules. Under the community system . . . the individual was punished for his misbehavior without repression of the ordinary activities of the mass of the prison population . . . the individual was punished according to his desserts, without the dehumanizing of all convicts in the process."[46]

In his annual report for FY1920, published on 1 July 1920, a few months after Osborne's departure from Portsmouth, Daniels was glowing in his praise of the Mutual Welfare League: "It has demonstrated its great improvement over all other prison systems. . . . Before the introduction of the new methods there was a marine detachment of 141 to guard 175 prisoners, men were not allowed to talk except during meals and a brief period following it and the old system of severe prison discipline was followed. . . . Education, athletics, and entertainment, with religious services, serve to give a new and hopeful atmosphere."[47] Daniels was accurate with his description of the improvements the League had brought to Portsmouth prison. Critics would argue that it also brought abuses that would lead to its undoing.

The Mutual Welfare League was the keystone for the reform architecture Osborne put in place at Portsmouth. It was implemented shortly after his arrival, was in operation the day of his departure, and continued for about one year after he left the prison. Osborne's immediate successor, Commodore Wadhams, USN, was a strong endorser of the League, but he only lasted a year in the job. Wadhams' relief, Lt. Col. Hamilton South, USMC, essentially took a sledgehammer to the League and totally demolished it within a few weeks after his arrival.

⸻

Osborne had been warden at New York's Sing Sing Prison (1914–15) and was a noted prison reformer when he arrived at Portsmouth at the start of the World War I. Clearly those in the Navy knew what they were getting when they hired him to be warden at Portsmouth prison. Many would think a prison administration based on prisoner self-government and open dealings between the warden and prisoners is a poor choice for a naval prison. Nevertheless, Osborne made it work quite well at Portsmouth prison—for a while.

In *Prisons and Common Sense*, Osborne described his prison operations through the eyes of a newly reporting officer who was amazed at what he saw: "During the first day he looked about; found upwards of 2000 prisoners, *most of them living in barracks outside the prison–with no bolts or bars and no wall around the grounds*; saw a number of prisoners go down to their work in the Navy Yard, accompanied by a few marine guards; *saw the rest going about their duties at the prison without any guards at all*; . . . saw the third-class prisoners entirely under the charge of their fellow prisoners of the first-class; saw, in short, *an unguarded prison run by the prisoners*" [emphasis added].[48] Successful implementation of the Mutual Welfare League had produced, in Osborne's own words, "an unguarded prison run by the prisoners." A prison without bolts, bars, and guards may have been Osborne's vision of a prison utopia, but it was hardly what the fleet had in mind when they sent courts-martialed prisoners to Portsmouth.

11

Reform Struggles at Portsmouth

In time of trouble a letter to "Dear Frank [FDR]" worked miracles, and disgruntled Navy officers discovered it was dangerous to bedevil the Commanding Officer at Portsmouth [Prison] too much.

—Rudolph W. Chamberlain, 1935, *There Is No Truce: A Life of Thomas Mott Osborne*

The Commandant disapproves fixing the temperature [90 degrees] which when reached working parties shall not be required to leave the Prison. . . . It is not expected that the war will mark time when that temperature is reached.

—Rear Adm. Clifford Boush, 1918

Osborne had little use for naval customs and traditions. Of Osborne's intolerance for naval protocol, Chamberlain wrote, "For the fetishes of the service, the rules of etiquette, and the sanctity of rank, he [Osborne] cared not a whit. They were useless, ridiculous, humiliating."[1] Daniels held similar sentiments about naval rank and traditions. Their lack of respect for naval protocol was an irritant to the naval officer community, which made for difficult and strained relationships. Is there any doubt that Osborne and his fellow officers would, in time, disagree on many issues?

Osborne's disregard for naval protocol caused his success to be challenged and his critics to multiply. He did not appreciate the necessity of gaining the cooperation of intermediaries between him and higher authority. Richard Lewis Alan Weiner in his Harvard University thesis, "Ideology and Incumbency: Thomas Mott Osborne and the 'Failure' of Progressive Era Prison Reform," suggested that Osborne's life would have been a lot easier and his accomplishments even more impressive had he gained that cooperation, "even if it meant feigning collaboration with those not disposed to his policies."[2] Osborne, however, preferred confrontation to compromise. His failure to build a consensus for his views on prison reform with his contemporaries and immediate superiors in the Navy yard, as well as officers of the operating fleet, contributed to his ultimate failure to implement permanent reform at Portsmouth prison.

Osborne often treated fellow officers with intransigence and intolerance and frequently overreacted to criticism of his practices or his prisoners in a manner that made adversaries of would-be supporters. Not one to ever back away from an argument, he frequently responded with self-righteous lengthy prose that belittled opposing views. He was insensitive to the military environment and traditions of which he was a part by virtue of being a lieutenant commander in the U.S. Navy. He showed contempt for the Marine Corps and its traditions, upon which he was dependent for prison guards and security. Finally, he had an utter disrespect and a total disregard for the time-honored naval chain of command. Rather than a tool for efficient administration of naval matters, Osborne viewed it as an obstacle to be ignored or worked around.

The following specific examples show how Osborne repeatedly challenged or avoided the Navy's way of doing things. These examples, perhaps not particularly damning as isolated incidents, had the cumulative effect of straining working relationships at the Navy yard and in the operating fleet. These strained relationships worked to the detriment of his reform efforts.

The chain of command became an immediate challenge for Osborne. Within a month of his arrival, Osborne revised the prisoners' daily schedule to incorporate more recreation and free time for the prisoners. He submitted the revised schedule to the yard commandant, Rear Admiral Boush, for his approval on 13 September 1917, only one day after Boush had assumed command of the shipyard. Among other things, the schedule proposed revisions to improve conditions for the after-meal smoke breaks: "The old schedule permits a considerable time for smoking and talk after each meal—thirty minutes. The custom has been to lock the men in the bathroom during this period [after-meal smoking]; but that is impracticable owing to the increase in numbers. The prisoners now have their smoking privileges in the open air on fine days and in the cellblock in bad weather. . . . The new schedule will permit a few moments for a smoke after each meal, in the cells."[3] Commandant Boush approved the new schedule "with the exception of smoking in the cells."[4] With this disapproval, the newly arrived commandant had given Osborne his first indication that he was not going to be able to routinely implement everything he wanted to do at the prison. Some resistance could be expected from his immediate superior in the chain of command. Finding ways to work around the inconvenient chain of command would become a high priority for Osborne.

Even though Boush was new to the job, he quickly understood that Osborne would be pushing for significant changes to the operation of the prison. Some of these changes could be implemented locally with Boush's approval whereas others required the concurrence of the office of the secretary of the Navy. In either case, Boush was in a position to exercise control over Osborne because official naval correspondence to activities outside the shipyard required the endorsement of the commandant; thus, naval regulations and correspondence procedures provided the bureaucratic structure needed to keep Osborne in check. Osborne, however, did not take kindly to bureaucratic controls. He skirted perceived roadblocks through personal appeals to his contacts at the highest level of the Navy Department. And he did so on numerous occasions. Such bypassing of the chain of command only served to frustrate and antagonize his critics.

More often than not, Osborne's requests of the office of the secretary of the Navy were through personal letters, telegrams, and conversations instead of using official Navy channels and correspondence. According to Chamberlain, "In time of trouble a letter to 'Dear Frank [FDR]' worked miracles, and disgruntled Navy officers discovered it was dangerous to bedevil the commanding officer at Portsmouth [prison] too much."[5] Osborne considered naval correspondence regulations to be bureaucratic "red tape." A diary entry during one of Osborne's earliest visits to the naval prison before he assumed command simply reads "endless red tape."[6] Osborne knew early on that his friendships with Daniels and FDR were critical to his success at Portsmouth. Without their help, he thought he would be mired in "endless red tape."

Daniels was sympathetic to Osborne's goals for the prison and very receptive to any requests for help. In his annual report for FY 1918, the secretary wrote, "Punishment for military offenses in time of war must be swift and sure, but even in war the policy has been to *mend, not to break, prisoners* [emphasis added]. The Navy is composed of boys and young men. Some of them violate regulations more from thoughtlessness than from intent to be violators of regulations of law. Desertion in times of war is a serious offense, and it is met with summary and stern punishment; but even for this grave offense hope of reformation to the guilty must not be denied."[7] Daniels' goal of mending and not breaking naval prisoners, with a total commitment to giving young wayward sailors every opportunity for restoration, was a page right out of Osborne's progressive reform manual.

Clearly, Osborne enjoyed a close personal relationship with both Daniels and FDR. Osborne met with Daniels in Washington four times between 17 March and 10 August 1917, when he assumed command of Portsmouth prison.[8] On one of those occasions, Daniels invited Osborne to his home after their meeting, and on another occasion, they had dinner and went to the theater. They met at least six more times while Osborne was at Portsmouth, including for dinner at FDR's residence on 25 November 1919.[9] Some of the meetings were quite long and involved, indicating that Daniels and Roosevelt had considerable interest in Osborne's work. For example, Osborne's personal calendar entry for 8 September 1917 reads, "Arr Washington am Breakfast Roosevelt Walk to Dept. [Navy]—Lunch—More Roosevelt & Daniels—Train 7 pm for Boston."[10] Here was a lieutenant commander putting in a full day of work in Washington, D.C., with the secretary of the Navy and his assistant. It is highly unusual for a lieutenant commander to have this kind of personal access to the most senior levels of the Navy. A more accommodating person might have balanced such access with personal habits and actions that would have defused others' resentment and criticism of that access; however, Osborne's attitude and methods were more defiant than accommodating. The result was that he became a target for critics.

The events surrounding the building of additional facilities needed to accommodate the increasing number of prisoners at Portsmouth illustrate Osborne's early manipulation of the chain of command. Despite being the most junior attendee at a Washington, D.C., meeting in December 1917, when decisions were made about needed prison facilities, Lieutenant Commander Osborne's views prevailed and the results of that meeting strongly reflect his influence. The meeting attendees included the secretary of the Navy, several admirals, and Osborne.

After the meeting, a directive was issued to the commandant of the Portsmouth Navy Yard, Osborne's immediate boss, ordering the erection of three barracks and a mess hall, the major portion of the work to be done by the prisoners under the supervision of the public works officer.[11] Osborne had apparently convinced the senior Navy officials that "his" prisoners were capable of such a task at a large cost savings to the Navy. Unfortunately, in this case Osborne knew little about the technical requirements and trade skills needed for the construction of buildings or the shipyard labor agreements covering such work.

In response to the Washington directive, the industrial manager of the shipyard, Cdr. H. L. Wyman, highlighted the undesirability of using inexperienced prison labor for construction requiring highly skilled laborers as well as "the likelihood of creating serious labor difficulties"[12] with local labor organizations if prison labor and yard labor were employed side by side. With only a few months on the job, Osborne's exuberance to advance his agenda had prompted him to make commitments for prison labor that not only exceeded their abilities but also were in conflict with existing union contracts. As with the chain of command, Osborne apparently considered unions and labor contracts merely obstacles to be ignored or worked around.

The industrial manager's $425,000 estimate for the project to erect three barracks and a mess hall prompted the commandant to recommend a much less expensive project. Boush also concurred with the industrial manager that the mixing of prison and shipyard labor for this project was highly undesirable.[13] Common sense prevailed when the Navy Department backed down and decided to provide temporary facilities for housing approximately five hundred men. The work was to be accomplished by a contractor; prison labor, if used at all, was to be limited to grading and site preparation.[14] (The temporary wooded barracks that were built are shown in photo 15.)

Under normal circumstances, a major shipyard construction project would begin with a proposal from those in the shipyard who were responsible for, and knowledgeable about, the work. In this case the Navy Department in Washington, under Osborne's influence, mandated the details of a project that would have been technically impossible within the proposed budget and a nightmare from the standpoint of labor relations. Osborne's bypassing of the chain of command frequently caused the tail [Washington] to wag the dog [Navy yard]—to the consternation of the Portsmouth Navy Yard department heads.

The industrial manager's concern about the use of prison labor was validated later on a different project, when the Metal Trades Council, American Federation of Labor, Portsmouth, New Hampshire, protested the use of prison labor for work ordinarily performed by civilian workmen.[15] The industrial manager replied in general concurrence with that policy, but noted a recent exception "on patriotic grounds," in order to complete repairs on an armored cruiser "needed for convoy duty for the protection of the lives of our fellow-country-men."[16] Despite this exception, the American Federation of Labor spokesman protested "against the continued employment of prisoners in any of the departments of the Portsmouth Navy Yard when civilian employees are daily being discharged from the service of the Government."[17] Osborne was obviously unaware, or uncaring, about such union agreements.

Osborne also used his Washington connections to get approvals for prisoners to go off the shipyard for drama club presentations and other performances. Osborne often orchestrated the receipt of telegrams from Daniels or FDR to gain permission for prisoner off-yard activities. For example, FDR personally approved naval prisoners traveling off-yard to give shows at the Portsmouth Opera House on 1 September 1919 and York Lancaster Harbor on 29 August 1919.[18] FDR also granted permission for fourteen Jewish prisoners to attend Jewish religious services in Portsmouth in September 1919.[19] Osborne routinely forwarded the Washington telegrams to the commandant for concurrence—after the fact—and approval of gate passes so the prisoners could leave and reenter the Navy yard. Having already received authorization from the assistant secretary of the Navy for such activity, the commandant was not about to disapprove Osborne's requests for gate passes.

With Osborne's background in theater and the arts, it is not surprising the prison drama club was one of his more innovative and ambitious programs. The interaction of prisoners with the local community during frequent performances in local theaters was another remarkable feature of Osborne's reforms. Consider the following drama club calendar for 1919:

Table 10	Portsmouth Prison Drama Club Calendar for 1919	
Date	*Location*	*Title*
25, 26 Apr	Portsmouth Music Hall	Easter Show [overture & dance program]
28 June	Portsmouth Music Hall	Summer Show [minstrel & one act plays]
16 Aug	Portsmouth Music Hall	Creatures of Impulse [play with chorus]
29 Aug	York Lancaster Hall	Creatures of Impulse [play with chorus]
1 Sept	Portsmouth Music Hall	Midsummer Night Dream in Old Madrid
11 Dec	Manchester Strand	Entertainment [dance & play]

Source: Programs filed in Box 270 of the Osborne Family Papers at the Syracuse University Bird Library, Syracuse, NY.

As many as forty or fifty prisoners might be involved with each production, complete with orchestra, costumes, scenery, makeup, and everything else required to stage a first-rate show. Several of the programs for these performances included as many as fifty advertisements from local vendors, an unusually high level of community interest and participation. On one occasion, ninety-eight prisoners traveled in thirteen cars to Manchester, New Hampshire, to give a dramatic performance.[20] One of the thirteen cars lost its way on the return to Portsmouth. With no guards in the car, the prisoners reportedly roamed all over the area into the early hours of the morning, never contemplating escape, "trying to find the right way back to prison."[21] In addition to performing at off-site venues, the drama club frequently entertained ship-yard officers and their wives on the shipyard.

Some time after Osborne's departure from Portsmouth, in a letter to the *New York Times* dated 24 December 1922, he explained that the value of prisoner performances was not in the entertainment provided the public, but rather in the trust shown the prisoners and the interruption in the monotony of prison life. Osborne's letter was motivated by the newspaper's report of the escape of an Auburn prisoner who had taken advantage of that trust. According to Osborne, "Some inmates . . . are unfit for trust; but the difficulty is that you can't tell the ones until you trust them." He cautioned readers not to condemn a program for one prisoner escape when hundreds of prisoners have proven trustworthy. Relating his experience at Portsmouth prison, Osborne wrote, "The prisoners not only got up remarkably good shows, but they gave them ten times in Portsmouth, once at York Harbor and once at Manchester (over sixty miles from the prison). Escape was absurdly easy; but, although there were among those taking part long-term as well as short-term prisoners, and even some 'lifers,' there was not a single case of bad faith. Not one single man attempted to escape; we returned with full numbers in every instance."[22] Osborne was a staunch defender of prisoner performances to civilian audiences. His two passions in life, prison reform and theatrical performance, met on the stage with each performance.

One might conclude from table 10 that some prisoners at Portsmouth prison enjoyed more evenings on liberty during the summer of 1919 than did sailors serving deployments on naval ships. This perception did not go unnoticed in the fleet. Later, a few unguarded prisoners' comments about preference for confinement at Ports-mouth over life at sea sparked an uprising in the fleet that eventually contributed to an investigation of conditions at Portsmouth prison. The fleet did not take kindly to the thought that prisoners were being treated better than sailors on sea duty.

Osborne was also quick to solicit the help of Daniels and FDR on policy and procedural matters. A few months after assuming command, he recommended changes to the Manual for the Government of United States Prisons to the secretary of the Navy. His recommended changes included reduced segregation of the classes of prisoners, increased cigarette smoking privileges, elimination of all rules of silence, and encouragement of prisoners to write to wives and parents.[23] The first change, reduced segregation of the classes of prisoners, was a frequently recurring theme during the Osborne era at Portsmouth.

Osborne, determined to streamline the cumbersome processes requiring many routine prisoner requests to be approved in Washington, D.C., was particularly irked by the slow approval for prisoners to travel home for funerals or serious illness of family members. He claimed that funerals were being missed because the system was too slow.[24] Responding to Osborne's criticism, Daniels approved local approval of such requests for prisoners in good standing, provided the family paid for prisoner and guard expenses.[25] Osborne repeatedly demonstrated his ability to cut through red tape to avoid bureaucratic delays.

Osborne never hesitated to forcefully remind Daniels and FDR of their lack of support if they failed to deliver on a promise. On one such occasion, Osborne took FDR to task for Daniels' failure to effect a change to Navy policy that would let his "graduates" qualify for honorable discharges. The Navy Department had "directed that no man who had been a General Court Martial prisoner should receive an honorable discharge," and Osborne sought to reverse that decision so his graduates, who had made good on his terms, could be placed "on an even keel with others."[26] Osborne reminded FDR that the secretary had assured him that the policy would be changed, but the matter was still unresolved. Osborne's tone with FDR was often that of an equal, lacking the deference normally expected of a lieutenant commander speaking to a senior official. Unfortunately, Osborne often exhibited this same lack of deference to admirals and captains who were much less accommodating and understanding than apparently were FDR and Daniels.

Osborne took advantage of his personal relationships in Washington to restructure shipyard organizational responsibilities and expand his authority within the Navy yard. He used the overcrowded conditions at the prison to justify moving the Marine guards off the prison grounds so their quarters could be converted to prisoner accommodations. Eager to minimize the influence and interference of the Marine guards by distancing them physically and organizationally from his prison, Osborne claimed the relocation of the guards could be done without "in any way decreasing safety." In fact, he argued, safety would actually be increased, as "it is very undesirable to have too close association between the prisoners and their guards."[27] The secretary of the Navy endorsed what appeared to be a blatant power grab on Osborne's part and encouraged Boush to support the move despite the latter's concerns and objections.

Six months later, in March of 1918, Osborne attempted to have the prison guard detachment placed under his direct command. He argued, "At present there is a double standard authority over the Prison Marine sentries which is certain, even under the most favorable circumstances, to result in misunderstandings, poor discipline, and loss of efficiency."[28] This issue was elevated to the headquarters of the Marine Corps in Washington, D.C., through the secretary of the Navy. The end result gave Osborne control over the daily assigned guards, but this was far less than the total control Osborne desired.[29] This conflict was just one of many incidents between Osborne and the Marines during his tenure at the shipyard.

No sooner had the dust settled from his attempt to gain control of the Marine guards than Osborne moved to gain total control of the operations on the *Southery*. Any debate about Osborne's request for total control of the *Southery* was cut short when Daniels sent a telegram to Boush saying, "Commanding Officer *Southery* should be regarded as an assistant to the Commanding Officer of the prison."[30] The commandant complied immediately with the secretary's order by issuing a local directive saying, "The Commanding Officer of the Naval Prison has full and complete authority over the Commanding Officer of the *Southery* in all matters affecting the prisoners on that ship . . . the Commanding Officer of the *Southery* will be regarded as an assistant to the Commanding Officer of the Prison."[31] Four months into his tour of duty at Portsmouth, Osborne obviously enjoyed the total confidence and backing of the secretary of the Navy. Anyone familiar with the time-honored tradition of naval command can appreciate the frustration Boush must have felt to have the secretary of the Navy routinely usurping his command authority.

A few months after gaining control of *Southery*, Osborne exercised it to the fullest when he chastised the commanding officer of the *Southery* for withdrawing the smoking privileges of prisoners after a disturbance. Osborne reminded him that "instructions from the Bureau of Navigation gives Commanding Officer Naval Prison entire responsibility for the discipline of the General Court Martial Prisoners on board the *Southery,* and this leaves no discretion in the matter . . . in punishing the prisoners by withdrawal of smoking privileges, in a recent case of disorder, you were overstepping the line which the Bureau of Navigation has drawn."[32] Osborne gained in stature with the inmates by routinely championing the causes of prisoners, but at what cost to his relationships with his fellow officers at the prison and shipyard? Osborne's aggressive power grabs and zealous commitment to improve prisoner living conditions made him unpopular with his contemporaries in the yard. In their minds he coddled prisoners while showing his colleagues little or no respect. Osborne's attitude and actions led to strained and outright adversarial relations that limited his ability to achieve lasting success.

Adversarial Relationships in the Shipyard

One can only imagine the consternation that resulted when an extremely liberal prison reformer was implanted in the traditionally conservative Navy yard officer corps. Osborne was a worldly, politically astute, fifty-eight-year-old lieutenant commander with no naval experience when he arrived at the yard. Worse yet, he was impatient when it came to prison reform. He never hesitated to flaunt his expertise on the subject. His destabilizing influence in the Navy yard made everyone's job, including his own, more difficult.

Osborne's propensity to generate a seemingly never-ending stream of miscellaneous requests to improve living conditions for his prisoners proved to be an irritant to the shipyard officers who were obligated to respond to the requests. These officers, who were working long hours to meet ship repair schedules and other wartime priorities, did not always share Osborne's sense of urgency for prisoner living accommodations or other prisoner needs. Osborne's priorities often differed from those of the rest of the shipyard. Frequently, after raising an issue or problem to be solved, Osborne debated the issue ad nauseam in written correspondence rather than resolve the problem through face-to-face confrontation.

Osborne was an excellent and prolific writer who was apt to launch into a written sermon or dissertation on prison reform at the slightest provocation. Frequently the provocation was a short letter from a senior naval officer drawing Osborne's attention to a shortcoming in his prison. The unsuspecting originator of the complaint might receive a six- to eight-page letter in response, which absolved Osborne of all blame and highlighted the officer's ignorance of the proper handling of prisoners. Such actions tended to rub salt in the wounds of a naval officer community that found liberalism, prison reform, and the policies of Daniels and Osborne troublesome to begin with. Osborne was unpopular with his contemporary officers at the yard, if not an outright irritant and nuisance.

Osborne's inclination to write about problems instead of solving them prompted his Navy yard adversaries to do the same. The official Navy files are filled with accusatory memoranda about trivial matters, generated by both sides. These did not have to be written. Too often the commandant found himself refereeing disputes between Osborne and his adversaries. On one occasion, the commandant received complaints from shipyard personnel about the conduct of several prisoners assigned to a work party. The prisoners had reportedly exhibited impertinent conduct toward officers' wives and women shipyard workers, conversed with civilian workers, and had been observed loafing on their jobs.[33] When queried, Osborne responded that he had received no such reports from the Marine guards. Further investigation revealed that the Marines were reluctant to report prisoner misconduct to Osborne because, they said, he never backed them up when they did so.[34]

A heated exchange of memoranda ensued between the commanding officer of the Navy yard Marine detachment, Maj. Lauren S. Willis, and Osborne, during which Willis assured Osborne that his Marines would continue to perform their guard duty as required by Marine Corps tradition. Willis suggested that Osborne should do the same, implying discipline and accountability were lacking in his prison command. As Osborne was prone to do, he lashed out in response saying, "If I were to attempt to dispense discipline according to the theories of the Marine force, . . . there [would] be nearly as many different kinds of discipline as there were sentries."[35] Osborne had little respect for the Marines and the Marines had even less respect for him and his methods. Osborne and the commanding officer of the Marines at the Navy yard maintained an ongoing adversarial relationship for the entire time Osborne was at Portsmouth.

Within a month after the work party incident, there was another similar report of prisoners marching in an unmilitary manner in the Navy yard. (Prisoners can be seen working and moving about the yard in photos 16 and 17.) Cdr. H. L. Wyman reported he had observed prisoners exhibiting "unduly slouchy appearance and habitually slow and unmilitary pace when marching in squad."[36] Wyman had observed prisoners talking and laughing in ranks with "their heads turned in various directions."[37] Osborne dismissed Commander Wyman's concerns by suggesting, "Prisoners of any sort are, as a rule, dull and dispirited in appearance and conduct. It is perfectly natural that they should be so."[38] Osborne took the opportunity to express his displeasure with his lack of control over the Marine sentries by indicating that he was "under serious disadvantage in dealing with the conduct of prisoners who are in the charge of Marine sentries over whom he has no authority."[39] Osborne suggested that the Mutual Welfare League could do a better job of prisoner surveillance than the Marine sentries.[40] He also suggested better-fitting uniforms would improve prisoner appearance. As so often was the case, Osborne did not assign any blame to himself or his prisoners. Instead, in this case, the Marine sentries and ill-fitting uniforms were at fault for the prisoners' impertinent conduct and slouchy appearance.

Osborne's relationship with Major Willis reached a low point in August 1919 when the secretary of the Mutual Welfare League, a court-martialed prisoner, wrote a letter to the Marine officer of the day requesting the attendance of eleven Marines as witnesses for a League trial. An angry Major Willis wrote the commandant, "It is considered subversive to discipline to require an enlisted man in a duty status, and especially a non-commissioned officer, to appear before a delegation of general court-martial prisoners for investigation."[41] Willis requested "disciplinary action be taken in this case and that steps be taken to put a stop to this practice."[42] Osborne considered the instance an inadvertent mistake and the request of Major Willis for disciplinary action to be "quite superfluous."[43] Osborne's disdain of Marine Corps tradition and discipline was a continuing source of disagreement and friction. Boush had much better things to do than referee an ongoing battle between the commanding officer of the prison and the commanding officer of the Marine detachment.

It is not surprising that another Marine, Lt. Col. H. L. South, quickly abolished the Mutual Welfare League and reversed most of Osborne's reform innovations upon assuming command of Portsmouth prison in 1921. South was one of many Marines who commanded the prison. The first seven commanding officers of the prison before Osborne were Marine Corps officers, as were all the commanding officers after Osborne's immediate successor, Commodore Wadhams. That Osborne was the first naval officer to command the prison after a series of Marines may have provided an interservice rivalry that added to Osborne's difficulties.

Osborne also had several run-ins with the Navy yard supply officer, Capt. F. T. Arms, USN, who relied on prison labor work parties to clean warehouses, move materials, and load ships. During the height of the war, as many as 250 prisoners were assigned daily to the supply department.[44] On one occasion, a work party of 40 prisoners assigned a high-priority job loading boiler tubes on the USS *Houston* refused to work in the rain alongside supply department personnel who were working in the rain to get the job done. Worse yet, the prisoners were guilty of "obscene language and contumacious conduct" when ordered to proceed with loading the boiler tubes.

Supply department personnel solicited the efforts of an active duty naval petty officer, Boatswain's Mate Kelly, to get the prisoners to proceed with the work, but Kelly's efforts were equally unsuccessful. Only thirty-five tubes, weighing 80 pounds each, were loaded on 23 September 1919 when an average of thirty five hundred tubes a day had to be loaded to meet the required load-out date of 13 October 1919. Captain Arms attributed the problem directly to Osborne. According to Arms, "The Supply Officer cannot extract from a subordinate duty which he is unable, by reason of the prison regulations, to accomplish. . . . No good end can be accomplished by continuing the employment of prisoners unless there is someone competent and with the necessary authority to make them work whether they desire to or not."[45]

Concerned about the high priority assigned to the work and the possibility that loading of the boiler tubes might not be completed as scheduled, Arms added, "In the event that the prisoners are taken away entirely from this work, it is recommended that a despatch [*sic*] be sent to the Navy Department, telling them why this work cannot be accomplished by the thirteenth of October, that is, the unwillingness of the prisoners to perform it, and the lack of funds to hire a sufficient number of *civilians, who, of course, could be made to work in the rain* [emphasis added]."[46]

Osborne seized the situation and replaced the contentious prisoners with some of his best performers; loading of the *Houston* was completed on 3 October, nine days early. Captain Arms, after complaining so bitterly about the lack of progress on the first day, felt compelled to send a letter of commendation for the two prisoners most responsible for the successful loading. Arms' compliment was wrapped around an overall criticism of Osborne's prison operation: "So many complaints have originated in this office, during the past year or so, concerning the dishonesty and shirking of Naval prisoners that the Supply Officer [Arms] feels constrained to invite the Commandant's attention to any special meritorious case. It was almost entirely through Hagarty's efforts that order was brought out of chaos. . . . Both of these men deserve, and have the highest approbation of this office. . . . The vile language used by the prisoners first employed, who are understood to have been of the criminal class, disappeared entirely when prisoners undergoing punishment for military offenses were substituted for them."[47]

Note the reference in the last sentence to improved performance because of the substitution of labor drawn from prisoners confined for military offenses rather than criminal offenses. Not only did Osborne disregard Navy regulations and mix the serious offenders with the less serious offenders in confinement, he permitted serious offenders to roam the yard as members of prison work parties.

Osborne, as might be expected, was not content to let the matter pass without comment. His response took issue with Arms, the supervisors on the job, and the Navy's definition of a criminal. All were at fault save Osborne and his prisoners: "The Commanding Officer of the Prison [Osborne] cannot let this occasion pass without calling attention to the unfortunate tone of the report of the Supply Officer [Arms] . . . hopeless failure awaits those who try to *drive* unwilling workmen, whether in or out of prison, and who regard a sailor boy sent up here for "sleeping on watch" or a few hours over leave," as a *convict*" [emphasis in original].[48] Boush was frequently called upon to referee disputes between Osborne and other shipyard managers regarding matters related to prisoner work parties.

Prisoner work programs were a large benefit to the shipyard during the war. Osborne believed "every crime is only misdirected energy"[49] and subscribed to the philosophy that "work could be the religion of the prison."[50] Numerous work parties involving over one thousand men were assigned tasks daily "excavating, laying concrete, [and] moving building materials and supplies, while others engaged in the hundred and one jobs required for the running of a large and growing Navy Yard."[51] Much of this work was done with minimal supervision. Prisoner work parties were a welcomed source of labor for the Navy yard. They provided valuable experience and training for the prisoners when they left the prison, as well as daily opportunities for prisoners to interact with others in the shipyard. These public encounters often resulted in criticism of prisoner behavior, which Osborne was required to address.

Shipyard managers, forced to rely on prison labor to meet wartime deadlines, often felt that neither the prisoners nor Osborne shared their concerns and priorities. The extremely democratic prison environment produced many lax and poorly disciplined prisoners. These prisoners, when assigned to work parties, were frequently cited for poor appearance, lackadaisical performance, and theft. When challenged, Osborne would almost always rally to a prisoner's defense.

In January 1920, shortly after the war ended, Captain Arms found himself pleading for prison labor, which was then in short supply. A precipitous postwar decline in prison population and a significant cut to the supply department's budget had reduced the department's operations to "the minimum consistent with keeping the store open at all."[52] After being cited in an inspection report by Rear Adm. H. O. Dunn, commander First Naval District, for the unsatisfactory state of stowage and cleanliness of his shipyard storage buildings, Captain Arms claimed that the unsatisfactory conditions were owing to the loss of prisoner labor: "All through the war large numbers of prisoners were employed in this department, averaging about two hundred and fifty per diem. . . . With the loss of these prisoners . . . the Supply Officer finds himself absolutely unable to arrange his stores in a neat and businesslike manner."[53] Captain Arms believed his department's need for prison labor was as great as at any time during the war because the number of ships in the yard to be unloaded was "larger than the number has been for a long period of years." Arms claimed that the workload exceeded the supply department's available postwar resources. Clearly the prisoner work parties Arms had been so critical of during the war had also provided a valuable service to his department.

A request from Commandant Halstead for additional funding from Washington confirmed that the loss of prison labor was a hardship for shipyard operations: "During the war the number of prisoners available for work at the prison was over 2000, but at present the number is less than 500, of whom not more than 100 are available for work. Furthermore, the number of marines has been so cut that not more than six sentries for prison working parties are available and this number is frequently reduced."[54] Osborne's prisoner work parties, so often the target of accusations and complaints during the war, were sorely missed immediately after the war.

Prisoner work parties were just one source of strained relations. There were others. In fact, Osborne seemed dedicated to keeping the commandant's in-basket and frustration level filled to the brim. For example, the commandant must have been shocked to receive an urgent request from Osborne in June 1919 for "one thousand (1,000) rifles for use at the Naval Prison for the purpose of holding battalion drill by the prisoners." Osborne reassured Boush, "Should the request be granted, the firing pins would be removed."[55] Boush, incredulous that any prison warden would ever

consider arming inmates, immediately disapproved the request.[56] Less than a year earlier, prison authorities thought that Sunday evening movies represented the cutting
edge of prison reform; now prisoners were running the prison under the Mutual
Welfare League and the warden wanted to give them rifles.

"Rifles for prisoners" was not Osborne's most controversial request. During the
summer of 1918, he requested that working parties not be required to leave the prison
when the temperature reached 90° F.[57] (Photo 18 shows Commandant Boush at the
christening the USS *O-1*, the yard's second submarine, on 9 July 1918, a few weeks
before Osborne's request.) When the commandant was actively involved with converting the yard's industrial processes to the construction of submarines to fulfill its
new mission, Osborne did not believe his prisoners should have to work when it was
hot. Boush immediately disapproved the request, noting that the war would continue
independent of the temperature at the Portsmouth Navy Yard: "The Commandant
disapproves fixing the temperature which when reached working parties shall not be
required to leave the Prison. Personnel, both service and civilian will undoubtedly
be required to work when the temperature reaches 90 degrees Fahrenheit and it is
not expected that the war will mark time when that temperature is reached."[58] Why
would Osborne make such frivolous requests of the commandant when the requests
seriously undermined his credibility with his boss and contemporaries in the Navy
yard? Possibly Osborne thought that knowledge of such requests, leaked to prisoners,
would enhance his reputation as "champion" of prisoner causes. If so, Osborne was
more concerned about his reputation with his prisoners than his reputation with his
boss and contemporaries.

Another example of Osborne's championing of prisoner causes involved a disagreement between shipyard officials and a representative for eighty prisoners who
were coaling the *Southery* in September 1919. According to Osborne, shipyard officials were "very disagreeable in their refusal" of a request from the prisoner representative who had suggested that "work would go better if coffee and sandwiches were
provided."[59] Osborne's memorandum to the commandant on the subject indicated he
just wanted to remind the commandant that "these prisoners, being human, will do
their work better if a little more consideration is shown them."[60] Osborne might have
raised this issue for discussion at his next meeting with the commandant; however, by
putting such matters in writing, Osborne could enhance his reputation as the champion of prisoners' rights. One cannot argue with Osborne's advocating for prisoners'
rights and privileges. However, one can question his wisdom in continually escalating
and giving visibility to prisoner issues that tended to alienate his contemporaries.

Boush and his staff unfortunately added to the dissension by contributing their
own memoranda about petty issues. The commandant's edict on unauthorized apple
picking by prisoners was a classic example of bureaucratic pettiness: "It has been
reported to the Commandant that apples on the government reservation have been
gathered by prisoners without the knowledge or consent of the Commandant. These
apples will be held subject to the Commandant's orders which will follow later."[61]
Apple picking should not have required a directive from the commandant.

On another occasion, the commandant took Osborne to task for shoddy shoe repairs. "The Commandant is in receipt of a communication in which it is stated that shoes needing only a little mending, sent to the prisoners to be mended are ordered to be thrown into the furnace. It is directed that this matter be investigated."[62] On yet another occasion when candidates for Mutual Welfare League offices had hung campaign posters around the prison grounds, the commandant wrote Osborne, "The sides of several buildings in the prison inclosure [sic] are very much disfigured by paper posters of various colors, sizes, and no particular design or merit."[63] The commandant directed that the posters be removed.

With pressing issues of national importance facing the Navy yard during the war, it is unfortunate that such time-consuming trivial matters received so much attention and debate. At times, the shipyard environment appears to have resembled that of the cargo ship in the 1955 film *Mr. Roberts*, lacking only the palm tree to be thrown overboard. Each of the above examples, as an isolated incident, is hardly worthy of mention; however, collectively they added turmoil to a busy shipyard environment and strained relationships.

SEGREGATION OF PRISONERS

Osborne and Boush also held vastly different opinions about the segregation of prisoners. Osborne's opinion on the subject differed from that of the entire Navy as well as society in general. Naval regulations required criminals to be separated from military offenders. Osborne argued and wrote prolifically—but not convincingly—against that practice. Much of Osborne's resistance was because he did not consider prisoners guilty of moral offenses to be criminals.

Allan Berube wrote in *Coming Out under Fire: The History of Gay Men and Women in World War II* (1990) that during the late nineteenth and early twentieth centuries the Navy's places of confinement were filled with hundreds of enlisted men convicted for the crime of sodomy. He wrote of the widespread practice of segregating homosexuals and the difficulty of controlling their behavior while in prison: "Their presence had a powerful impact on Navy prisons and federal penitentiaries because of long sentences and the difficulty of controlling homosexuality among inmates. Prison administrators decided early on to set policies and establish procedures for managing their 'sodomist' population. Segregation was the primary means of dealing with homosexuals in United States penitentiaries in the first decades of the twentieth century."[64] Osborne was lax to the point of ignoring the segregation requirement, and he failed to control the behavior of homosexual prisoners at Portsmouth prison.

The major revision to the "Manual for the Government of United States Naval Prisons and Detention Systems," directed by Daniels in June 1917, stressed the requirement to separate criminals from naval prisoners with only the latter able to advance through the class system to gain privileges and probation. Osborne believed prisoners should be judged and evaluated for clemency on their record and performance while at Portsmouth prison. He chose to put less emphasis on the seriousness of the misconduct that had caused prisoners to be sentenced to prison in the first place. According to D. J. Rothman, most reformers concurred with the separation and classification of prisoners "to remove the troublemakers from the general prison population, thereby isolating the hard-core offender"[65] in order to improve rehabilitation opportunities for a high percentage of the prisoners. Osborne was in the minority when it came to the segregation of prisoners. Being in the minority never troubled him, once he was convinced his was the right position.

Osborne's superiors, even Daniels, had difficulty with his refusal to follow regulations regarding segregation of prisoners. In March 1918, Daniels alerted Osborne that he would soon have a total of fifty-seven prisoners guilty of acts of moral turpitude and that these prisoners should be kept totally isolated from other prisoners. Daniels, unlike Osborne, believed prisoners guilty of moral turpitude should be confined at the state prison. His 27 March 1918 letter to Osborne stressed this fact. "There are at present 25 prisoners of this character [moral turpitude] at the Naval Prison, Portsmouth in whose cases ultimate transfer to the State Prison at Concord, N.H. has been directed. . . . There are also . . . 21 additional men who . . . would likewise be committed. . . . Also, there are 11 additional cases . . . who have not yet been received at Portsmouth."[66] Osborne resisted all attempts to force him to physically separate prisoners on the basis of the nature of their offense. His system for prison administration based everything, including a prisoner's confinement accommodations and privileges, on the prisoner's performance and behavior after his arrival at Portsmouth prison.

Osborne responded to Daniels with a five-page dissertation that criticized the Navy policy for the separation of prisoners: "The moment the policy of reform rather than retaliation is adopted some methods heretofore in force become not only obsolete but harmful. . . . For instance, the classification of prisoners by their court-martial offenses, . . . should be superseded by a classification based upon their conduct in prison. . . . It is an interesting fact that the seriousness of a man's offense . . . is no index of his conduct in the Naval Prison . . . *the best results can be obtained by mixing together the good, bad, and indifferent.* . . . It would be a mistake to segregate too strictly those prisoners who are sentenced for the more serious crimes" [emphasis added].[67]

Boush's written endorsement to Osborne's letter indicated that he "failed to see the necessity of mixing the 'good, bad, and indifferent'"[68] and that Osborne's argument was "certainly not convincing."[69] Regarding the restoration of criminals, especially those prisoners convicted of moral turpitude, Boush wrote, "The service does not want them back and there is no necessity for putting them back." Osborne, who saw the potential for restoration in every prisoner, regardless of the seriousness or nature of the offense, felt otherwise. And he did not hesitate to voice his views.

Daniels eventually, after a three-month debate through the exchange of letters, directed Osborne to segregate prisoners because "the Department's instructions are not being carried out at the Naval Prison."[70] Osborne reluctantly complied, but fired one last broadside on the subject: "The crowded conditions at the Naval prison make it impracticable to obtain a complete segregation of the less desirable prisoners. . . .

The placing of the so-called 'criminals' with this segregated group has been put in force; but it is desirable that as such men show themselves trustworthy they should be allowed to advance to other grades [not be segregated]. It is an error to assume that a man convicted of a criminal charge is necessarily more criminal than many others convicted of lesser offenses" [emphasis in original].[71] Senior naval authorities were not accustomed to having their orders challenged by a lieutenant commander and certainly did not expect to receive a lecture while being disobeyed.

An examination of the wide range of offenses committed by prisoners indicates that Osborne's desire to mix the good, the bad, and the indifferent could have had serious consequences. During Osborne's tenure, the crimes and military offenses for which prisoners had been sent to Portsmouth varied from failure to salute an officer to murder. Table 11 illustrates the breakdown of sentences handed down toward the end of Osborne's tenure ranging from three months to death. This extreme range in sentences suggests that prisoners had committed offenses varying from minor violations to serious crimes. The integration of prisoners for a short three-month stint

Table 11	Portsmouth Sentence Durations (1919–20)		
Sentence Length	*16 Aug 1919*	*17 Oct 1919*	*29 Feb 1920*
3 months	1	0	2
6 months	96	23	8
1 year	147	123	67
2 years	136	95	63
3 years	240	163	44
4 years	50	39	35
5 years	118	90	63
6 years	9	9	7
7 years	19	20	17
8 years	3	2	5
10 years	23	22	22
12 years	2	3	3
13 years	1	1	1
14½ years	1	0	0
15 years	7	4	5
20 years	1	1	2
25 years	1	1	1
Life	4	4	4
Death	0	0	1
TOTAL	859	600	350

Source: Commanding Officer Portsmouth Naval Prison letters, 22 August 1919, 20 October 1919, and 2 March 1920, NARA Waltham, RG 181, Portsmouth General Collection.

could expose them to hardened criminals serving much longer sentences—up to and including death sentences. Table 11 also highlights the marked change in prisoner demographics at the end of the war. The prison population was reduced by 50 percent between August 1919 and February 1920 with essentially no reduction in the number of serious offenders—those with sentences longer than five years. Recall that the state prison was emptied of military prisoners at the end of 1918; the more hardened criminals were moved back to Portsmouth prison. This contributed to a high percentage of serious offenders at Portsmouth.

As long as Osborne's controversial actions were confined to the Navy yard or the offices of the Navy Department in Washington, where Daniels and FDR could moderate their impact, Osborne and his prison reforms survived and prospered. When his reform initiatives were exposed to senior officers of the operational fleet, however, his fortunes began to turn. Once the fleet began to question Osborne's methods, events moved quickly toward his decline and departure from Portsmouth.

What's Going on
at Portsmouth Prison?

These men apparently regard confinement at Portsmouth as in the nature of jest—they are in a home so good that they would not even try to escape . . . strongly recommend that steps be immediately taken by the Department.

—Vice Admiral Sims, 30 April 1918

Osborne was not shy about taking on senior officers in the fleet when he thought that a prisoner had been wrongly sentenced to Portsmouth prison. The first of these instances, which occurred a few months after his arrival at Portsmouth, involved a dispute with the commanding officer of the battleship *New Jersey* concerning prisoners he had sentenced to Portsmouth. Other disputes involved senior naval officers, including Vice Adm. William S. Sims, who challenged Osborne's restoration practices and lax administration of the prison. Some critics accused him of being a zealous and unreasonable defender of the rights of prisoners. The last straw was an accusation by a discontented ex-inmate of improper fiscal accountability at the prison. This resulted in a JAG investigation that quickly turned to concerns about Osborne's condoning of rampant immoral and homosexual activity at the prison. An on-site investigation led by FDR himself ultimately acquitted Osborne of all charges. Although acquitted, Osborne's days were numbered at Portsmouth.

OSBORNE'S CRITICS MOUNT

In September 1917, Osborne wrote the secretary of the Navy challenging the case of three firemen from the USS *New Jersey* convicted of moral offenses and sentenced to Portsmouth.[1] The men had been convicted of sodomy solely on the testimony of Fireman Bott, who also had been convicted of the same offense and sentenced to Portsmouth prison. While there, Bott confessed that he had given false testimony to get even with the other three men against whom he held a past grudge. This situation closely resembled the case at Sing Sing that had caused Osborne so much grief and ultimately led to his departure. In that case, Osborne alleged a prisoner had given false testimony about sodomy that led to the conviction of twenty-one fellow inmates.

Firmly convinced that the other sailors had been exonerated by Bott's confession, and perhaps recalling his experience at Sing Sing, Osborne wrote Daniels recommending a new court-martial trial: "While Bott is a wretched little degenerate he is neither an imbecile nor a lunatic; he knows and understands perfectly what he is doing and saying. . . . The only witness whose testimony was conclusive has voluntarily and without any outside pressure made a confession which exonerates the other three men."[2] Asked by Daniels to reconsider the cases of the three firemen, the commanding officer of the *New Jersey* had replied that he was convinced of their guilt.[3]

Not content to let the matter drop, Osborne responded with a four-page letter detailing a legal defense of the three firemen, complete with testimony from witnesses that included a former deputy attorney general of New York State and a local psychiatrist. In the process, Osborne compared the case of the three sailors to the Dreyfus affair in which a French artillery officer was falsely accused of a crime and imprisoned for many years before the accusations were determined to be baseless:

> It is not so many years ago that the unimportant case of an obscure Captain in the French Army refused to be smothered; and it grew until it shook the whole civilized world. Poor Paddy Flynn [one of the three prisoners] is no Dreyfus; but there is the same underlying question in his case; whether in face of a most important confession exonerating the convicted man—the case shall remain closed. It cannot be for the best interests of the United States Navy that three men shall stand convicted of a heinous crime if they are innocent.[4]

Probably still puzzled by Osborne's reference to Captain Dreyfus, the commanding officer of the *New Jersey* read on to find that the lieutenant commander was accusing him of operating on hearsay evidence and affidavits that in "no way reach the heart of the matter."[5] Too often Osborne refused to let an issue drop or to let well enough alone, if he thought he was in the right. This habit of constantly reopening issues that senior officers considered minor and closed did not win him many friends.

With the war in progress and thousands of prisoners passing through Portsmouth prison, it was inevitable that rumors about the prison would reach the operating fleet. Admirals who had sentenced sailors to Portsmouth prison were enraged when the imprisoned sailors wrote shipmates that conditions at their new Portsmouth "home" were better than shipboard life. S2C Slim Morton, a prisoner at Portsmouth prison, wrote to Seaman Speed on the USS *Yamacraw*, which was operating in the European waters during the war, describing his favorable conditions of confinement at Portsmouth:

> There is something doing every night, either boxing, wrestling or moving pictures. . . . There are only a few Marines here now. The prisoners are doing all the guarding themselves . . . no one wants to run away because it is too good a home. . . . We are never locked up. . . . This Mr. Osborne is a square fellow. . . . If they are going to keep you over there

don't be afraid to get a general court martial for it is a lot better here than it is over there. . . . I will be able to write you often, as we can write anytime we want, and the best of it is they don't read any of the mail.[6]

Similarly, FM John F. Cody, USCG, wrote Fireman Edso on the same ship, "We are waiting for Washington to cut down on the sentences, they all get cut down over on this side."[7] Rear Adm. A. P. Niblack, commander Squadron Two, Patrol Force, U.S. Atlantic Fleet, and his boss, Vice Adm. William S. Sims, commander U.S. Atlantic Fleet, were furious when they became aware of these letters from men whom they had sentenced to five years in prison. Rear Admiral Niblack wrote Vice Admiral Sims: "With the strict censorship of all correspondence on the part of the officers and enlisted men engaged in active operations in the war zone to friends and relatives at home, it is with a deep sense of chagrin and dismay that it has resulted that two men who have demonstrated their criminal unfitness to serve their country in time of war, have been permitted to write uncensored letters from Naval prisons to ships from which they have just left."[8]

On 30 April 1918, Vice Admiral Sims redirected Niblack's letter to the secretary of the Navy with the following endorsement recommending the Navy Department immediately rectify the lax and too comfortable conditions at Portsmouth: "These men apparently regard confinement at Portsmouth as in the nature of jest—they are in a home so good that they would not even try to escape . . . strongly recommend that steps be immediately taken by the Department, which will for all time dispel any illusion that prisoners convicted of serious military offenses in time of war are sent to a home from which they can attempt to seduce men on active service from the strict and faithful performance of duty demanded by the nation in time of war."[9] Sims and Daniels did not see eye to eye on a number of issues involving naval matters, and it was certainly not out of character for Sims to find fault with one of Daniels' initiatives.

Osborne's four-page response of 3 July 1918 to Sims and Niblack acknowledged the admirals' concerns, but then asked the officers to weigh the foolish, frivolous, and inaccurate writings of two uninformed sailors against the long-term importance of the new system of penology at Portsmouth prison. He specifically cautioned Sims and Niblack not to rush to hasty judgments, but instead to give his new system a chance to be proven. "It must be obvious that the only thorough test of a system of penology, like the test of [a] battleship, lies in its ultimate results . . . that those in the Service who doubt the wisdom of experiment should at least be willing to have it given a fair trial, and should not form hasty conclusions from incomplete premises, but postpone judgment until the actual results can be correctly ascertained."[10]

With regard to Seaman Morton's claim that "they don't read any of the mail," Osborne advised that all the prisoners' mail was censored. He then stressed the challenge he faced owing to the excessive population at the prison. He cited a need for additional resources to accomplish satisfactory censorship reviews: "A system that is effective and satisfactory when the prison population is one hundred and seventy (January 1917) breaks down completely long before it reaches twenty-three hundred

(January 1918)." He went on to explain that, with his present limited resources, reviewing a calculated workload of ninety-two hundred letters a week meant "a steady task of censoring over three letters a minute for every minute of every eight-hour day." He concluded, "Is it any wonder that any foolish and inaccurate letters sometimes get past the censors . . . is the Commanding Officer of the Prison to be held responsible for every false or inaccurate statement which slips by the censor? Would it be practicable to hold any officer of the prison ship or of a battleship, to such accountability?"[11]

Finally Osborne closed by noting that he always welcomed advice; however "it is only by careful consideration of all the facts and suggestions attainable that the best methods can be determined."[12] In other words, Osborne was not to blame. The admirals did not have all the relevant facts. They were guilty of making hasty decisions, and the issue was still open. As was his practice, Osborne attached several copies of testimonial letters from restored prisoners to make his case that his system worked, despite a few indications to the contrary, which he labeled misunderstandings. All of this came from a lieutenant commander who had been asked by a vice admiral to fix a problem at Portsmouth prison.

About the same time Osborne was fending off Vice Admiral Sims, he was also defending himself against another Navy Department accusation regarding three enlisted men at Portsmouth prison who, allegedly, had deliberately committed offenses "so as to be sent to a Naval prison rather than perform duty within the War zone."[13] Osborne replied in a four-page letter, stating that his investigation found no such prisoners at Portsmouth. That would have sufficed; however, he added, "If there were any such prisoners, would it not be better for the country to have them in prison than on the firing line?"[14] Using a tactic rarely seen in naval correspondence, he quoted Shakespeare to make his point:

> According to Shakespeare, King Henry V, before the battle of Agincourt, proposed to pay the expenses home of those soldiers who did not wish to go into battle:
>
> > *Rather proclaim it, Westmoreland, through my host,*
> > *That he which hath no stomach to this fight,*
> > *Let him depart; his passport shall be made*
> > *And crowns for convoy put into his purse*
> > *We would not die in that man's company*
> > *That fears his fellowship to die with us.*
>
> King Henry's policy was sound and justified by the event. If there are cowards in the Naval Service of the United States, it is better they should be in Portsmouth Naval Prison than in the fleet.[15]

One could almost hear the admirals thinking, "Who is this lieutenant commander who quotes Shakespeare, treats prisoners better than sailors at sea, and keeps returning great numbers of marginal sailors to the fleet?"

In *1920: The Year of Six Presidents*, David Pietrusza wrote of the fleet's discontent with Osborne's restorations: "Regular Navy officers questioned Osborne's approach, discerning a direct correlation between ex-convicts aboard and personal property disappearing ('Nobody could own a watch. They'd steal you blind'). Years later, Adm. Richard L. Conolly recalled: 'Only two or three [of the twenty-three Portsmouth Prison inmates on his ship] were any good at all. Maybe only one was rehabilitated. And they blamed Franklin D. for that.'"[16] Osborne's infamy spread as his practices attracted increased attention and notoriety in the fleet.

The fleet's dissatisfaction with Osborne eventually found its way to the office of the secretary of the Navy. At first, Daniels attributed complaints about Osborne to a conservative naval leadership unwilling to adjust to the changing times. He noted in his diary that some of the old-timers mourned for "the good old days of long terms without a ray of hope for youths, guilty mostly of offenses not criminal."[17] There is no doubt that many "old-timers" had problems with Osborne's methods. As had been the case at Sing Sing a few years earlier, Osborne had become a lightning rod for his critics.

The end of the war on 11 November 1918 did not bring an end to Osborne's problems with fleet commanders. A brief entry in Daniels' diary for 7 May 1919 indicates that concerns about his friend's practices at Portsmouth had continued to bubble up through the Navy Department to his level: "Talked with officers Clark [Judge Advocate General] and Robertson about sending Ensign to Portsmouth to report on Osborne."[18] E. David Cronon, the editor of *The Cabinet Diaries of Josephus Daniels*, notes for Daniels' entry, "There had been some criticism in and out of the Navy over Osborne's reforms at the Portsmouth Naval Prison, especially his relaxation of traditional discipline and his emphasis on rehabilitation rather than punishment."[19] By late 1919 the number of prisoners being sent to Portsmouth prison had dropped significantly. However, the fleet's concerns about Osborne's methods remained high.

Despite the increased pressure on Daniels to look into conditions at Portsmouth prison, it was not until a discontented ex-prisoner made accusations about graft—awarding contracts and receipt of supplies in the supply and commissary departments at the shipyard—that a JAG inspection was scheduled in mid-1919. The JAG investigations continued through the fall of 1919, and a report was issued on 9 December 1919. The focus of the investigation quickly turned from concerns about irregularities with contracts and the accounting for supplies to alarm about rampant homosexual activity at the prison. The report started a chain of events that eventually led to Osborne's undoing. On 17 March 1920, three months after the JAG report, Osborne was gone from Portsmouth prison. It was a tumultuous three months.

The discontented ex-prisoner who started the chain of events was Albert G. Von der Leith, a former yeoman third class, USN. Convicted of desertion and sentenced to three years' confinement at Portsmouth prison, he was released on 18 April 1918, after which he quickly ran afoul of the law, was detained in the Portsmouth city jail by local police, and charged with passing fraudulent checks. Convinced he had been set up by enemies he had made while working as a prisoner-clerk in the commissary department at the shipyard, he retaliated with a letter to the department of justice accusing shipyard employees of fraud involving the purchase and receipt of supplies. He also provided information regarding the lax administration of discipline at the prison along with allegations that immoral practices were common and tolerated by prison officials.[20] The justice department responded by sending agents to Portsmouth to investigate the charges several times during July, August, and September 1919.

It did not help Osborne's case when a whiskey still was discovered in an unused prison mess hall in late November 1919. The incident was reported in the national press. According to the *New York Times*, "An improvised still in which inmates of the naval prison here have been distilling liquor from apples, raisins, and prunes was discovered by members of the Mutual Welfare League today. The still had been set up in an unused mess hall. It was made principally of coffee cans."[21] The good news was that members of the Mutual Welfare League had done their job and reported the still to authorities for investigation. The bad news was that this was even more evidence of lax supervision and discipline at the prison.

The JAG investigation report of 8 December 1919 did find minor irregularities in the shipyard's supply department, summarized in one short paragraph of the ten-page report. The bulk of the report was devoted to prisoner and guard testimonies describing a rampant lack of discipline at the prison, including conditions of "a vile and extraordinary nature."[22] One ex-prisoner claimed "unimaginable conditions of depravity and immorality among large number of prisoners." This prisoner claimed to have witnessed other prisoners performing unnatural acts of sexual depravity in front of large audiences on numerous occasions. One report told of a prisoner being caught in a compromising position with a telephone operator in Osborne's office. Worse yet, there were accusations that Osborne was aware of these incidents and did not discipline the offenders. The inflammatory report concluded with a recommendation that "a Court of Inquiry be convened by the Department to inquire into the foregoing matters."[23]

The investigation, initially prompted by accusations of fraud in the purchase of prison commissary supplies, had expanded to serious concerns about Osborne's methods and the "general administration and discipline" at the prison.[24] The allegations of rampant homosexual activity and other immoral practices were especially damning.[25] The JAG report marked the denouement of Osborne's reign. It was only a matter of time until the Navy's experiment with progressive prison reform would unravel and regress.

On 15 December 1918, one week after the JAG report was issued, Osborne obtained Daniels' permission to free 200 prisoners with dishonorable discharges so they could reach home by Christmas. The following week, 120 additional prisoners received releases. In the face of mounting criticism and challenges to his command, Osborne remained true to his commitment to his prisoners.[26]

On 27 December 1918, Osborne's life became even more hectic when he was sued for $25,000 by Julia V. Mullane Duffy of Portsmouth. The woman claimed Osborne had persuaded her husband, Osborne's chauffer CPO William J. Duffy, to leave her. To further complicate matters, Duffy had married another woman on 10

June 1918. Osborne, again taking care of his men despite his own difficulties, supplied a $1,000 bail for Duffy, who had been arrested for having two wives.[27] This case was not settled until three years later, long after Osborne's departure from Portsmouth. On 2 February 1922, the *Boston Daily Globe* featured a four-tier encapsulated headline that added another chapter to the Osborne serial: "Defense Opens for Osborne, Woman Witness Faints in Juryman's Arms, Duffy Intoxicated When Wed, Says Lawyer, Gives Three Reasons Why His Client Should Not Pay."[28] Finally, on 8 February 1922, the *New York Times* reported that a jury in Concord, New Hampshire, had returned a verdict in favor of Osborne.[29] Two years after Osborne left Portsmouth, his exploits continued to attract sensational coverage in national newspapers.

Sensing his fortunes were about to change at Portsmouth, Osborne explored the possibility of returning to the New York prison system. On 27 December 1919, the *New York Times* reported that the Mutual Welfare League at Sing Sing had received a telegram from Osborne in which he offered encouragement and hinted at his return.[30] After meeting with Governor Smith on 2 January 1920, Osborne said he "would not accept the wardenship of Sing-Sing again," but that he "would not be averse to accepting the post of Superintendent of Prisons." The last line of the article indicated "those close to the governor say that he has no intention of appointing Mr. Osborne."[31] Osborne had apparently burned too many bridges in New York state, and his bridge at Portsmouth was about to go up in flames.

The extensive coverage of Osborne's exploits in the *New York Times* began with his political activity at the turn of the century, peaked during his time at Sing Sing Prison, and peaked again with the investigation at Portsmouth prison. On 6 January 1920, under the headline "Assistant Secretary Roosevelt to Examine Conditions at Portsmouth," the newspaper reported a number of charges and allegations that reflected negatively on Osborne's management of the prison:

> The charges embrace allegations of depravity, use of stolen property and misappropriation of funds, also demoralization of personnel. . . . It is alleged that Sunday night parties are among the features of the prison that came under the eye of the investigators. Trusty prisoners are allowed to have girl friends visit them on Sunday evenings, and on certain other occasions other entertainment is allowed. . . . A short time ago a whiskey still was found in a vacant room at the prison. It is alleged also that during the recent New York election a dozen or more prisoners were allowed liberty to go to New York and vote, and that three of them came back some days later in an intoxicated condition.[32]

Although it was difficult at times to separate fact from fiction at Portsmouth prison, it was obvious that this article had not originated at Osborne's desk, as had so many others. Rumors were running rampant, and Osborne was a target of opportunity for many of his critics. Despite the long list of grievances against Osborne, the article maintained that Daniels considered conditions at the prison to be "better than ever." Osborne's friends in high places were not about to abandon him—not just yet.

A 9 January 1920 *New York Times* article with the headline "Osborne Courts Inquiry, Denies Reports Alleging Lax Conditions at Portsmouth Naval Prison" quotes Osborne as saying "Everything that goes on is open to all persons, there is nothing to conceal. . . . It is an open book."[33] A JAG team spent several months uncovering the charges that FDR's team was about to investigate—apparently prisoner activities were not quite as transparent as Osborne was advertising.

JAG investigation leaks and continued fleet concerns about conditions at Portsmouth prison received considerable controversial coverage in the *Army and Navy Journal*, which began with an article in the 3 January 1920 edition that was very supportive of Osborne's practices at Portsmouth. The article suggested commanding officers of naval ships were favorably disposed toward Osborne's practices, which restored thousands of prisoners to operating ships. The article had the effect of waving a red flag in front of a herd of bulls. Commanding officers with opposing views charged forward to state their case.

Capt. Joseph K. Taussig, senior commander of the first U.S. destroyer division to reach Europe and head of the Division of Enlisted Personnel of the Bureau of Navigation at the time, responded to the article with a letter to the editor published on 10 January 1920, which took strong exception to the pro-Osborne article. Taussig maintained commanding officers were being burdened with a lot of riffraff and disciplinary problems under the guise of restored prisoners. He was especially disturbed by the restoration of sodomites. He wrote, "The good men of the fleet must, of necessity, owing to the intimate way of living on board and the requirements of working in the same confined spaces, associate to a more or less extent with these moral perverts, and thereby be exposed to contamination."[34] Osborne's growing reputation for returning moral perverts and marginal performers to the fleet fueled the fires of discontent already existing between Daniels, Sims, and other senior naval officers.

On 24 January 1920, just two weeks after Taussig's letter was published, a letter from FDR himself appeared in the journal claiming Taussig was mistaken. Taussig responded in a personal letter to Daniels, saying FDR had questioned his veracity, impugned his motives, and publicly discredited him.[35] Taussig went on to write, "This procedure by the Assistant Secretary of the Navy in publicly denouncing a Naval officer is . . . unprecedented and unjustified."[36] Taussig sought redress for the damage to his reputation through a court of inquiry, to validate the truth of his statements. A few weeks later, after FDR had met with Taussig and attempted unsuccessfully to reconcile their differences, Daniels denied the request for a court of inquiry.[37] The exchange between FDR and Taussig put even sharper focus on Osborne and his prison. FDR, despite mounting evidence to the contrary, remained a staunch supporter of Osborne and his methods until the bitter end. However, not even Roosevelt's support could save Osborne.

Captain Taussig had other issues with the Daniels administration. His testimony before the Senate Naval Affairs Committee in March 1920 fully corroborated Admiral Sims' charges that the Navy Department was unprepared for war because of mismanagement on the part of Secretary Daniels. Taussig testified that the Navy's personnel situation in 1914 was "entirely inadequate for peace" and "deplorably deficient" for the approaching war. According to Taussig, this "deplorable and unsatisfactory" condition was "not only ignored," but steps were taken "to prevent the unsatisfactory personnel conditions from being made public." The controversy at Portsmouth prison, fueled by criticism from Sims, Taussig, and Fiske, was a microcosm of a much larger rift between the Daniels administration and these same officers.[38]

The FDR-Taussig feud was but one of several major distractions for the Daniels-Roosevelt administration in January 1920, a disastrous month for them. Much of their difficulty emanated from Newport, Rhode Island, where Sims was serving his second tour as commanding officer of the Naval War College. His 7 January 1920 letter to the Senate prompted the Senate Naval Affairs Committee to begin an investigation into Daniels' wartime administration of the Navy Department. This investigation brought a great deal of negative exposure of Daniels and his administration in the national press over the next several months, concurrent with events unfolding at Portsmouth prison.

On 22 January 1920, a naval court of inquiry convened at Newport to investigate charges that a naval team of investigators had employed inappropriate procedures to entrap sailors and civilians in an effort to rid the city of homosexuals. Twelve sailors had stood trial in December 1919, five of which were found guilty of homosexual crimes and sentenced to Portsmouth prison for terms of five to thirty years. Because the entrapped civilians included a local minister, Rev. Samuel Neal Kent, other clergy rallied to his defense and wrote a letter to President Wilson requesting an investigation into the Navy's investigative methods. Team members had reportedly engaged in homosexual acts with targeted suspects to obtain evidence, and Daniels and Roosevelt were accused of condoning such practices. In response to the clergy's letter, Daniels established a court of inquiry that convened on 22 January 1920, one week after FDR's court of inquiry convened at Portsmouth prison. Daniels and FDR were obliged to defend themselves during the Newport court of inquiry and a subsequent Senate Naval Affairs Committee investigation of the same subject.[39]

The Navy's Newport sex scandal investigation was a major distraction for Daniels and Roosevelt from late 1919 until the Wilson administration left office in March 1921. Early in the Harding administration they found themselves under attack again when the Senate reported its findings. With John R. Rathom, an archenemy of Daniels and Roosevelt and editor of the *Providence Journal*, writing inflammatory articles condemning the two, the Newport sex scandal attracted national media coverage. Rathom fueled the fire by writing similar articles deploring conditions at Portsmouth prison. The Newport scandal had ties to, and involved personalities associated with, the Portsmouth prison investigation.

To add to their woes, the personal relationship between Daniels and FDR became strained when the politically ambitious FDR, according to historian Geoffrey C. Ward, sought "to separate himself somehow from Daniels to make the Secretary's enemies continue to consider him an ally rather than an adversary. . . . On 1 February 1920, Franklin cut himself loose from the beleaguered man, . . . without warning."[40]

During a speech he boasted that he had acted independently and illegally ordered material before the war started because he recognized the Navy's unpreparedness for war. The implication was that he shared Sims' view that the nation was ill prepared for war and had acted aggressively to improve conditions when Daniels and Wilson were reluctant to do so. Self-promotion was not out of character for the politically motivated undersecretary, who had his eyes on loftier political prizes. Some even suggested that he wanted Daniels' job. The secretary's job remained secure; however, FDR did gain enough exposure during his undersecretary tour to be nominated as the 1920 Democratic candidate for vice president along with Ohio governor James C. Cox as the presidential candidate.

FDR's latest betrayal may have been the last straw. "Astounded at this attack from the young man with whom he had been patient for so long . . . Daniels could barely bring himself to speak to his assistant."[41] Daniels, who continued to stew over FDR's comments, called on the White House on 21 February "wishing to discuss with the President at least the possibility of having to replace his disloyal subordinate."[42] Wilson, bedridden and distraught, was having little success recovering from a stroke he had suffered on 25 September 1919 in Pueblo, Colorado, while campaigning to promote his League of Nations.

Wilson's erratic and offensive behavior had recently caused some cabinet members to abandon him. Secretary of State Robert Lansing, angered by a Wilson "brutal and offensive message," had resigned, and others were finding reasons to leave.[43] Wilson's fragile state of health and concern about his reaction, should another name be added to the list of departures, caused Daniels not to mention his disappointment with FDR. Ward wrote, "Daniels backed off. With three Cabinet members [Secretary of the Treasury Carter Glass; Secretary of the Interior Franklin Knight Lane, and Secretary of State Robert Lansing] gone from the government since the first of the month, and the president's mental state now a matter of public debate, perhaps he thought the sudden departure of a fourth prominent official . . . might be more than the beleaguered administration—or the sick President—could handle."[44] Ward maintains FDR was fortunate not to have been fired by Daniels in the middle of the Portsmouth investigation. Daniels' patience with his assistant was rewarded. Their relationship improved and thrived for the remainder of their tenure and continued. President Roosevelt appointed Daniels ambassador to Mexico in 1933, a post he held with distinction until 1945.

The Volstead Act, better known as the National Prohibition Act, was passed on 29 October 1919, setting the starting date for nationwide prohibition: 17 January 1920. At midnight on that date, Daniels, Bryan, and other prominent temperance advocates gathered at the First Congregationalist Church in Washington, D.C., to celebrate the arrival of the prohibition era.[45] Prohibition, one of Daniels' lifelong campaigns, was coming to fruition at the same time that his dream for prison reform was beginning to fade . . . and he was involved in the early stages of the Newport sex scandal . . . and Admiral Sims was mounting an attack that would lead to a Senate investigation. January 1920 was not a very good month for Josephus Daniels.

Investigation into Conditions
at Portsmouth Prison

The whole aim of the investigation and of the charge is apparently the
old trick: Throw enough mud and some of it will stick.

—Lieutenant Commander Osborne, 24 February 1920

The investigation by the said agents was superficial and perfunctory. . . .
In particular no facts were developed to indicate conditions of lax discipline
or immorality existing in the Naval Prison.

—Assistant Secretary of the Navy Franklin Delano Roosevelt, 1920

With the Daniels-Roosevelt administration seemingly under attack from
all sides, the FDR team convened at Portsmouth on 14 January to investigate conditions at the prison. In addition to FDR, the court of inquiry
included Rear Adm. H. O. Dunn, commandant First Naval District, and Rear Adm.
A. S. Halstead, commandant of the Portsmouth Navy Yard. Halstead had relieved
Rear Admiral Boush.[1] Dunn had also been appointed by Daniels to head the court
of inquiry for the Newport sex scandal, which became known as the Dunn Court
of Inquiry.

The Portsmouth investigating board, headed up by Osborne's good friend FDR,
was skewed in Osborne's favor from the start. In addition, Rear Admiral Dunn was
indebted to FDR for a personal favor. Lawrence R. Murphy notes in *Perverts by
Official Order,* "He [Dunn] was especially close to Franklin Delano Roosevelt, with
whom he had vacationed in the Azores during the summer of 1918. The month the
[Newport] inquiry began, Dunn secured Roosevelt's assistance in obtaining admis-
sion to the Annapolis Naval Academy for his wife's nephew."[2] FDR could count on
Dunn to protect him from his critics at the Newport inquiry and to cooperate with
him during the Portsmouth investigation.

FDR's board primarily focused on Osborne's 8 December 1919 rebuttal letter
to the JAG's report. In his massive rebuttal of one hundred and eight pages, Osborne
noted:

There never has been any claim that the Naval Prison was a paradise without evil . . . its inmates are far from perfect; were they inured with a passion for righteousness the chances are they would not be in the Naval Prison. . . . On the other hand it is [underline is Osborne's] claimed that no prison has ever been managed with less friction and with less wrong-doing on the part of the inmates . . . no strikes, no riots, no severe punishments, no brutality. It is claimed that a very large proportion of the men . . . have lived clean, sober, industrious lives while here; and left its walls wiser and better men.[3]

He concluded, "The whole aim of the investigation and of the charge is apparently the old trick: Throw enough mud and some of it will stick."[4] Despite FDR's subsequent efforts to clean up or cover the mud, some of it indeed stuck.

Osborne's rebuttal, which suggests he recognized the seriousness of the charges against him, included 47 exhibits, totaling about 225 pages, which consisted of letters and affidavits from rehabilitated prisoners, shipyard workers, community leaders, and others testifying to the effectiveness of his methods. Exhibit 36 consisted of approximately 100 letters from rehabilitated prisoners expressing their appreciation for Osborne and the "wonderful workings of the [Mutual Welfare] League."[5] Excerpts from some of the letters follow:

Under your system I learned to be considerate and thoughtful of my friends. . . . I grew from boyhood into manhood in those six months [of confinement].[6]

I am well with my little family and my wife always speaks to me about you, for the way you tried to help me while I was there and I also wish to tell you that my family has been increased with another little girl.[7]

A thing I am proud to tell you is that I haven't touched a drop since I left Portsmouth.[8]

You should have heard my old dad, when I first went home after being restored. He praised you more than I will ever be able to describe. . . . And I will thank you from the bottom of my heart, for sending me back to the Navy.[9]

These letters are glowing in their praise of Osborne and the Mutual Welfare League. Most were not spontaneous letters, but instead letters written in response to correspondence received from Osborne some time in the past. The dates on the letters range from January 1918 to January 1920. It appears that during his entire time at Portsmouth, Osborne routinely sent letters to rehabilitated prisoners inviting comments about their experience at Portsmouth prison and inquiring about their lives after they had been released. Thus, Osborne had a ready file of testimonial letters from rehabilitated prisoners praising him and his Mutual Welfare League. He frequently included copies of prisoners' letters in correspondence responding to critics or, in this case, to rebut the charges of a JAG investigation. This practice can be traced to his experience at Sing Sing, where he learned the importance of protecting himself at all times in the event of criticism.

It should not be concluded that Osborne's sole purpose for collecting these letters was to prepare an advance defense for his critics. In many cases Osborne had the best interests of the rehabilitated prisoner in mind; he was sincerely concerned about their welfare. Therein is the riddle that was Osborne. At times his sincerity and altruism overlapped with his egotism and pride, making it difficult to find the truth of the moment. In this case, his prolific letter writing served both purposes well.

Osborne was a master politician and a skilled debater of prison reform. These talents are evident in his defense of the conditions found at Portsmouth prison. Osborne's defense was comprehensive, convincing, and overwhelming in comparison to the documentation supporting the charges against him. His critics grossly underestimated his capacity to respond to their complaints, as well as the backing he would receive from FDR. The board of inquiry found Osborne's defense convincing.

The board's report discredited the JAG investigation. Referring to the investigation as a "so-called investigation by the Department of Justice," the board's report of 26 February concluded "that the investigation by the said agents [of the JAG investigation of early December 1919] was superficial and perfunctory, and that it was based almost wholly on hearsay evidence and unreliable witnesses."[10] The report claimed that no facts were developed to support the accusations of lax discipline and immorality at the Naval Prison.

In a matter of a few days, the *New York Times* reported, "Osborne Cleared by Inquiry . . . [the board of inquiry] has given a clean bill of health to Thomas Mott Osborne."[11] With a backhanded compliment, the article concluded, "He put into effect there the honor system and other innovations that he had tried at Sing Sing. Citizens of the towns adjacent to the Portsmouth Navy Yard did not appreciate his efforts." Apparently the local residents still had concerns about a prison operating in their own back yard.

A few weeks later, on 13 March, the secretary of the Navy implemented another recommendation of the board that effectively eliminated the chain of command that Osborne detested and sought to avoid. Daniels directed that the commanding officer of the naval prison report directly to the Navy Department: "In order that the Department may exercise a more immediate control over the matters of internal management of the U. S. Naval Prison at Portsmouth, N.H., such prison will, so far as matters as concerned, be directly under the cognizance of the Navy Department (Office of the Judge Advocate General). Correspondence concerning such matters will hereafter be carried on directly between the Department and the Commanding Officer of the Prison."[12] This organizational restructuring meant that Osborne was no longer under the direct authority of the commandant of the Navy yard. Consequently, his correspondence no longer had to go via the commandant and his staff. More important, Osborne's visibility would be greatly reduced as well as his exposure to critics.

After an exhaustive six months of investigations, which consumed considerable resources in manpower, money, and time, FDR's board of inquiry exonerated Osborne of all charges. It enthusiastically endorsed his reforms and initiated a reorganization whereby the office of the secretary of the Navy could exercise direct control over Osborne. He could not have hoped for a better result. But this was by no means the end of the matter.

Some viewed the findings of the board, and FDR's direct participation in the investigation, with suspicion. Even biographer Rudolph W. Chamberlain, a strong Osborne supporter, thought FDR might be biased because "he was investigating his friend and was already a believer in the system under fire."[13] In the immediate aftermath of the war, with massive manpower reductions and organizational realignments taking place within the U.S. Navy, it was questionable whether the assistant secretary of the Navy should have assigned himself to lead any investigation, let alone an investigation of a friend who personally owed his assignment at Portsmouth prison to him.

FDR could not have been more determined to personally involve himself in the affairs at Portsmouth prison. Shortly after receiving the JAG's scathing report of mismanagement and rampant immorality at Portsmouth, he immediately declared, "In case a further personal or official investigation is recommended, the Assistant Secretary will either appoint a Court of Inquiry or *do it himself* [emphasis added]."[14] True to his word, two weeks later FDR and the board met at Portsmouth to review conditions at the prison.

Daniels' biographer, Joseph L. Morrison, had a different, and much more positive, view on the outcome of the investigation: "After interviewing Osborne at length in what was anything but a whitewash, the Board found that the preponderance of evidence—including disproven charges by a lying ex-convict—showed that the prison was being run in an efficient and enlightened manner."[15] *Providence Journal* editor John Rathom, however, was equally convinced that the investigation was a "whitewash" and "the culmination of the political chicanery."[16] As usual, there were great differences of opinion regarding events surrounding Osborne.

It is clear that the tone of the final report and the conclusions of the board differ remarkably from the JAG report that precipitated the inquiry. In stark contrast to the JAG's initial assessment, the board totally absolved Osborne of all blame and praised conditions at Portsmouth prison. It is difficult to reconcile the two reports. Events that took place behind the scenes suggest that the board's report may have been inappropriately influenced by Roosevelt.

As mentioned, Rear Admiral Dunn and FDR were close friends and Dunn was somewhat indebted to FDR for a recent appointment to the Naval Academy for his wife's nephew. According to Geoffrey C. Ward, at the start of the investigation, Dunn agreed with FDR that "we can work out [the] Portsmouth Prison trouble if we of the service can only get together on these things and not air our dirty linen in public."[17] If nothing else, it appears that FDR's team went into the investigation with a bias toward a quick resolution with minimal publicity. They were successful with the former, but not the latter.

An innocuous entry in Daniels' diary casts suspicion on FDR's involvement in the investigation. His Monday, 9 February 1920, entry indicated, "FDR came in as usual. Osborne coming on Wednesday [assumed to be 11 February 1920]."[18] The fact that Osborne traveled to Washington on 11 February 1920 to meet with Daniels, and probably with FDR, while he was the subject of an investigation was inappropriate, to say the least. The rapid closure of the investigation began with Osborne's official response to the JAG report on 24 February, concurrent with the board's second visit to Portsmouth, and the issuance of the board's final report just two days later. All of this points to a well-orchestrated event between Osborne, FDR, and Daniels. It is quite obvious that they were eager to get this embarrassing episode behind them.

The findings were signed by the three members of the board—FDR, Rear Adm. H. O. Dunn, commandant First Naval District, and Rear Adm. A. S. Halstead, commandant of the Portsmouth Navy Yard. Neither Dunn nor Halstead was particularly enamored with Osborne's methods, as evidenced by their actions after Osborne's departure. The evidence suggests FDR rallied to the defense of his friend and used the authority of his position to dominate the other two members of the board.

The End

The following summary of events shows how besieged Daniels and FDR were with the Portsmouth investigation, the Sims-Daniels controversy, and the Newport sex scandal during this period:

December 1919	Five Newport sailors convicted of homosexual crimes and sentenced to Portsmouth prison
9 December 1919	JAG report issued alleging gross mismanagement of the Portsmouth prison.
9 December 1919 to early January 1920	JAG report evaluated at Navy Department and forwarded to Portsmouth Navy Yard.
7 January 1920	Vice Admiral Sims writes letter (Certain Naval Lessons of the Great War) to Senate Naval Affairs Committee criticizing the administration of the Navy Department under Josephus Daniels.
14 January 1920	FDR Board of Inquiry convenes at Portsmouth prison.
22 January 1920	Naval court of inquiry [Dunn Inquiry] convenes at Newport to investigate the Navy's pursuit of homosexuals (Newport sex scandal).
24 January 1920	FDR responds to Taussig's letter with a letter to the editor of the *Army and Navy Journal* defending Osborne.
21 February 1920	Daniels meets with President Wilson planning to discuss firing of FDR for insubordination and decides to drop the issue.

24 February 1920	Osborne officially responds to the accusations with his lengthy defense. The Board of Inquiry visits the prison for the second time.
26 February 1920	Board issues its final report absolving Osborne of all blame.
13–25 March 1920	Senate Naval Affairs Committee convenes to investigate charges made by Sims in his 7 January 1920 letter.
17 March 1920	Commodore Wadhams relieves Osborne.

Subsequent events suggest that Daniels, under attack from several different quarters, decided to cut his losses by cutting his ties to Osborne.

Events moved quickly toward Osborne's resignation after the board published its findings. On 26 February, the date the board's final report was issued, Osborne wrote Daniels a three-page letter imploring him to approve his most recent list of recommended restorations. This list included some criminals, as well as military offenders, over the objections of the JAG. Even though FDR's report had dismissed the JAG's charges against Osborne, it was becoming increasingly difficult to protect Osborne from the JAG, whose responsibilities supposedly encompassed all naval legal matters including prisoner pardons. Osborne wrote, "Believe me, Mr. Secretary, this job has been a much harder one than I have ever let you know—and if you throw us over now I cannot be held responsible for the results—the whole thing will go by the board. . . . To yield now is to give away the game."[19] Osborne's confidence was waning; he was far less sure of himself and Daniels' continued support.

Daniels' equally long response was the beginning of the end for Osborne. In a letter that has all the earmarks of having been prepared by the JAG for Daniels' signature, Daniels denied Osborne's request. Daniels' letter read, "In the long run it is better that we should not restore those guilty of the offenses of which I have spoken [immorality, theft, forgery]."[20] In other words, Daniels was telling Osborne that his practice of routinely restoring prisoners classified as "criminals" was over. Mounting criticism of Osborne from the fleet and his own staff had motivated Daniels to switch sides. With a stroke of the pen Osborne's powerbase had been eroded.

Events had taken a toll on Osborne. He admitted to a friend in a 1 March letter, "I have been under a great strain physically and mentally am not able to do much."[21] On 3 March 1920, Osborne met with Daniels and complained again that not all prisoners involved in the board's investigation were getting a "square deal" as some were not being restored on reduced sentences. Daniels again noted, "All who had not been guilty of crime were restored & sentences reduced [and] Clark [JAG] would not recommend the others."[22] At this point, it had to be obvious to Osborne that Daniels was now more inclined to accept the JAG's advice than his.

Osborne, discouraged with the increased scrutiny of restoration requests, and interpreting that scrutiny as a change in policy, indicated that he wished to be relieved "since his policy is not wholly approved."[23] A 9 March 1920 *New York Times* article reporting Osborne's resignation stated that Osborne felt "the only friction during his administration developed not from the prisoners, but from politicians [naval officers] on the outside."[24] In a letter to his good friend Austin MacCormick, Osborne confirmed Daniels' waning support as the reason for his resignation: "Daniels proclaims his intention to keep on and yet he allowed the Bureau of Navigation to overrule me on the vital matter of the restoration of men charged with criminal offenses. That was where we split."[25] Osborne was totally dependent on the secretary of the Navy for his success, and with Daniels no longer willing to routinely do his bidding, Osborne saw no future for himself and his dreams of prison reform in the Navy. He had built no consensus short of the secretary's level that would permit him to continue with his reform initiatives.

On 6 March 1920, Lieutenant Clifford, Osborne's executive officer, hand-delivered a letter to Daniels from Osborne confirming his desire to be relieved. Osborne's letter spoke to the continued pressure he was under: "Admiral Halstead was up here on Sunday afternoon with a 'friend,' paying a somewhat perfunctory visit to the prison. I have since then been informed that his companion was the head of the Naval Intelligence Bureau in Boston. Whether this means a new attack I do not know, but if so they seem to be losing no time."[26] On 5 March Osborne wrote a similar letter to FDR. In it he lamented that Daniels was "making a great mistake and putting himself in a false position by a switching of policy now while he is under fire." A discouraged Osborne closed his letter to FDR with a plea for one last favor. His request was to "get me out of here quickly."[27]

An entry in Daniels' diary confirms Osborne's extreme disappointment with the recent turn of events: "Osborne is almost heart-broken—feels that his work is not permanent and has not had a fair chance. It is depressing. Too many Naval officers lack willingness to meet new measures & cling tenaciously to old rules which lack the human touch and comradeship."[28]

The next day, 7 March 1920, Daniels sent for Commodore Wadhams and "talked to him about going to Portsmouth to succeed Mr. Osborne who has resigned."[29] Though Daniels never formally asked him to resign, Osborne had correctly interpreted Daniels' actions as a reversal of policy, which would undermine his reforms, leaving him no option but resignation. The noticeable lack of effort on Daniels' part to attempt to convince Osborne to stay on the job, coupled with the immediate move to find a replacement, suggests Daniels was ready to have Osborne move on.

Despite the board's favorable findings, the fleet kept pressure on Daniels to do something about Osborne and Portsmouth prison. Around the time Osborne was moving toward resignation, Daniels received a letter from the chief of the Bureau of Navigation that noted, "A majority of the officers charged with important commands within the fleet believe that the reputation of the Naval Prison did not constitute a sufficient deterrent against the commission of offenses."[30] Furthermore, Portsmouth prison was "having an adverse effect upon the discipline of the Navy."[31] The cumulative effect of Osborne's policies and practices had resulted in a strong "no confidence" vote from fleet commanders, who considered Osborne a failure. If events in late February 1920 had prompted Daniels to consider replacing Osborne, the fleet's 3 March letter must have pushed him even further down that path.

The fleet commanders' negative reaction to Osborne had more to do with the affect his methods were having on fleet operations than the offenses he was alleged to have committed at the prison. They expected the threat of prison confinement to be a deterrent for potential offenders in the fleet. They also expected prison sentences to be a permanent solution to shipboard discipline problems. In their eyes, Portsmouth prison met neither of these expectations. The prison was not a deterrent if some found confinement at Portsmouth prison more desirable than duty on board ship in a war zone. And it was not a permanent solution to discipline problems when habitual offenders were returned to the fleet after serving only a small part of their sentences. Any lingering thoughts Daniels had about keeping Osborne must have been quickly dismissed with the realization that the fleet was not about to back off on its campaign to "fix" Portsmouth prison.

On 16 March 1920, one day before he was relieved of command, and anticipating a reversal of his policies once he departed, Osborne recommended clemency for more than eighty prisoners with sentences over four years who had served at least one year of confinement:

> Practically all of these men were tried and sentenced during war-time, when discipline was rigid and punishment severe; moreover, the majority of them were new to the Naval Service and had not adapted themselves to the rigorous discipline of the service. . . . The punishments awarded them, as compared with peace-time punishments in the Navy, or corresponding punishment in civil life, in many cases are extremely severe. . . . Their entire records at this institution are such as to lead the Commanding Officer to believe that the exercise of clemency in their behalf at this time would be both judicious and fully warranted.[32]

True to form, Osborne refused to accept any changes to his liberal restoration practices. Right up until a few hours before the end of his command, Osborne fought for a "square deal" for his prisoners. He went out as he had come in, a champion of prisoners' rights.

Three weeks after receiving the ringing endorsement of the board of inquiry, Osborne was gone from Portsmouth prison. Osborne completed his assignment at Portsmouth on 17 March 1920 with a glowing endorsement from Daniels: "You have taught the Navy and the country that prisons are to mend the prisoners and not to break them. It must be a source of gratification to you that so many young men, who have violated Navy regulations or been convicted of wrongdoing, have found themselves through your friendship and leadership, . . . making good."[33] Daniels words of support were still good; his actions were much less supportive.

Osborne did not return to civilian life immediately after his departure from Portsmouth. Instead, he was tasked to conduct an investigation of naval prisons and detention camps on the East Coast. This extended his naval service until June 1920. His resignation as a lieutenant commander in the naval reserve was effective with his submission of the report for that investigation.[34] With Osborne's departure, the progressive reform experiment at Portsmouth prison immediately began to wane. Within a few years, few remnants of Osborne and his dream remained.

The Aftermath

The issuance of the board's report and Osborne's resignation were not the end of FDR's involvement in the matter. Later in the year, the investigation and his support of Osborne came back to haunt FDR when he was running as the Democratic candidate for vice president. Roosevelt had been nominated on 6 July 1920 at the convention in San Francisco, a few weeks after Osborne had returned to civilian life. During the summer and fall of 1920, as Osborne was recovering from the traumatic conclusion of his Portsmouth experiment, FDR was back on the campaign trail.

An open letter to FDR, written by his *Providence Journal* nemesis, John R. Rathom, and published in the *Journal* a few weeks before the November election, accused Roosevelt of covering up conditions at Portsmouth prison. Geoffrey C. Ward credits Sims with sending Taussig to Rathom "with details of the Portsmouth controversy" and notes Sims was "highly pleased by the editor's letter" because "the *Providence Journal* has all the goods [on FDR]."[35] Rathom's accusations included the sequestering or destroying of Navy Department records and returning men to active service convicted of unnatural crimes and sentenced to Portsmouth prison. (Photo 19 shows Sims and FDR during more friendly times, prior to their Newport and Portsmouth controversies.)

Rathom claimed that the *Journal* had on file "the records of eighty-three separate and distinct cases of men convicted of crimes who have been returned to honorable duty by either you or Mr. Daniels."[36] To stress his point, Rathom recounted the story of EMC Clarence A. Parker, convicted of unnatural crimes and scandalous conduct, whose sentence to Portsmouth had been reduced from ten years to seven years, and finally to one year and seven months, at which time he was placed on probation and permitted to return to active duty in August 1919. According to Rathom, "Under Mr. Osborne, discipline at the Portsmouth prison became a joke."[37] The closing paragraph of Rathom's public letter to FDR was especially harsh, "You, even more than Josephus Daniels, have been the evil genius of that department and you have earned the detestation and contempt of every patriotic and skilled naval officer with whom you came in contact."[38] FDR was having a difficult time putting the events at Portsmouth prison behind him.

Rathom's accusations against FDR in late October 1920 were the culmination of attacks on FDR and Daniels that began in January and were related to the Dunn Inquiry into the Newport sex scandal. Rathom, who was displeased that Daniels had appointed FDR's good friend Dunn to head the court, expressed outrage that the Navy would attempt to use the court to justify, instead of to investigate, the appropriateness of its methods. He was especially critical of Daniels' and FDR's efforts to escape responsibility for the scandal by singling out subordinates for blame. In early January editorials in the *Providence Journal*, Rathom wrote regarding Daniels, "Never in all its history has the Navy been subjected to such a reckless administration as has been imposed on it during the Daniels period. . . . [Conditions in the Navy are] rotten beyond conception. . . . Mr. Daniels with full knowledge of these degrading and vicious plots personally attempted to cover with infamy the names of subordinate men. . . . [Daniels and FDR had] known of these methods for several months."[39]

FDR's formal statement in Associated Press dispatches dated 22 January challenged Rathom's criticism: "In view of the circumstances [Rathom's criticism is] a deliberate and malicious effort to create trouble, in addition to being false."[40] In *Perverts by Official Order*, Lawrence R. Murphy wrote, "Roosevelt's statement interjected him into the dispute while spurring Rathom to intensify his criticism. Thus a prolonged debate over the anti-gay scandal would be aired in the nation's press for month's to come."[41] The prolonged debate extended over the summer of 1920 until the national election in November.

FDR claimed the late October accusations about Parker's restoration to active duty were merely the renewal of a series of unfounded attacks by Rathom orchestrated by the Republican National Committee Political Bureau. In addition, it was reported that FDR intended to file a suit against Rathom to recover $500,000 for libel.[42] In responding to the accusations, Osborne claimed Parker's sentence was reduced as the result of an admirable record at Portsmouth and Osborne's personal investigation of the case, which convinced him that the man was framed by his shipmates.[43] Acting as judge and jury, Osborne had found the man innocent and restored him to duty.

Parker's case summarizes well Osborne's modus operandi. Parker was a naval prisoner convicted of a morals crime and, as required by naval regulations, he should have been separated from the other prisoners and sent to the state prison. Instead, he remained at Portsmouth and was given every opportunity to reduce his sentence and be returned to active duty. As he did so often, Osborne personally involved himself in Parker's case and determined to his satisfaction that Parker had been framed. Based on his own investigation, and dismissing the court martial judgment of a ten-year sentence at Portsmouth prison, Osborne recommended to Daniels that Parker be restored. FDR, in Daniels' absence, approved the recommendation. Parker's restoration in August 1919, during the initial JAG investigation of the prison, came back to haunt FDR in October 1920 shortly before the national election that year.

Daniels and the JAG, Capt. George R. Clark, prepared their annual reports in June 1920 with the recent events at Portsmouth fresh in mind. Clark made no mention of the investigation of Osborne in his report. He appeared eager to put the Portsmouth controversy behind him with minimal visibility. Clark's diminishing enthusiasm for Osborne can be found in his three annual reports during Osborne's tenure. In 1918, ten months after Osborne assumed command, he wrote very positively about the Mutual Welfare League, "[The absence of serious disorder] is believed to be due in large measure to the system of partial or modified self-government known as the Welfare League, in the exercise of which the qualities of leadership of selected men are enlisted on the side of the authorities in developing the better instincts of the men and in encouraging them in such behavior as will lead them to restoration to duty or, at least, to a shortening of the term of confinement."[44] The next year, he did not comment at all about the Portsmouth reforms, but he did write positively about naval prisons in general: "The spirit of the prisons is excellent. There is a noticeable absence of the prison hang dog air."[45] Perhaps having Osborne in mind, his 1920 report expounded on the need to maintain separation of prisoners. He wrote, "Although the best possible means are employed by the prison author-ities to segregate the classes, it is believed that it would be better for all concerned, both light and grave offenders, if separate places of confinement were provided for them."[46] Clark's waning enthusiasm for Osborne, coupled with Daniels' increasing tendency to turn to Clark for assistance in the face of the fleet's mounting criticism of Portsmouth prison, no doubt contributed to Osborne's departure.

Unlike Clark, Daniels closed the book on Osborne with considerable praise. In his 1920 report, Daniels acknowledged Osborne's departure and credited him with setting an example in prison reform for others to emulate. Daniels wrote, "The world is following the Navy in modernizing and humanizing prison life."[47] Daniels' con-clusion was hasty and inaccurate. Looking to the future with hopes for continuing the Osborne reforms under Commodore Wadhams, Daniels added, "Equal commen-dation is due to Commodore Wadhams who succeeded Commander Thomas Mott Osborne, as head of the naval prison at Portsmouth, NH."[48] Though the Osborne era at Portsmouth was over, Daniels still thought that the future remained promising with Wadhams in charge.

14

Osborne's Results at Portsmouth

But some of the OldTimers mourned for 'the good old days' of long terms without a ray of hope for youths, guilty mostly of offenses not criminal.

—Secretary of the Navy Josephus Daniels, 1917

His results were as astounding as was his daring.

—Frank Tannenbaum, 1933, *Osborne of Sing Sing*

O sborne commenced his assignment at Portsmouth prison on 10 August 1917, just as the United States involvement in World War I was ramping up. The United States declared war on Germany on 6 April 1917, the first U.S. troops arrived in France in June 1917, and General Pershing requested the U.S. armed services personnel strength be increased to one million in July 1917. Osborne's plan to rehabilitate large numbers of misguided sailors could not have been better timed. The U.S. Navy needed sailors, and Osborne was determined to restore as many prisoners as possible to active duty.

He got off to a good start. During an address to the War Work Council of the Unitarian Church in Cambridge, Massachusetts, on 15 June 1918, Osborne summarized the first ten months of his tenure at Portsmouth: "When I went to the prison there were 304 prisoners, 170 in the main prison. There were 160 guards for the 170, forty of them on duty at a time. We have now 1,814 persons in the main prison and only ten guards at a time . . . 538 men have been returned to active duty, an average of about two a day. . . . Of the 538 only twelve have been returned to the prison [2.2 percent].[1] Osborne returned about four times as many sailors to active duty (538) during his first ten months as warden at Portsmouth than had been restored since the founding of the prison eight years earlier (about130). Overcrowded prison conditions, Daniels' charge to reform the prison, and Osborne's eagerness to practically demonstrate the effectiveness of his prison reform theories combined perfectly, accelerating prisoner rehabilitation to unprecedented levels.

Daniels' annual report for FY 1920, published 1 July 1920, provides a convenient summary of Osborne's record of accomplishments while at Portsmouth. Written just a few months after Osborne had been relieved by Commodore Wadhams, Daniels reported with considerable pride the successes of Osborne and his Mutual Welfare League:

> Since the Mutual Welfare League system has been introduced . . . [between] August 1, 1917 and June 30, 1920, the prison has handled 7,011 prisoners. The following table shows as of July 1, 1920, the distribution of these men:

Count on 1 Aug 1917	464
Received between 1 Aug 1917 and 30 June 1920	6,547
TOTAL	7,011
Restored to duty	2,509
Restricted to ship or station	173
Ordinary discharges	68
Transfers to Hospital for Insane and the Federal Prisons	125
Escaped (at large)	9
Died	37
Dishonorably discharged	3,778

> Latest figures show that approximately 50 per cent of the men who were restored to duty made good. This would indicate that 1,255 trained men were restored to the Navy during the war, when trained men were badly needed. The records of the naval prison show that out of the total number (2,509), who were restored to duty, only 403 were actually returned to the naval prison, Portsmouth, the others who failed to make good being discharged.[2]

At first glance, the figures are quite impressive. During his tenure, Osborne was responsible for more than 7,000 prisoners and restored more than 2,500 [36 percent], which resulted in an additional 1,255 trained men for the fleet. However, it can be argued that Daniels' analysis of the results is a "glass half full" interpretation, whereas Osborne's critics saw the "glass half empty." If 50 percent of the restored men "made good," Daniels' concluded that a very valuable contribution had been made to the Navy during wartime when men were badly needed. Critics argued that a 50 percent "made good" rate meant twice the number of men were restored to the fleet than should have been. From the viewpoint of the commanding officer of a ship, if he sent 10 sailors to Portsmouth prison with sentences that would remove them as shipboard discipline problems for, say, 2 years, he could roughly expect 4 (36 percent) of the sailors to be restored to his ship in a matter of months with the probability that only 2 of those (50 percent) would "make good." Commanding officers did not find those odds attractive.

The 403 prisoners returned to Portsmouth prison that Daniels considered successfully low, gives a recidivism rate of 16 percent. No civilian prison would be proud of such a high rate of recidivism. Worse yet, this rate is based on a population (2,509) of prisoners thought to be rehabilitated with high potential to "make good." The other

3,778 prisoners with less potential were dishonorably discharged. As with so many issues where Osborne was involved, success of or failure was a matter of viewpoint.

Figure 7 permits a closer examination of Osborne's performance and helps break down further the figures in Daniels' 1920 annual report; it compares the number of prisoners received and restored annually (fiscal year from 1 July to 30 June) with those dishonorably discharged during the Osborne era. Clearly, something extraordinary took place at Portsmouth in 1918 and 1919. Figure 7 invites several observations:

1. The number of prisoners received and processed annually at the prison increased more than 500 percent (600 versus 3,229) between 1917 and 1918, remained high in 1919 (2,710), and dropped off dramatically to 751 in 1920. The administrative workload at the prison was huge during 1918 and 1919.

2. Dishonorable discharges did not change much between 1917 and 1918 (333 versus 396) while the number of prisoners restored to the Navy increased ten-fold (69 versus 743). During the first year of the war, the fleet's need for sailors would have discouraged dishonorable discharges if restoration was a possibility. At the same time, the fleet's numbers could be increased even more if the penal system were more conducive to restorations. Osborne had arrived at Portsmouth with a new penal system tailor-made for the times.

3. Restorations peaked in 1919 at 1,563, but so did the dishonorable discharges at 2,003. The latter was the result of a decreased need for restorations in late 1918, with the approaching end of the war. A Navy directive of mid–September 1918 encouraged early releases of prisoners because of overcrowded conditions and excessive costs to maintain those prisoners: "All men [at Portsmouth prison] who have been tried for minor military offenses involving absence without

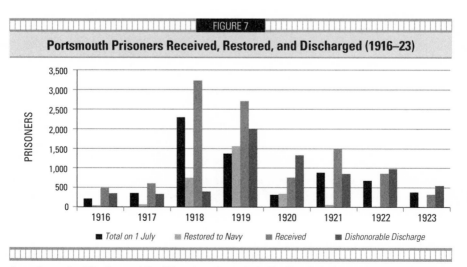

FIGURE 7

Portsmouth Prisoners Received, Restored, and Discharged (1916–23)

■ Total on 1 July   ■ Restored to Navy   ■ Received   ■ Dishonorable Discharge

Source: Commanding Officer Portsmouth Naval Prison, *Annual Reports for the Fiscal Years Ending 30 June 1916–1922,* NARA Waltham, RG 181, Portsmouth General Collection.

leave and who have served a reasonable part of their term of confinement and whose conduct has been satisfactory during such confinement, should be immediately discharged ... as the prison is overcrowded with 2,400 prisoners, at great expense to the government."[3] The war ended on 11 November 1918, and the Navy was no longer interested in incurring the costs of maintaining and possibly rehabilitating prisoners not needed in the fleet. Cost reduction was achieved by increasing the number of dishonorable discharges.

4. A decreased need for restorations continued in the years 1920–22, and dishonorable discharges greatly exceeded restorations. During this post-Osborne period, the prevailing philosophy of prison administration was to rid the Navy of malcontents and marginal performers rather than devote time to the restoration of prisoners not needed in the fleet. Restorations after the war quickly dropped below prewar levels.

Clearly, the Osborne years at Portsmouth were the most active and challenging period in the life of the prison up to that time—and for the entire life of the prison as it turns out. Activity again peaked at the prison during World War II when there were more prisoners confined but far fewer restorations and much less controversy.

An analysis of prisoner escapes and deaths gives even more appreciation of the challenges Osborne faced (table 12).[4] The most startling figure in the table, twenty-eight deaths in 1919, was primarily because of the worldwide Spanish influenza epidemic. This plague caused "more deaths (50 million) than had resulted from the First World War which lasted four years."[5] The shipyard medical officer reported, "During the months of September and October the universal epidemic of the so called 'Spanish Influenza' broke out at this station. Out of a complement of approximately two thousand men there were three hundred fifty-nine cases. The severe cases were transferred to the U.S. Naval Hospital for treatment where twenty-two deaths [at the time of the report] occurred among the prisoners. In February a secondary epidemic followed in the wake of the first and there were two hundred and twenty cases out of a complement of approximately two thousand men."[6] The number of deaths might have been higher had a fully staffed shipyard hospital not been available just a few blocks from the prison.

The percentage of received prisoners who were restored annually (figure 8), confirms the uniqueness of the Osborne years at Portsmouth prison. The year 1919

Table 12	Portsmouth Prisoner Escapes and Deaths (1916–23)							
	1916	*1917*	*1918*	*1919*	*1920*	*1921*	*1922*	*1923*
Escapes	0	0	0	5	4	0	0	0
Deaths	1	0	6	28	3	1	0	0

Source: Commanding Officer Portsmouth Naval Prison, *Annual Reports for the Fiscal Years Ending 30 June 1916–1923*, NARA Waltham, RG 181, Portsmouth General Collection.

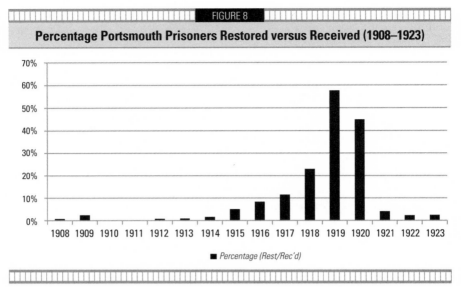

FIGURE 8

Percentage Portsmouth Prisoners Restored versus Received (1908–1923)

■ *Percentage (Rest/Rec'd)*

Source: Commanding Officer Portsmouth Naval Prison, *Annual Reports for the Fiscal Years Ending 30 June 1908–1923,* NARA Waltham, RG 181, Portsmouth General Collection.

was a banner year for Osborne and Portsmouth prison when nearly 60 percent of the prisoners received were restored. Prisoner restorations increased slowly from 1915 to 1917 as the result of Daniels' increased attention and commitment to reform, accelerated significantly in 1918 and 1919 under Osborne's reign, and began to decline in 1920 with the decreased need for naval personnel at the end of the war. Restorations dropped precipitously in 1921 after Osborne's exit. The negligible restoration percentages before 1915 and after 1921 attest to a status quo that was only interrupted by the reform initiatives of Daniels and Osborne. Figure 8 visually presents the wave of progressive prison reform that crested in 1919 as it passed through the Portsmouth prison during World War I.

By any standard, Portsmouth prison and the Portsmouth Navy Yard were a hotbed of activity from 1918 to 1920. In the midst of a full-scale wartime Navy yard industrial mobilization, the prison saw an influx of about 3,000 prisoners annually and had about 2,000 prisoners confined on 1 July each year. Shipyard civilian employment peaked at about 5,100 employees, making naval prisoners a significant percentage of the total population within the physical boundaries of the shipyard. Included in all this activity were the deaths of 34 prisoners and the escape of 9 others. With all this activity, Osborne's repeated pleas for expanded facilities and support are understandable. At the same time, one can also question the wisdom of introducing progressive reform into such a chaotic prison environment. Critics might find Osborne guilty of piling chaos on top of chaos.

As warden of Portsmouth Naval Prison, Osborne rehabilitated many prisoners and generated much controversy with his methods. His reform crusade frustrated shipyard managers and disrupted shipyard operations. Similarly, the naval officers in the fleet who court-martialed and sentenced offenders to Portsmouth, only to have them returned to the fleet after serving a small part of their sentence, were equally frustrated by Osborne's methods. Osborne's perceived know-it-all attitude and his penchant for working around the traditional naval chain of command undercut the support of his fellow naval officers at the yard and the fleet support he so critically needed to be successful. Senior naval officers did not readily accept the progressive prison reform espoused by Osborne and enthusiastically endorsed by Daniels and FDR. Support for progressive naval prison reform at the top and the bottom of the chain of command, with very little acceptance from the links in between, made for considerable debate and dissension within the U.S. Navy.

ANALYSIS OF THE OSBORNE YEARS AT PORTSMOUTH PRISON

Any analysis of the Osborne years at Portsmouth prison must include a disclaimer, as it is difficult to remain impartial when he is concerned. As stated previously, Osborne attracted either avid supporters or severe critics. With that acknowledgment, and having examined the Osborne years at Portsmouth prison in detail, several observations can be drawn about the man and his methods.

Osborne was an altruist with an ego. Judgment about which attribute dominated depended on whether one was a supporter or a critic. Daniels and FDR saw him as an altruist with the capability of bringing much-needed change to naval prisons. Portsmouth Navy Yard officers and naval officers in the fleet, who were the recipients of his Shakespearian quotes and dissertations on prison reform, undoubtedly believed that his ego interfered with his job performance and his responsibilities to the U.S. Navy. Supporters perceived him to have achieved remarkable success. Critics perceived him to be an abject failure. There was not much middle ground. In the long run, Osborne's inability to create and exploit this middle ground kept him from achieving lasting reforms in naval prisons.

Osborne's personality was complex and confusing. Neil D. Novello's video *TMO @ the Castle* presents Thomas Mott Osborne in a very positive light. However, the narrator, historian David Connelly, at various times admits to Osborne's complex personality. He begins the film with, "Osborne was either a nut or a visionary" and concludes with, "Who was this man, . . . I have to tell you I still don't quite know."[7] Connelly is one of many who do not know how to categorize the man—saint, sinner, nut, visionary, savior, adversary—these terms all appear to fit Osborne, depending on one's viewpoint and the situation.

Rudolph Chamberlain wrote, "It is inaccurate to say that Osborne possessed ideas. Ideas possessed him." He also observed, "He was practically incapable of compromise. At critical moments in his career, refusal to concede a minor point lost him the chance of preferment."[8] Chamberlain was referring to earlier lost opportunities, but this attribute was fully exposed at Portsmouth. When his ideas were challenged or his methods criticized, compromise was never an option. Instead, he preached his gospel of prison reform even louder and stronger to some naval officers who did not care to hear the sermon. They just wanted the sermon to end.

On the other hand, Daniels, FDR, and many civilians shared his sympathies for prison reform and were eager to hear his sermons. Some even thought Osborne intended to use his Portsmouth experience and pulpit to launch a nationwide campaign for prison reform. On 18 December 1919, a *Boston Daily Globe* headline proclaimed, "Osborne to Stay at Naval Prison, Denies Plan to Reform Whole Country." The article noted that Osborne had been "making trips to New York and as far west as Chicago to lecture on prison reform." He reportedly denied "recent interviews attributed to him" that suggested grandiose plans to reform prisons from coast to coast. Knowing Osborne's passion for reform and publicity, it would not have been out of character for him to advance such an idea and then deny it.

The above episode highlights one of Osborne's problems at Portsmouth. His objectives were much loftier and more long-range than what he was doing for the Navy. His Portsmouth experience was intended to be the shining example of the potential of progressive prison reform—the launching pad for bigger and better things. The irritating criticism from the fleet was something to be endured and explained away so he could get on with his grand plan. Needless to say, the fleet's objectives were much more immediate and pragmatic.

It was not only the fleet that was critical of Osborne's methods. In an article written for the *Journal of the American Institute of Criminal Law and Criminology* in May 1922, two years after Osborne left Portsmouth, Sanford Bates criticized Osborne's Mutual Welfare League. The author was commissioner of the Massachusetts Department of Corrections (1919–29) and superintendent of Prisons, U.S. Department of Justice (1929) and went on to become the first director of the Federal Bureau of Prisons (1930–37). Writing about an "Honor System for Inmates of Prisons and Reformatories," Bates considered the Mutual Welfare League, established by Osborne at Auburn, Sing Sing, and Portsmouth to be "the most advanced example of the system." Still, he could not approve Osborne's system "unless allowed to impose certain qualifications." Bates took issue with the widespread application of an honor system to a group that had not previously demonstrated its trustworthiness. "The honor system as exemplified by the Mutual Welfare League possesses one serious defect in that it attempts to confer the privileges and duties of citizenship and self-government on those who have by their very position [serving prison sentences] shown their inability to accept them."[9] Bates argued that prison management should always remain the absolute responsibility of prison officials. Any increase to inmate responsibilities and privileges must be earned. Bates thought that Osborne was too quick to give prisoners the benefit of the doubt without requiring them to prove their trustworthiness. Indeed, Osborne always saw the good in every man. When his blind trust was rewarded, his results were often spectacular. When that trust was misplaced, disaster struck as it did in his final days at Sing Sing and Portsmouth.

Osborne's finale at Portsmouth was a replay of his previous experience at Sing Sing. Both his experiments terminated in a dark cloud of accusations of rampant homosexuality and sexual depravities. Osborne, more or less, invited these accusations. He was much more tolerant of homosexual prisoners than either the authorities who sentenced them to prison or the naval regulations that governed his prison. Osborne considered homosexuality an inevitable consequence of men closely confined for long periods of time, such as inmates in prison and sailors on board a ship. Osborne wrote on this subject in *Prisoners and Common Sense*, "One of the inevitable results of men being thrown together, either in prison or the Navy, is the prevalence of unnatural vice; and if it is hard to control in the Navy it is impossible to exterminate in prison."[10] Immorality, a black-and-white issue to fleet commanders, was a gray issue for Osborne. He believed "the only thing the head of such an institution as a prison can do, is . . . reduce such immorality to a minimum."[11] His critics were not convinced that he attempted to do so. Instead, the JAG charges alleged rampant and undisciplined immoral practices at the prison.[12] Osborne's insistence on mixing prisoners guilty of immoral offenses with those convicted of lesser offenses, despite regulations against doing so, angered his critics even more. A prison population with large numbers of homosexuals provided conservative critics all the ammunition they needed to mount an attack.

Clearly, Osborne was a caring and compassionate man. He preached the need for compassionate treatment of prisoners, and he practiced what he preached. Tannenbaum thought Osborne's compassion bordered on sainthood. "There was something of the saint about Thomas Mott Osborne, something about his love for his fellows that reminds one of Saint Francis of Assissi [*sic*]. . . . Men whose lives had been seared and embittered, human beings who had touched the bottom of depravity, of degradation, of sorrow, of failure, could turn to him in perfect frankness, in affection, in adoration almost. . . . Surely no man of our day and generation was so loved by the outcast and persecuted of the underworld."[13] Was Osborne a saint or a devil? Once again the judgment is in the eye of the beholder. And once again there is no middle ground.

The compassion, sincerity, honesty, and openness that characterized his relationships with prisoners proved effective in gaining their trust and confidence. On the other hand, Vice Admiral Sims, Captain Taussig, and other senior naval officers thought these attributes contributed to lapses in discipline that challenged the Navy's concepts of command and control. Senior naval officers believed the lack of discipline that accompanied progressive reform was incompatible with the hierarchal structure and good order and discipline required of a military environment.

If Osborne found reform difficult at Sing Sing, it was an even more challenging task at a naval prison. Austin MacCormick spoke of this challenge when he wrote to Osborne as things were unraveling at Portsmouth in late February 1920, "Until the Navy has changed radically, democracy can have no place in it, and you and I will leave it with the realization that we have backed up against a blanker wall than the bigotry of the civil population with regard to state prisons."[14] MacCormick was suggesting that he and Osborne had tried to introduce democracy into a naval prison when the Navy itself was not a democracy. The realization that the Navy is not a democracy would come as no surprise to anyone who has served in the Navy or any branch of the military. He also suggested that the Navy's bigotry and lack of compassion had made their job at Portsmouth more difficult than it would have been at a state prison. In retrospect, the challenge of reforming Portsmouth prison was much larger than either Osborne or MacCormick had anticipated.

Both MacCormick and Osborne underestimated the inertia of the U.S. Navy and its resistance to change. About their efforts to institute permanent reform at Portsmouth, MacCormick observed, "We tried to chew solid stone and only a rock crusher can do that." Even with the crushing influence and power of Daniels and FDR behind them, they were not able to dent the solid stone that was the U.S. Navy. Finding consolation in having fought the good fight, MacCormick added, "But they can't take away from us the hundreds of decent men we turned back into the Navy, and the hundreds discharged and restored who were better for having gone to Portsmouth. They may tear down your whole structure, . . . but, they can't nullify the results in the lives of your few thousand 'boys.'"[15] As unpopular as Osborne and his practices were to some, there is little doubt that he was a positive influence on the lives of hundreds of prisoners.

Osborne firmly believed that his most important contribution at Portsmouth prison was the positive effect and lasting influence he had on the thousands of prisoners' lives he helped restore to respectability. He continued to maintain contact with ex-prisoners long after they had left his prison, evidenced by the hundreds of letters contained in official Navy files and Osborne's personal collection. Most are letters of appreciation from young men who benefited from Osborne's compassion during their stay in prison:

> "Look, could anyone else in this wretched world have done what you have done for a poor unfortunate like me? . . . How can I repay you for all this?"[16]

> "I have not touched liquor once since my discharge, and never will again."[17]

> "I now realize that the legitimate is a better game than the old one; and the returns are larger. If a man will only place the same amount of cleverness and ingenuity that he used in robbing people? It is a good world after all; and I am thankful that I am in it."[18]

> "This may be my last opportunity to write you. I admire and respect you more than I could express in a thousand letters and know that I owe a debt to you that can never be paid. . . . Pray do not consider this an attempt at flattery; I wouldn't lower myself in your eyes by attempting such. . . . Things have 'broke' wonderfully for me. And in another month or two, the girl that has been loyal through everything will be my wife, and I will be doubly strengthened to fight life's battles successfully."[19]

Austin MacCormick was right. Their critics could not take away the many changed lives that had resulted from their vision and actions. Osborne salvaged the lives of hundreds of young men, not just for the Navy, but also for society. He claimed his vision was not to convert bad prisoners to good prisoners. Instead, his goal was to prepare prisoners to be good sailors and good citizens, so they could rejoin society outside the prison walls.

In Osborne's eyes, he had turned Portsmouth prison into more of an asset than a liability for the Navy. He believed his prison to be the shining example of prison reform—and so did Daniels. Daniels said Osborne "made the Navy prison as near a model one as humanly possible."[20] As noted earlier, Osborne sincerely believed that his principles of prison reform were "thoroughly and brilliantly vindicated at Portsmouth."[21] Many did not share his view or Daniel's opinion that Osborne had made Portsmouth a model prison. The restoration numbers were impressive, but many naval officers believed that Osborne was too soft on prisoners and much too eager to return marginal performers to the fleet. Osborne's attitude and methods, especially the routine bypassing of the traditional naval chain of command to achieve his ends, were particularly disturbing and frustrating to those who did not share his views and passion for prison reform.

Osborne was the champion—if not the savior—for the needy and the destitute who found themselves at Portsmouth prison. Researching his personal files, one is impressed with the time and effort he routinely devoted to individual prisoners. If he was convinced a prisoner had been falsely convicted and sentenced, he was relentless in his pursuit of a reversal of the sentence. Letters from graduates requesting his assistance or recommendations for employment were most often answered quickly. During the height of the investigation at Portsmouth, when he was under severe attack by critics and stressed to the maximum, he answered many letters from low-ranking ex-prisoners. Most responses began with a brief apology that attributed his delayed response to a busy schedule. He was not one to dwell on his own problems when others needed his help.

Osborne did something else during the investigation that demonstrated yet another dimension to his caring and character. On 18 February 1920, in the middle of all the turmoil and controversy that surrounded his investigation and imminent departure, he wrote a personal letter to Daniels recommending World War I service awards (medals) for Admiral Boush and three other shipyard officers. Osborne wrote, "I may be intruding where it is none of my business, but . . . these four men should not be overlooked."[22] Under attack from all quarters, he took the time to do something for these men who were included among his adversaries during his time at the Navy yard. It is unfortunate that Osborne's actions never demonstrated some of the apparent hidden respect he had for his contemporaries at the Navy yard. Had he done so, he would have had a good start building the consensus he desperately needed.

In *Crime and the Community* Frank Tannenbaum summarized Osborne's approach to penal administration as one that stressed mutual cooperation between the prisoners and the warden: "The penal administration developed by Osborne had as its base the co-operation of the prisoners. It operated on the assumption that the prison could be treated as a community. . . . It consisted of a system of semi-self government within the prison, and had as its most useful instrument open and public dealing between the warden and prisoners on all issues affecting the men."[23] Osborne's experiment at Portsmouth was indeed based on open communications, mutual cooperation, and the prisoners' faith that he could deliver on his promises. That faith was well placed.

Prisoner faith in Osborne was the keystone of the Osborne system, and he often went to extremes to reinforce that faith. Visits to the prison by FDR and Daniels reinforced prisoner faith and confidence by showing that Osborne enjoyed the backing of senior Navy officials. His frequent challenging of improper sentences, and what he believed to be invalid criticism of his prisoners, reinforced prisoners' belief in his leadership. Being very visible in petitioning for prisoners' rights and small privileges also enhanced prisoners' faith in him. Faith was a two-way street. Osborne constantly told his prisoners of his faith in them and frequently relayed favorable impressions of others to them. His philosophy for the care of prisoners was not far removed from the parental philosophy that claims the child will become what you repeatedly tell him he is.

If faith in Osborne was the keystone, the possibility of hope and forgiveness was the mortar that kept it all together. Osborne was relentless in keeping those two attributes continuously in front of his prisoners. Every speech or talk he gave offered the possibility of restoration and release as the natural consequence of demonstrated good conduct and performance of duties. Names of men recently approved for restoration were read at assemblies and published weekly in the *Mutual Welfare News*. Inmates frequently saw convincing evidence that Osborne could deliver the promised restoration if they fulfilled their part of the bargain. Osborne used the *Mutual Welfare News* to remind prisoners of their individual responsibilities. At the end, when it became obvious he could not routinely deliver the promised restorations, Osborne correctly assumed his system would unravel. And unravel it did.

Some penal scholars think the Portsmouth prison experiment in progressive reform was a microcosm of the movement as a whole. According to one scholar, these reformers were victims of their own naiveté about their abilities to mold public opinion and delusional in thinking that the best of intentions would guarantee practical results. "Progressive penal reformers were victims of their own assumptions, sacrifices to naïve faith in the power of public opinion . . . proper methodology does not insure practical results. While such delusion may have intensified the reformer's own self-purpose, the notion naively assumes dutiful malleability—of inmates, of politicians, of public—based on the exemplification of obvious good."[24] Osborne fits this mold well. He was indeed a victim of his own naïve assumptions about the malleability of inmates, politicians, and naval officers. The latter, who were heavily involved in the day-to-day realities of the mobilization of resources needed to win a war, found it difficult to accept Osborne's belief in the inherent goodness of man and most prisoners. Deluded by his own visions of the ultimate prison environment, Osborne's zealous championing of prisoners' rights attracted notoriety and criticism of his methods. This undermined the support needed to achieve his goals.

Tannenbaum believed that Osborne's experiments in prisoner self-government eventually failed because of "the hostility of [subsequent] wardens, the indifference of the public, and the ingrained belief that external discipline is the safest road to reformation."[25] As will be seen, the warden who reversed Osborne's practices, Lt. Col. H. L. South, could not have been more hostile to prisoner self-government nor could he have been a more ardent believer in external discipline. And the officers at the shipyard were more than indifferent to Osborne's reforms. Another prison reform scholar, David J. Rothman, argues in *Conscience and Convenience* that the tension between conscience-driven reformers and a convenience-driven society always evolved toward the more practical and organizational needs of society.[26] Osborne, FDR, and Daniels provided the "conscience" for reform at Portsmouth prison. Those reforms waned quickly after these actors left the stage amid "convenience-driven" concerns for fiscal and organizational challenges under the new leadership of Secretary of the Navy Edward Denby and Lt. Col. H. L. South.

Any fair criticism of Osborne and his methods must be balanced with an objective acknowledgment of the results he obtained. For two and a half years at the height of World War I, Osborne burst on the scene and briefly made Portsmouth prison a shining example of progressive prison reform. With the personal involvement and backing of the secretary of the Navy, and with World War I providing an overwhelming need for manpower, Osborne delivered restorations to the Navy at a phenomenal rate. FDR summarized things well when he said that Osborne was a man of "vision" but also a "voice crying in the wilderness."[27] Osborne was an idealist with visions that others could not see and did not share. Yet, his dedication and perseverance made progressive reform work very well, for a while, at Portsmouth prison.

15

Portsmouth Post Osborne

These sexual perverts being members of the "Mutual Welfare League" were permitted to mingle freely with other prisoners. . . . It is my belief that these immoral practices have continued among this class of men generally throughout the prison for a long time.

—Lt. Col. Hamilton South, 1921, Commanding Officer, Portsmouth Prison

Osborne's immediate successor, Commodore Wadhams, did his best to continue Osborne's reforms. When Daniels learned of Osborne's desire to resign, he immediately offered the job to Wadhams, who was no novice to prison administration. Wadhams had served "for several years as a member of the board of parole of the New York state prison."[1] Daniels encouraged Wadhams to continue Osborne's efforts, and the commodore arrived at Portsmouth determined to maintain much of what Osborne had put in place.

Wadhams graduated from the U.S. Naval Academy in 1868 and retired in 1907 after forty-three years of service.[2] "During the war, Commodore Wadhams was called from the retirement list of the navy and assigned duty in Washington, D.C., as the representative of the navy department at the national headquarters of the American Red Cross. On 1 November 1919, Commodore Wadhams was again placed on the retired list, but was recalled to active duty 8 March 1920."[3] Wadhams relieved Osborne on 17 March 1920.

Wadhams gained valuable experience with prison management during his twelve-year hiatus from the Navy. "Upon his original retirement from active duty, Commodore Wadhams was appointed by Governor Charles E. Hughes of New York, as a member of the Board of Pardons and Parole for State Prisons in New York. He served as commissioner in this capacity for five years."[4] In a rare change of command that may have established a record for the cumulative age of the two change-of-command participants, a sixty-one-year-old lieutenant commander was relieved by a seventy-five-year-old commodore.

Osborne's first impressions of Wadhams were quite favorable. In a 17 March 1920 letter to Austin MacCormick, who was no longer assigned to the prison, Osborne wrote, "Commodore Wadhams is here and he is A-1—filled with enthusiasm for the League which he really thinks is the greatest thing ever; determined to carry on and see the thing through."[5] As pleased as Osborne was to be relieved by Wadhams, he must have been overjoyed the next month when MacCormick received orders to return to the prison to assist Wadhams.[6] With the tide turning against reform at Portsmouth prison, Daniels and FDR were doing all they could to stem that tide by assigning pro-Osborne men to the prison.

Wadhams quickly assumed Osborne's role as spokesman for the League and Portsmouth prison. Within a month after assuming command, he addressed the annual meeting of the National Committee on Prisons and Prison Labor at Columbia University. There he "told of conditions in his institution and of the workings of the Mutual Welfare League."[7] A month later he spoke at the same organization in New York City where other notable speakers included author Frank Tannenbaum, who spoke on "Prison Cruelty." Another speaker, George Hodson, who had spent some time at Portsmouth prison, was advertised as the secretary of the "outside" branch of the Mutual Welfare League.[8] Wadhams was off to a good start. He had taken a page out of the Osborne playbook and garnered a lot of publicity for the League; in the process he had established himself as Osborne's successor.

Wadhams published a pamphlet early in his new assignment in which he proudly described a number of Osborne-initiated prison facilities and organizations: "Among the recreational activities of the prisoners may be counted the Farragut Club, which is like any Y.M.C.A. but, having a gymnasium complete with all kinds of athletic gear. . . . We also have a library, which contains over 4,000 volumes, fiction and non-fiction. . . . There are also two other activities . . . a literary club . . . also a Bible Study Club."[9] There was no doubt that Wadhams was determined to preserve as many of these prisoner amenities as possible.

Meanwhile, Osborne continued to make the news. The 7 June 1920 *New York Times* reported that he was back at Portsmouth prison after conducting an investigation of naval prisons and detention camps along the Atlantic coast.[10] Osborne's resignation from the Navy was effective upon the completion of that investigation. He returned to Portsmouth for one last visit to offer advice and counsel to Wadhams and MacCormick.

The next week Osborne made a triumphant return to Sing Sing, where he was greeted with a band playing and twelve hundred convicts cheering. The new warden, Lewis F. Lawes, invited Osborne to address the convicts. Osborne urged the men to "play straight" with the new warden "who is playing straight with you." When asked of his plans for the future, he replied, "I expect to devote my life to prison reform, not in New York state alone but wherever the occasion arises. I will act in the capacity of a consultant expert." Ever the optimist about his Mutual Welfare League, Osborne predicted, "The League is going to spread all over the United States." He added, "They are anxious for leagues of prisoners in Japan" and that he had been invited "to go to England to organize it there." He failed to mention that the League was under attack at Portsmouth Naval Prison and its future tenuous.[11]

Wadhams' efforts to continue Osborne's initiatives were resisted by higher authorities. Local interest in continuing Osborne's reforms had greatly diminished with his departure. When Wadhams sought to continue competition between the prison baseball teams and outside teams, the Navy yard commandant, now Rear Adm. A. S. Halstead, denied the request because it was not "proper to permit games between prisoners and men in good standing in that it tends to lessen the distinction between them and loses sight of the mission of the Naval Prison."[12] Halstead was one of the three members of the board of inquiry that had absolved Osborne of all charges. Halstead was not willing to continue to run the prison under Osborne's rules, now that he was out from under the thumb of FDR.

The above incident, which occurred in August 1920, illustrates how quickly naval protocol returned to Portsmouth prison after Osborne's departure. Wadhams' request for permission to have the prison baseball team play outside teams got no further than the commandant because the chain of command had been restored. Gone were the days when the prison commander could bypass the shipyard commandant and get permission directly from Daniels or FDR for prisoners to participate in outside activities. In this case, "outside teams" meant other shipyard baseball teams outside the immediate walls of the prison. Under Osborne "outside" often meant outside the shipyard's gates. There could be little doubt in Wadhams' mind that change was in the air.

Further evidence of Halstead's harder line was his denial of funds to the naval prison for moving pictures, entertainments, and athletics. Wadhams appealed to a higher level for this funding only to have another member of FDR's board, Rear Adm. H. O. Dunn, commandant of the First Naval District, deny the request.[13] Halstead also denied a request from Wadhams to improve lighting in the cells; it was his opinion that the prison cells were only occupied by "bad cases" and he was not inclined to provide "extra comfort" for such prisoners.[14] Times indeed had changed.

The hard line taken by Halstead and Dunn concerning proposed prisoner amenities is inconsistent with the much softer line taken toward Osborne when both were investigating officers on his board of inquiry. Their actions immediately after Osborne's departure lend credence to the argument that FDR had dominated the board and unduly influenced these two board members to accept his views. Free of FDR's influence, Dunn and Halstead did not hesitate to oppose the conditions they had found at Portsmouth prison.

The tide continued to turn away from reform during Wadhams' short tenure. With Osborne gone and Daniels less directly involved with prison affairs, shipyard authorities were more outspoken about the way Osborne had run the prison. For example, Cdr. J. H. Sypher, a member of the clemency board under Osborne, was disturbed because, in his opinion, the orders for release of two prisoners who had committed serious offenses had misrepresented the facts of the case. Sypher claimed the orders indicated the release was in accordance with the recommendation of the clemency board when no such recommendation was made. This accusation cast even more aspersions on Osborne and his loose and dictatorial management of the prison.

Commander Sypher claimed that one of the prisoners was "a murderer, sentenced to be hanged," whose sentence was first commuted to life imprisonment and then further reduced until he was eventually "released after serving about two years of his sentence."[15] The second released prisoner was "an embezzler of approximately $30,000, who was sentenced to ten years imprisonment, mitigated to eight years, and released after eight months."[16] Sypher requested that the orders for release of these men be revised to remove any reference to a clemency board recommendation. The commander considered it "a perpetual record of dishonor upon the members of the Clemency Board"[17] that their names were associated with the release of these two prisoners. Sypher considered the radical sentence reductions and eventual pardons of these most hardened of criminals appalling. He did not want to be identified in any way with such a travesty of justice. Sypher's concerns bolster the earlier accusations of senior naval officers that Osborne restored many marginal performers to the fleet. If Osborne, as Commander Sypher claimed, arranged early pardons for a murderer and an embezzler, it seems highly probable he also arranged to have less serious offenders pardoned far sooner than they deserved.

Contrary to naval regulations, Osborne apparently not only mixed but also restored the "bad" with the "good" and the "indifferent." Osborne's ability to work around the chain of command facilitated such restorations. Much as FDR had dominated the board of inquiry, Osborne had dominated the local clemency board. He routinely sent the "board's" recommendations, heavily skewed in favor of his view of things, on to Daniels, where they were approved without question. After Osborne's departure, a new procedure was instituted that required the JAG to make periodic visits to the prison to review each case for restoration. This procedure eliminated any possible local manipulation of the clemency board and also reduced the direct involvement of the secretary of the Navy in prisoner restorations.

Wadhams' tour of duty was short, 18 March 1920 to 4 July 1921. The relief of Wadhams by Lt. Col. Hamilton South, USMC, a hard-line strict disciplinarian, unquestionably marked the end of reform at Portsmouth prison. The sharp turn toward conservatism at Portsmouth prison during and immediately after Wadhams' fifteen months of service closely paralleled a similar move toward conservative values on the national scene during approximately the same timeframe.

From the summer of 1919 to the summer of 1920, the Red Scare swept the nation and raids approved by Attorney General A. Mitchell Palmer to identify and deport radical aliens were in full swing. By February 1920 Palmer's name was "anathema to every progressive and liberal (and many a conservative) in the country."[18] On 2 June 1920, an anarchist bomb demolished Palmer's house (and the anarchist), directly across the street from FDR's house in northwest Washington, D.C. Punctuated by a neighborhood bomb blast, it could not have been more obvious to FDR that progressivism was in full retreat nationwide—including the progressive reforms at Portsmouth prison.

President Wilson's Democratic reform–oriented government was replaced with the conservative Republican administration of Warren Harding on 4 March 1921, less than one year into Wadhams' short tenure. The Republican ticket of Harding and Calvin Coolidge defeated the Democratic nominee for president, James C. Cox, and his running mate for vice president, FDR, who had resigned as assistant secretary of the Navy on 26 August 1920.

The Newport sex scandal plagued Daniels until his final hours as secretary of the Navy. He signed his endorsement to the report of the two-year investigation at 7:30 p.m. on the evening of 4 March 1921, his last day in office. His endorsement again denied any wrongdoing on his part.[19] According to Lawrence R. Murphy, "The Navy's official interpretation was that with only minor exceptions the Dunn Court had found that charges lodged against the Department from [Bishop] Perry, the Newport ministers, and Rathom were either disproved or not proved, in whole or in part."[20] There were a lot of similarities between the report of the Dunn Court and the report of the FDR Board of Inquiry. Both dismissed the original accusations and exonerated the accused parties—some called both a "whitewash."

The Senate's report of its investigation of the Newport sex scandal, issued four months into the Harding administration on 19 July 1921, was much more critical of the Navy. It contained "a strongly worded rebuke of nearly every navy official" associated with the case. While the report of the Dunn Court considered FDR's actions "unfortunate and ill-advised," the Senate's report termed them "most reprehensible." The report considered Daniels' and FDR's sanction of the entrapment methods a "most deplorable, disgraceful, and unnatural proceeding." The Senate's report essentially concurred with the charges originally submitted by the clergy and Rathom. FDR, initially very disturbed with the report, soon wrote Daniels, "In the long run neither you nor I have been hurt by this mudsling, and it is best to file this whole thing away."[21] Both men were apparently eager to put the seemingly never-ending Newport sex scandal behind them.

Daniels' successor in the incoming Republican administration was an ex-Marine, Edwin Denby, who had been a Michigan congressman from 1904 to 1911. (Photo 20 shows secretaries Denby and Daniels.) Denby enlisted in the U.S. Marine Corps shortly after the outbreak of World War I. Married, forty-six years old, and weighing in at two hundred fifty-four pounds, Denby had to obtain age, weight, and marriage waivers in order to enlist in the Marine Corps.[22] He rapidly rose from the rank of private to major during the two years he was in the service. As an ex-officer in the Marine Corps, it was obvious where Denby's allegiance would fall if there were any future disagreements between the administrators at Portsmouth prison and the Marine Corps detachment at the yard. Had Osborne continued at Portsmouth, he would have had little success bypassing the chain of command with his complaints about the shipyard Marines.

On 6 March 1921, a few months after Denby's having assumed office, it became obvious to the fleet that he did not share Daniels' liberal philosophies when he relieved two commanding officers for what was described as a growing tendency to introduce "soviet" methods in the Navy. One commanding officer was relieved for permitting the crew to vote on what port they preferred for dry docking the ship;

another, Capt. D. Sterns, was relieved of command of the battleship *Michigan* for "permitting the enlisted men to elect a committee to pass upon disciplinary measures among members of the crew."[23] If flogging was as far right as the pendulum of naval discipline could swing, "discipline by committee" was certainly on the far left arc along with Osborne's reforms at Portsmouth. Denby was not willing to tolerate disciplining crewmembers by committee or Portsmouth prisoners through the Mutual Welfare League.

The *Providence Journal*, the longtime critic of the Daniels administration, delighted in the new Navy Department regime. According to the *Journal*, "During the time that Josephus Daniels ruled the destinies of the U.S. Navy, certain commanding officers, with the knowledge and consent and probably under his direction, instituted onboard ships in active service a Soviet form of control." The use of the word "soviet" to describe a commanding officer's leadership style and Daniels' organizational management of the Navy hints at the Red Scare paranoia so prevalent at the time. With the relieving of the two commanding officers, the *Journal* thought that Denby had reversed any soviet initiatives and made Daniels' policies merely an "echo of an old regime."[24]

On the day Denby assumed office, an article in the *New York Times* affirmed that the Navy was still plagued with foolish young sailors destined for Portsmouth prison. The paper reported the sentencing of a young sailor, Harold Hammond, to Portsmouth for the rare offense of bigamy. Hammond, who supposedly admitted to having fourteen wives, had also deserted. A follow-up article two months later humorously reduced the number of wives to eleven: "The romantic wartime career of Harold Hammond, a twenty-year-old naval apprentice, who is alleged has already married eleven girls . . . is serving a sentence in Portsmouth prison for bigamy." Hammond's lawyer said that his only explanation for Hammond's conduct was that "he was having a lot of fun."[25] Hammond would not find much fun at Portsmouth prison, where Lt. Col. Hamilton South would soon relieve Wadhams.

It did not take long for the "old timers" and other critics of Daniels and Osborne to convince the new "no-nonsense" secretary of the Navy that Commodore Wadhams should be replaced. Wadhams was gone four months after the presidential inauguration. The last obstacle to the full reversal of Osborne's reforms had been removed. Wadhams' replacement, Lieutenant Colonel South, arrived at Portsmouth on 4 July 1921. His personal philosophy about prison management was in sharp contrast to that of Osborne and Wadhams. As with Osborne's successor at Sing Sing, South was a prison professional who proclaimed a return to "iron discipline."[26] South led the prison with a firm hand until 6 June 1925.

South immediately restored a more traditional prison system.[27] Two weeks after he assumed command, headlines in the *Boston Daily Globe* proclaimed, "Prison Reform Killed at Portsmouth, New Commandant Throws Out Osborne System."[28] The crown jewel of Osborne's reform architecture, the Mutual Welfare League, was abolished nine days after South assumed command of the prison. Most of the rest of the reforms were abolished within a few weeks. South quickly reduced prisoner freedom to within the bounds of the prison, restricted civilian access to the prison, and increased guard surveillance during prisoner recreation periods.[29] Any question about where the prison baseball teams would play their games was no longer an issue; South answered that question when he prohibited the playing of baseball.[30] He increased the discipline associated with work details, including the maintenance of silence during assembly and marching to and from worksites.[31] Should his crackdown on prisoners' privileges encourage escape attempts, he instituted new harsher procedures for the handling of such attempts.[32] The result of South's actions left no doubt that confinement at Portsmouth prison was much less appealing than a sailor's life at sea.

Most noteworthy was the sudden change in attitude with regard to prisoners guilty of moral offenses. The new prison commander stressed that "moral perverts" and unreliable prisoners were not to be mixed with other prisoners at work or in the cellblock.[33] Naval regulations were to be strictly adhered to in this regard. Osborne considered homosexuality an inevitable consequence of situations where men were closely confined for long periods of time. He not only tolerated those convicted of such behavior, but refused to brand such offenders with derogatory labels and punishments. The tone used by Osborne and South in discussing homosexuality could not have been more different. Osborne's correspondence on the subject exhibited understanding, tolerance, and compassion. South's correspondence showed repugnance, anger, and disgust. He labeled them sexual perverts and degenerates.

Just two weeks after his arrival, South recommended general courts-martial trials for twelve prisoners on charges including sodomy, scandalous conduct tending to the destruction of good morals, and assault: "There are prison records here to show that men who have been guilty of 'sodomy' within the prison, during their incarceration, have been dealt with in an astoundingly light manner. . . . These sexual perverts being members of the 'Mutual Welfare League' were permitted to mingle freely with other prisoners. . . . It is my belief that these immoral practices have continued among this class of men generally throughout the prison for a long time. . . . The nature of punishments awarded formerly for offenses of this kind at this prison can only have resulted in prisoners of this perverted character being led to believe that they can practice their vicious immoral acts without restraint."[34] South's accusations against the twelve prisoners were an indictment of the Osborne years and specifically the Mutual Welfare League.

South expressed his disdain for the League in his first annual report: "Under the Mutual Welfare League system there were no prison guards, the prisoners going freely about their work on the prison reservation and throughout the prison. . . . The prison Detachment moved into the prison proper. . . . The cell-block containing 320 cells which had been practically empty under the Welfare system was [now] filled with prisoners convicted of Scandalous Conduct (perverts) and those guilty of the *higher crimes*" [emphasis in original].[35] South's view of the conditions preceding his arrival were much akin to those described in the JAG report of December 1919, which bore little resemblance to the conditions cited by FDR's team.

The *New York Times* continued to follow events at Portsmouth prison. This time, however, the reporting was in sharp contrast to the previous optimistic reports about Osborne's valiant reforms at the prison. The newspaper reported eighty-two prisoners, all members of the League, had been locked in their cells for offenses against the rules. According to the paper, "It was said to have been the first time in years that men were locked in cells during daylight hours."[36] The actions taken by the new warden demonstrated to the world that the reform experiment at Portsmouth prison was over.

There was one exception to the new hard line toward prisoners convicted of homosexual offenses. Denby ordered the five men sentenced to Portsmouth from the Newport sex scandal freed with dishonorable discharges on 3 September 1921. The Senate's report on the sex scandal, which was critical of the Navy's failure to protect the rights of the entrapped men, recommended naval regulations be revised to better guard defendants' rights. Denby's action, which was consistent with the Senate's recommendation, recognized that the rights of the five defendants had not been protected.[37] This action was also a well-intended slap in the face to the Daniels-FDR administration that had imprisoned the men in the first place.

The clemency list of December 1921 provides clear evidence of the change that had taken place in prison administration. Lieutenant Colonel South recommended 147 prisoners for immediate dishonorable discharge, only 3 for restoration to duty, 1 for immediate bad conduct discharge, and 2 for reenlistment (good discharge). South stressed that he had personally interviewed all prisoners appearing on the lists, along with supervisors and guards, to determine if the prisoners' conduct was deserving of his recommendation.[38] Under Osborne, prisoners were given the benefit of the doubt and were liberally restored to duty; under South, the onus was on the prisoner to prove his worth beyond a shadow of a doubt. Obtaining South's favorable recommendation for restoration was difficult to achieve. Under Osborne, hundreds were returned to the naval service each month. Under South, three were restored to duty during December 1921. The change in prison administration could not have been more dramatic.

Osborne relied on peer pressure and the Mutual Welfare League to control noncompliant prisoners. South resorted to more physical means. On 19 January 1922, South resorted to the use of leg irons to restrain a prisoner who had been involved in a fight with another prisoner.[39] Similarly, he restrained two other prisoners with irons in June 1923 after they had assaulted another prisoner.[40] No reference to the use of irons could be found in any of Osborne's correspondence. Under South, confinement conditions bore more resemblance to those on a nineteenth-century man-of-war than to the conditions at Portsmouth prison a few years earlier.

Several factors contributed to South's actions to end progressive reform. First, as noted earlier, there was a dramatic change in the criminal nature of the prisoners sent to Portsmouth after World War I. Wadhams stated in his 1920 annual report that both the seriousness of the sentences and the length of confinement had increased. He provided the following gross breakdown of the prison population in the 1920 annual report:

Military offenders	108
Criminals	146
Scandalous conduct / sodomy	57
TOTAL	311

The Portsmouth prison population of 1920 was a far cry from the pre–World War I population, which had been dominated by young deserters with a small percentage of criminals and moral degenerates.

The number and percentage of serious offenders confined at Portsmouth increased significantly at the end of 1918, when the last of the naval prisoners were relocated from the state prison to Portsmouth. The number of prisoners serving sentences of more than five years was twice as large in 1920 as in 1919. At the same time, the total number of prisoners dropped from 2,295 in 1918, to 1,367 in 1919, to 311 in 1920. Thus, by 1920 the prison population consisted of a much smaller group with a much higher percentage of serious offenders. This increase alone might have been cause for a move toward more rigid prison controls.[41]

Typical of the more serious offenders was SM Frederick Henry, who was convicted by the American Consular Court in Alexandria, Egypt, of second-degree murder of an Egyptian seaman. He was sentenced to a twenty-year term at Portsmouth prison in July 1922. Henry, who started his sentence at Hadra Prison in Alexandria, was one of the few who might find better confinement conditions under Lt. Col. H. L. South at Portsmouth.[42]

Clearly, South had more desperate characters serving sentences at the prison during his watch than did Osborne. Take, for example, the dramatic escape in July 1924 of four serious offenders: George M. Maher, serving ten years for manslaughter; Frank O'Neal, serving ten years for theft and robbery, breaking arrest, and assaulting a sentry; Joseph Whitney, serving six years for theft and robbery and breaking arrest; and James S. McCord, serving five years for desertion. The four prisoners lowered themselves on a rope over the prison wall seventy feet to the ground, and, "after stealing clothes of Mrs. Frank P. Wallace, wife of gunner Wallace, USMC, and his uniform, they appropriated a car belonging to Lieut. W. D. Baker" and drove through the main gate. Three were dressed as women and one as an officer. Several days later, on 8 July 1924, all four were arrested in Norwich, Connecticut, while "holding up automobile parties at the point of a .38 caliber revolver."[43] The prisoners were returned to their cells at Portsmouth prison on 10 July 1924.[44]

The second factor contributing to the end of progressive reform at Portsmouth prison was postwar budgetary cutbacks. In the summer of 1921, the Navy Department reported, "The allotment . . . for the expenses of prisons and prisoners is 43 percent less [than] expended last year . . . this allotment *must not be exceeded* [emphasis in original]. The necessity for the strictest economy in every detail is therefore evident."[45] Funds were simply not available to continue the prisoner comforts that Osborne had provided and that Commodore Wadhams had requested and been denied. South's crackdown on prisoner comforts was a good fit with the new budgetary constraints.

The third factor was South's personal "hard-line" views on prison management. Had it not been for this factor, ways might have been found to work around some of the budget cuts to continue selected reform programs. The Mutual Welfare League was disbanded because South felt "shrewd prisoners got control of the system and manipulated it to their advantage."[46] He "believed that prisoners did not have the scientific attitude or technique for dealing with violations of their own regulations." Furthermore, he thought, "they were likely to be crueler and less judicious in their treatment of difficult prisoners than were the prison officers themselves."[47] South's lack of confidence in the ability of prisoners to govern themselves was only exceeded by Osborne's faith and confidence in those same abilities.

Finally, any discussion about factors that contributed to the quick reversal of progressive reform at Portsmouth prison must include the administration change that brought President Warren Harding and the Republican Party to power in 1921, with Denby as the secretary of the Navy. Had Daniels continued in power, reform might have survived longer than it did. Instead, by mid-1922, only two years after Osborne's departure, progressive reform was a distant memory at Portsmouth prison.

16

Osborne Post Portsmouth

> You [Osborne] have taught the Navy and the country that prisons are
> to mend the prisoners and not to break them.
>
> —Secretary of the Navy Josephus Daniels, 1920

Osborne continued to be a strong voice for prison reform and his Mutual Welfare League from the time he left Portsmouth in 1920 until his death in 1926. After his death, his former assistant at Portsmouth, Austin MacCormick, picked up the mantle of prison reform and gained worldwide fame as an expert in prison education. The Osborne Association, founded by a group of his supporters in 1931, continues to the present day to advance Osborne's goals, offering compassionate opportunities to prisoners to redeem and transform their lives. We will examine more closely these three subjects—Osborne after Portsmouth, MacCormick after Portsmouth, and the Osborne Association.

Osborne took to the lecture circuit after he left Portsmouth and continued to preach his prison reform ideology. At times he appeared to be in denial of his experiences at Sing Sing and Portsmouth. For example, at a King's Chapel lecture in Boston, on 17 September 1923, he said, "Some . . . methods of treating prisoners were first laughed to scorn, then carefully studied, and finally made the basis of many modern prison systems."[1] In fact, at that time, his methods were in decline, never to regain the popularity they once enjoyed.

In *Prisons and Common Sense* (1924), Osborne drew on his experiences at Sing Sing, Auburn, and Portsmouth prisons to expound on his views on prison reform. Those views had changed little since his first experiments with prisoner self-government at Sing Sing in 1913. Some in positions of authority judged his prison experiments to be failures, but Osborne argued that the results achieved had validated his thesis that society is best served by a prison system that restores a prisoner's self-worth and dignity. Osborne continued to tout the merits of the League: "In spite of the imperfect conditions under which it had been tried, . . . the Mutual Welfare League has proved itself. We do not need to see it under perfect conditions; when we studied geometry, we learned that only three points in the circumference are needed to draw a complete circle."[2] After extreme criticism and mounting pressure from authorities had forced him to vacate his positions as warden at Sing Sing and Portsmouth prisons, Osborne remained firmly convinced he had proven his concepts of penal reform.

At the same time, Osborne understood that his efforts to convert authorities to his views had fallen short: "For ten years now, I have been hammering away at the endeavor to make understood a few simple propositions relating to prisons; but in spite of the wide-spread interest in prison reform, it is still very difficult for people to comprehend them. . . . I begin to feel that it must be my own fault—that I somehow fail to make clear my meaning."[3] After all the trials experienced, both literally and figuratively, Osborne remained convinced his life's work, his crusade for prison reform, remained as valid as ever. With death just a few years out, he firmly believed the problem was not his message but rather his inability to convincingly deliver the message. Having explored his commitment to the cause and the power of his personality, one might ask, "If Osborne could not deliver the message—who could?"

In the early 1920s Osborne became the president of the New York State Prison Council and chair of the National Society of Penal Information. As a result of the latter, he personally inspected and reported on more than thirty prisons in the United States, Great Britain, and Greece. He spread his message of prison reform worldwide through lectures, which often included showing a film he produced titled *The Right Way*. After one of those lectures, Victor Nelson, one of Osborne's former prisoners at Portsmouth, and at the time an escapee from the Charlestown, Massachusetts, jail, identified himself to Osborne. Nelson, sentenced to five years for assaulting and robbing a manicurist, had recently seen *The Right Way* in a Cincinnati theater and was motivated to atone for his mistakes. Nelson later spent some time with Osborne at his home in Auburn, New York, where Osborne convinced him to return to the Charlestown jail.

When testifying at Nelson's trial, Osborne was asked by the judge why he had not informed the authorities immediately of an escapee; Osborne explained his philosophy for dealing with prisoners. He had not reported Nelson because the man "spoke to me in confidence and I have never violated a confidence yet." Asked if he thought it necessary to punish offenders who escape and return voluntarily, Osborne responded, "No, I do not. If a prisoner treated in this manner gets away, he won't come back." Osborne's personal philosophy of rewarding deserving prisoners who had demonstrated proper behavior never wavered.[4]

With his Mutual Welfare League concept losing favor, he took advantage of his last work, *Prisoners and Common Sense* (1924), to argue that the League would have proven itself beyond a shadow of a doubt "if it were given a trial under entirely favorable conditions." Lamenting efforts under way to eliminate the League, he blamed its decline primarily on politics: "At Auburn, politics and official stupidity have almost completely smothered it; at Sing Sing, politics of the foulest kind drove one warden from office, and it has seriously curtailed [the] League. . . . At Portsmouth, the League is gone; as soon as the present Naval administration came into power it hastened to undo what a former administration had created. So it is unfortunately true that a fully developed Mutual Welfare League can be seen nowhere at present."[5] By 1924 Osborne had begun to accept reality. The League's future was in a decline, if not a death spiral. Many predicted the demise of the League; however, Osborne believed the League could never die because "the principle [faith in the goodness of man] upon which it rests is eternal."[6] The reformer, who had dedicated his life to prison reform and so aggressively defended his beliefs before a host of critics, remained true to his beliefs and battled those critics right up until his death.

Osborne died on 20 October 1926. His death was as bizarre as much of his life. He died while walking home from an Auburn theater, where his son Lithgow had performed in a play. Osborne had attended the performance disguised as a whiskered old man so that he could sit unrecognized in the audience and hear honest appraisals of his son's performance. Consequently, when he collapsed and died on the street, he was not immediately recognized.[7] In addition to the false whiskers, "false teeth were fitted over his real ones; small coils of wire distended his nostrils; [and] a milky glass eye starred up at a night sky."[8] This strange ending to his life seemed somehow appropriate: This impersonator extraordinaire, who enjoyed center stage whenever he could get it, had spent the final evening of his life incognito at the theater.

Osborne was buried next to his wife in a large family plot at Forest Hill Cemetery in Auburn, New York, following a funeral service at the Auburn prison chapel. His final resting place is not far from the prison at which he first introduced progressive reforms. As a final tribute to the importance he attached to his time at Portsmouth prison, and in one final act of impersonation, he went to his grave wearing a Portsmouth Naval Prison uniform.[9]

The Osborne Legacy

The Mutual Welfare League lasted longer at Sing Sing than it did at Portsmouth, but it too finally died in 1929 when a riot "gave guards and other critics the occasion to eliminate it."[10] The 11 December 1929 riot resulted in nine deaths and a trial of seven conspirators that concluded with three electric chair executions. One set of critics believed that had Osborne been alive, there would have been no riot. Another set of critics believed that Osborne's methods of mollycoddling prisoners was the cause of the riot.[11] Three years after his death, Osborne continued to be a controversial champion for progressive penal reform and a lightning rod for its critics. The governor of New York who received the Sing Sing riot reports in December 1929 was none other than Osborne's dear friend, Franklin D. Roosevelt.

The acting warden at Sing Sing, another hardliner in the mold of Lieutenant Colonel South, blamed the uprising on lax discipline and vowed, "This is going to be a tough prison . . . so long as I am in charge."[12] Sing Sing officials had joined a groundswell of reactionaries who had backed away from—if not run away from—Osborne's teachings. Less than ten years after Osborne's grand experiment with prisoner self-government at Portsmouth and just a few years after his death, his bold concepts of penal reform were in full retreat.

The Norfolk Massachusetts Penitentiary experimented with the League in the early 1930s without success.[13] By 1938 Osborne's concept of prison self-government had run its course. In discussing the demise of the Mutual Welfare League, David J. Rothman wrote, "The one reform that might have fundamentally altered the internal organization of the prison, Osborne's Mutual Welfare League, was not implemented to any degree at all. Wardens were simply not prepared to give over any degree of power to inmates. After all, how could men who had already abused their freedom on the outside be trusted to exercise it on the inside? . . . In brief, the concept of a Mutual Welfare League made little impact on prison systems throughout this period."[14] The rejection of progressive reform at Portsmouth prison in 1920 was a harbinger of things to come. South's hard line and refusal to empower inmates became the rule rather than the exception at other prisons.

The popularity of Osborne's Mutual Welfare League may have waned, but Austin MacCormick's memories of his old boss did not. Ten years after his experiences at Portsmouth prison, he retained the highest regard for Osborne and his concepts. MacCormick wrote, "This writer believes in the principle of inmate community organization, not only because it is consistent with sound educational, penal, and social philosophy but also because he has had experience under this system as an official of a large institution and has seen it work successfully . . . [at] the United States Naval prison at Portsmouth, New Hampshire, the commanding officer was Mr. Osborne himself, the foremost exponent of the system of inmate community organization. His contribution of this idea to prison practice is probably the most significant contribution of this generation."[15] MacCormick, like his boss, considered the experience at Portsmouth to have been a success.

More of a realist than Osborne, MacCormick wrote, "The idea of inmate community organization has been subjected to sweeping and usually uninformed criticism."[16] As a result of this criticism, he observed that the practice had ceased by 1933, with one exception, "In its more complete forms it is found today [1933] only in the reformatories for women, where it is accepted as standard practice and has demonstrated its value beyond any shadow of doubt. . . . As a result of the disorders in the New York State Prison at Auburn, the prisoner's organization there has recently been temporarily suspended."[17] The Massachusetts Reformatory for Women at Framingham, Massachusetts, under the direction of Miriam Van Waters (1932–57), was one of the women's reformatories that continued to operate as an "inmate community organization."

MacCormick became one of the nation's leading penologists and an expert on prison education. In the spring of 1927, MacCormick, then assistant director for the Bureau of Prisons, chaired a study of educational programs in American prisons for the American Association for Adult Education and the National Society of Penal Information. The goal of the study was to develop a standard educational program for all penal institutions. After visiting 110 institutions, MacCormick concluded, "Taking the country as a whole, we are tolerating a tragic failure. . . . Not a single complete and well rounded educational program, adequately financed and staffed, was encountered in all the prisons in the country." MacCormick's *Education of Adult Prisoners: A Survey and a Program* (1931) became the bible for prison education programs. The work was dedicated to Osborne and cited his "epochal work" in prison reform.

MacCormick went on to build a distinguished career in criminal justice and law enforcement until his death in 1979. His positions included assistant superintendent of federal prisons (1929–34), commissioner of the New York City Department of Corrections (1934–40), special assistant to the undersecretary of war for matters concerned with military law and corrections (1944–47), and professor of criminology at the University of California at Berkeley (1951–60). The young man who was incarcerated with Osborne at Portsmouth prison in 1917 committed his life to prison reform and the Osborne legacy. His mentor would have been proud.

The Osborne Association, founded in 1931 to provide prisoners and ex-prisoners the personal support and encouragement embodied in Osborne's reform endeavors, is active today. The association's mission is to "offer opportunities for individuals who have been in conflict with the law to transform their lives through innovative, effective, and replicable programs that serve the community by reducing crime and its human and economic costs."[18] The association preserves the Osborne legacy by serving more than 5,500 people annually in the greater New York region.

MacCormick was heavily involved in the Osborne Association. He served as the executive director of the association during World War II and later made important surveys of prison systems for the association between 1944 and 1951, when he joined the faculty at the University of California at Berkeley. Following his retirement from Berkeley in 1960, he again served as full-time executive director of the Osborne Association, until his death on 24 October 1979.

For over half a century, Austin MacCormick continued the legacy of Osborne and the principles of prison reform they had implemented at Portsmouth Naval Prison during World War I. Thanks to his efforts, and those of others associated with the Osborne Association, Osborne's legacy survives a century after he first introduced the Mutual Welfare League at Sing Sing and Portsmouth prisons. That legacy is reinforced daily by statues of Osborne's likeness, which adorn the lobby of the Corrections Museum at the New York State Department of Corrective Services Training Academy in Albany, New York, and the entrance of the Auburn, New York, Police and Fire Departments.

17

Conclusion

Thomas Mott Osborne had courage; even his enemies admit that;
he had vision . . . [but his] was a voice crying in the wilderness.

—Franklin Delano Roosevelt, 1933

Portsmouth Navy Prison continued to play a major role in the Navy's prison system until its closure in 1973. Throughout the late 1920s and 1930s the prison population declined dramatically from the peak of World War I (see figure 9). As a result of disarmament conferences and strong national neutrality sentiments, the size of the U.S. Navy was significantly reduced, and the naval prisoner population declined accordingly. Selective recruiting practices delivered higher-caliber sailors to the Navy, reducing the prison population even more. During those years in the 1930s when Portsmouth had minimal prisoners, Josephus Daniels was ambassador to Mexico, a position FDR had appointed him to in 1933. After some disagreements and strained relationships near the end of their tenure in the Navy Department, the relationship between the two had survived and prospered. Daniels was relieved as ambassador a few weeks before the attack on Pearl Harbor. He returned to North Carolina to resume his position as editor of the Raleigh *News and Observer* until he died on 15 January 1948.

Recalling that on 1 July 1918 Osborne had about 2,000 prisoners confined at Portsmouth prison, consider figure 9, which shows the prison population for the decade leading up to World War II. In May 1940 the prison population was 85, the lowest in the history of the prison up to that time.[1] Between the wars, the naval prison system was a shadow of its former self. According to Allan Berube, author of *Coming Out Under Fire*, a high percentage of the prisoners during this period were homosexuals: "By 1929, the Navy judge advocate general, to further segregate and more carefully supervise sodomists, had specifically designated Portsmouth Naval Prison as the place of confinement for moral perverts regardless of length of sentence." As a result, in the decade before World War II, "more than 40 percent of all new admissions to Portsmouth were men convicted of sodomy, oral coition, and sexual crimes other than the rape of women."[2] On the eve of World War II, as was the case during World War I, the confinement and control of homosexual prisoners

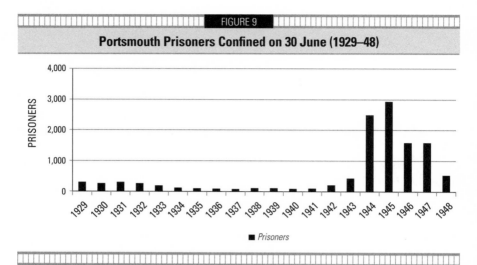

FIGURE 9

Portsmouth Prisoners Confined on 30 June (1929–48)

Source: Commanding Officer Portsmouth Naval Prison, *Annual Reports,* NARA Waltham, RG 181, Portsmouth General Collection, Folder A9–1.

challenged the administrators at Portsmouth prison, and segregation continued to be the Navy's policy to achieve that end.

Immediately before World War II, the total number of naval prisoners was fewer than two hundred, with most confined to Portsmouth and Mare Island prisons.[3] Organizationally, not much had changed since the reorganization under Daniels in 1914 that established these two prisons as the cornerstones of the naval prison system. During World War II, as was the case in World War I, the number of inmates at Portsmouth increased significantly as the population of the Navy increased and the war progressed. The following table summarizes prisoner activity at Portsmouth from 7 December 1941 to 30 November 1945:[4]

Received	5,894
Dishonorably discharged	575
Bad conduct discharged	734
Restored to duty	1,576

The highest count in the history of Portsmouth prison was reached in April and August of 1945 when 3,088 prisoners were confined as compared with a peak of 2,295 prisoners in 1918 under Osborne's tenure. Bear in mind that the prison was physically much larger during World War II. A comparison of photos 2 and 9 (prison, circa 1910 and circa 1970, respectively) will highlight the changes.

Osborne's restoration record during World War I is astonishing when compared with restorations at the same prison in World War II. With approximately 25 percent less prisoners during peak operations, Osborne restored 1,563 prisoners in one year (1919) as compared with a total of 1,576 prisoner restorations during all four years of World War II. The restoration rate was 27 percent during World War II as compared with 58 percent in 1919. Is it any wonder the fleet thought that Osborne's prison was fitted with revolving doors?[5]

At the end of World War II, the prison population included German prisoners of war from the U-boats brought to Portsmouth Navy Yard for inspection and disposal. Under strict CNO guidance and in accordance with the Geneva convention, four German submarines, U-805, U-873, U-1228, and U-234, were escorted into Portsmouth Navy Yard by U.S. destroyers between 15 and 19 May 1945 for observation, selective stripping, and processing of prisoners. The prison commanding officer, Col. A. Woods Jr., USMC, wrote in his annual report for 1945, "During the month of May 1945, there were confined in this institution a total of two-hundred and five (205) German prisoners of war, who were released to Naval Intelligence, Navy Yard, Portsmouth, NH for disposition."[6] Woods' report made no mention of the treatment and interrogation of these prisoners, a process that resulted in what was probably the most shameful chapter in the entire history of the prison.

The inspector general's report of alleged abuses of the German prisoners included 383 pages of testimony showing that U-805 had been looted by sailors and Marines, U-boat liquors "breached," and German prisoners robbed of Swiss francs, wristwatches, uniform ribbons and decorations, and other personal effects. Most grievously, an intelligence official, Mr. Alberti, dressed as a lieutenant commander, USN, had interrogated the U-873 commanding officer, Lieutenant Commander Steinhoff, in a humiliating manner. Acting under Alberti's direction, an enlisted man had slapped the prisoner to obtain information. The inspector general's report concluded "that the supine attitude of the Commanding Officer of the Naval Prison, Colonel Rossell, USMC, and of Lieutenant Commander Hatton, USNR, Office of Naval Intelligence, in permitting Mr. Alberti to conduct himself in the manner which he did, with the German prisoners of War, is most reprehensible."[7] The slapped and humiliated German prisoner, Lieutenant Commander Steinhoff, later committed suicide after he had been transported to Boston.

In a classic case of holding the commanding officer responsible for the actions of his subordinates, the naval inspector general found the commandant of the shipyard, Rear Adm. Thomas Withers, responsible for dereliction in the performance of his duties, "that the Commandant of the Navy Yard, Portsmouth, Rear Admiral Withers, U.S Navy, was derelict in his performance of duty in that he failed to recognize and accept his command responsibility to issue clear, concise instructions to his subordinates with regard to receiving, securing, safeguarding, and stripping U-boats surrendered in the Navy Yard, Portsmouth, New Hampshire, and to safeguard the persons and property, both private and public, of German prisoners who were in his custody. He further failed to take effective action when violations of the Chief of Naval Operations' order and the Geneva Convention were brought to his attention."[8] Appropriate administrative or disciplinary action was recommended for Withers, Capt. Clifford H. Roper, five other officers of the naval prison, and the intelligence official, Mr. Jack Henry Alberti.

In March 1944 the secretary of the Navy transferred the correctional duties and functions, other than legal, from the judge advocate general to the Bureau of Naval Personnel. The naval prison system was restructured under the administration of the Corrective Services Branch of that bureau. Portsmouth and Mare Island prisons were retained for intermediate to long-term confinements. Brigs and retraining commands provided short-term confinement and restoration.[9] This organization continued until 1959, when the correctional effort was concentrated at the local command level and Portsmouth prison was retained as the major place of confinement. The next major revision occurred in 1973 when the Portsmouth prison was closed.[10]

It took over one hundred years, but the Army prison system now processes and confines long-term naval prisoners as originally proposed by Secretary of War William W. Belknap in 1870 when he was seeking congressional support to build Fort Leavenworth prison. Long-term confinement of males of all services is now a responsibility of the Army, administered at the U.S. Disciplinary Barracks, Fort Leavenworth. The Army also serves as the Defense Department gateway for transfers to the Federal Bureau of Prisons. The Naval Consolidated Brig at Miramar, California, serves as the Defense Department's designated place of confinement for female offenders of all services.[11] The correctional systems for all the services now share consolidated facilities. Portsmouth Naval Prison, at one time the centerpiece of the entire naval prison system, is a distant and fading memory.

Although closed and crumbling inside, the exterior of Portsmouth prison remains a formidable structure. With its castlelike towers and high walls standing proudly, it continues to dominate the skyline of Portsmouth Harbor. The prison currently has no future, although a local developer and philanthropist spearheaded an initiative around the turn of the twenty-first century to turn it into condominiums. That initiative died with the developer. Other proposals for the prison's use have been advanced, but none have met with Navy approval. The features that made the site so attractive for a prison—located on an island and only accessible through the gates of a high-security naval shipyard—render it essentially useless for nonmilitary purposes.

The imposing structure, locally known as the "castle," is observed by residents and tourists wondering what stories are buried behind the thick walls and high turrets. We have resurrected some of those stories; research brought that dead prison back to life. Thomas Mott Osborne walked the prison grounds once again with Franklin Delano Roosevelt and Josephus Daniels. Thousands of prisoners roamed between opened cells and through unlocked gates. Prisoner work parties moved about the shipyard. All were prime actors in one of the most ambitious experiments in the entire history of progressive prison reform with Osborne, as usual, playing the leading role.

NOTES

1. Commanding Officer Naval Prison, Navy Yard Portsmouth, NH, 16 March 1920 letter, National Archives and Records Administration in Waltham, MA, Record Group 181; Portsmouth Naval Shipyard General Collection (Central Files). Hereafter referred to as Commanding Officer Portsmouth Naval Prison and NARA Waltham, RG 181, Portsmouth General Collection.
2. Commanding Officer Portsmouth Naval Prison, *Annual Report for the Fiscal Year Ending 30 June 1919,* NARA Waltham, RG 181, Portsmouth General Collection.
3. Robert J. Verge, *A History of the U.S. Naval Prison at Portsmouth New Hampshire* (Portsmouth: U.S. Naval Print Shop, 1946), 18, 38.
4. Archivist Alma R. Lawrence memo to Chaplain Drury, 12 April 1945, National Archives and Records Administration in Washington, D.C., RG 45, Subject File U.S. Navy 1775–1910, RP Prisons, Shore and Ships, Box No. 605, 1872–1908, "Prisons, Miscellaneous Material Relative to," Folder 7. Hereafter referred to as NARA, Washington, D.C.
5. Richard Lewis Alan Weiner, "Ideology and Incumbency: Thomas Mott Osborne and the 'Failure' of Progressive Era Prison Reform" (history thesis, Harvard University, 1981), Harvard University Archives at Cambridge, MA.
6. Geoffrey C. Ward. *A First-Class Temperament: The Emergence of Franklin Roosevelt* (New York: Harper & Row, 1989), 474n.
7. *TMO @ The Castle*, Neil D. Novello, Producer, The Iguana Division, LLC (2011).
8. Rebecca M. McLennan, *The Crisis of Imprisonment: Protest, Politics, and the Making of the American Penal State, 1776–1941* (Cambridge: Cambridge University Press, 2008), 421.
9. Thomas Mott Osborne, *Prisons and Common Sense* (Philadelphia: Lippincott, 1924), 96.
10. James E. Valle, *Rocks and Shoals: Order and Discipline in the Old Navy 1800–1861* (Annapolis, MD: Naval Institute Press, 1980), 5, 18.
11. George T. Davis, *A Navy Second to None: The Development of Modern Naval Policy* (New York: Harcourt, Brace, 1940), 11.
12. Ibid., 40.
13. Quoted in E. B. Potter and Cheater W. Nimitz, *Sea Power: A Naval History* (Englewood Cliffs, NJ: Prentice Hall, 1960), 464.

CHAPTER 1. NATIONAL PRISON REFORM (1790–1917)

1. See Rudolph W. Chamberlain, *There Is No Truce: A Life of Thomas Mott Osborne* (New York: MacMillan, 1935); Frank Tannenbaum, *Crime and the Community* (Boston: Ginn and Company, 1938) and *Osborne of Sing Sing* (Chapel Hill: University of North Carolina Press, 1933); and Sanford Bates, "Honor System for Inmates of Prisons and Reformatories," *Journal of American Institute of Criminal Law and Criminology* 13, no. 1 (May 1922).

2. D. J. Rothman, *The Discovery of the Asylum: Social Order and Disorder in the New Republic* (Boston: Little, Brown, 1971), 89.

3. Thomas Mott Osborne letter to Secretary of the Navy Josephus Daniels, 10 February 1917, Osborne Family Papers Collection, Syracuse University Bird Library, Syracuse, NY.

4. Thomas G. Blomberg and Karol Lucken, *American Penology: A History of Control* (New York: Aldine De Gruyter, 2000). 53.

5. Ibid.*,* 53–54.

6. D. J. Rothman, *Conscience and Convenience: The Asylum and Its Alternatives in Progressive America* (Boston: Little, Brown, 1980), 118.

7. Auburn Correctional Facility, www.prisontalk.com

8. Ibid.

9. Ibid.

10. Gustave de Beaumont and Alexis de Tocqueville, *On the Penitentiary System in the United States and Its Application in France* (Carbondale: Southern Illinois University Press, 1979), 79.

11. Thomas Mott Osborne, *Within Prison Walls: Being a Narrative of Personal Experience during a Week of Voluntary Confinement in the State Prison at Auburn, New York* (Montclair, NJ: Patterson Smith, 1969), 1.

12. Blomberg and Lucken, *American Penology*, 59.

13. Ibid., 27.

14. Rothman, *The Discovery of the Asylum,* 248.

15. Eric C. Monkkonen, "The Organized Response to Crime in Nineteenth- and Twentieth-Century America," *Journal of Interdisciplinary History* 14, no. 1 (Summer 1983): 115–16.

16. Rothman, *The Discovery of the Asylum*, 240.

17. H.R. Doc. No. 8, 46th Cong., 1st Sess. (1879). Prisons and Prison Systems of the United States. Letter from Secretary of the Navy, 6 May 1879, forwarding "Report of Examination of the Prisons and Prison Systems at Albany, Auburn, and Sing Sing, N.Y.; Boston, Mass.; Wethersfield, Conn.; and Philadelphia, PA." by Lt. Col. J. L. Broome, USMC, 25 December 1872.

18. Ibid., 2.

19. Ibid., 2–20.

20. Ibid., 2–4.

21. Ibid., 4–7.

22. Ibid., 7–10.

23. Ibid., 10–16.

24. Ibid., 16–20.

25. Ibid., 14.

26. Executions in Auburn prison, www.correctionhistory.org

27. Raymond T. Bye, "Recent History and Present Status of Capital Punishment in the United States," *Journal of the American Institute of Criminal Law and Criminology* 17, no. 2 (August 1926): 235.

28. Blomberg and Lucken, *American Penology*, 59.

29. Rothman, *The Discovery of the Asylum*, 63.

30. Bye, "Recent History," 237, 240.

31. Ibid., 234

32. *Christian Science Monitor*, 11 July 1919, "Naval Discipline in War and Peace."

33. Valle, *Rocks and Shoals*, 279.

34. Auburn Correctional Facility, www.prisontalk.com

35. Rothman, *Conscience and Convenience*, 3.

36. Ibid.

37. H.R. Doc. No. 1059, 62nd Cong., 3rd Sess. (1913). Letter from Acting Secretary of the Navy to the House of Representatives, 31 January 1913, 2.

38. Annual Report of the Judge Advocate General for the Fiscal Year 1915, 23; Annual Report of Secretary of the Navy for the Fiscal Year 1915, Navy Department Library, Naval History Heritage Command, Washington Navy Yard, Washington, D.C. Hereafter referred to as Navy Department Library.

39. *Reports of the Warden, Chaplain, and Physician of the New Hampshire State-Prison to the Governor and Council, June, 1880*, 13. Special Collections, University of New Hampshire Library. Hereafter Special Collections UNH Library.

40. Ibid.

41. *Reports of the Warden and Inspectors of the New Hampshire State-Prison, June Session, 1878*, 34. Special Collections UNH Library.

42. *Reports of the Warden and Inspectors of the New Hampshire State-Prison, June Session, 1879*, 31. Special Collections UNH Library.

43. *Biennial Report by the Prison Committee, Warden, Chaplain, Physician and Parole Officer, New Hampshire State Prison, To the Governor and Council 1910–1911— 1911–1912*, 484. Special Collections UNH Library.

44. *Report of the Warden of the N.H. State Prison for the Year 1866*, 9. Special Collections UNH Library.

45. *Reports of the Warden and Inspectors of the New Hampshire State-Prison, June Session, 1891*. Special Collections UNH Library.

46. *Biennial Report by the Officers of the New Hampshire State Prison, 1916*, 7. Special Collections UNH Library.

47. *Reports of the Warden and Inspectors of the New Hampshire State Prison, 1887*, 26. Special Collections UNH Library.

48. *Biennial Report by the Officers of the New Hampshire State Prison, 1918*, 3. Special Collections UNH Library.

49. *Report of the Warden of the N.H. State Prison for the Year 1866*, 10. Special Collections UNH Library.

50. Ibid., 8.

51. Ibid., 9.

52. *Biennial Report by the Prison Committee, Warden, Chaplain, Physician and Parole Officer, New Hampshire State Prison, To the Governor and Council 1910–1911—1911– 1912*, 483, 489. Special Collections UNH Library. These numbers, from the state prison annual reports, reflect inmate populations on 31 August each year, as opposed to the annual JAG figures cited throughout this book, which account for prisoner populations on a fiscal year basis ending on 30 June.

53. *Biennial Report by the Prison Committee, Warden, Chaplain, Physician and Parole Officer, New Hampshire State Prison, To the Governor and Council 1912–1913— 1913–1914*, 8, 532. Special Collections UNH Library.

54. Ibid., 516.
55. Ibid., 517.
56. Ibid.
57. *Biennial Report by the Officers of the New Hampshire State Prison, 1916,* 4. Special Collections UNH Library.

CHAPTER 2. THE END OF FLOGGING (1850–62)

1. N. H. Farquhar, Cdr. USN, "Inducements for Retaining Trained Seamen in the Navy, and Best System for Rewards for Long and Faithful Service," U.S. Naval Institute *Proceedings* 11, no. 2 (30 March 1885): 175–76.
2. Ibid.
3. Valle, *Rocks and Shoals,* 280.
4. Harold D. Langley, *Social Reform in the United States Navy, 1798–1862* (Urbana: University of Illinois Press, 1967), 140.
5. "Rules for the Regulation of the Navy of the United Colonies," quoted in Gardner W. Allen, *A Natural History of the American Revolution* (Boston: A Scholar's Bookshelf, 2005), 686–95.
6. "A Plea in Favor of Maintaining Flogging in the Navy," essay by anonymous naval officer in the 1840s. Navy Department Library.
7. H.R. Doc. No. 157, 28th Cong., 2nd Sess. (1845). Report of Secretary of the Navy to the President, 25 February 1845, 1.
8. Ibid., 2.
9. Langley, *Social Reform,* 171.
10. Ibid., 173.
11. Ibid.
12. Valle, *Rocks and Shoals,* 166.
13. Ibid., 174.
14. Thomas P. Lowry, *The Story the Soldiers Won't Tell: Sex in the Civil War* (Mechanicsburg, PA: Stackpole Books, 1994), 109.
15. Myra C. Glenn, "The Naval Reform Campaign Against Flogging: A Case Study in Changing Attitudes Toward Corporal Punishment," *American Quarterly* 35, no. 4 (Autumn 1983): 409.
16. Ibid.
17. Langley, *Social Reform,* 164–65.
18. Ibid., 148.
19. Ibid., 227.
20. Ibid., 38, 164–65.
21. Thomas R. Lambert Papers, Manuscript Section, New Hampshire Historical Society, Register. Hereafter Lambert Papers.
22. Valle, *Rocks and Shoals,* 140–41.
23. Langley, *Social Reform,* 164, n84.
24. Lambert Papers.
25. Valle, *Rocks and Shoals,* 190–91.
26. Glenn, "Naval Reform Campaign," 422.
27. Langley, *Social Reform,* 192–93.

28. Glenn, "Naval Reform Campaign," 422.

29. Langley, *Social Reform*, 194–95.

30. Ibid., 253, 190.

31. Quoted in Langley, *Social Reform*, 190.

32. S. Doc. No. 12, 31st Cong., 2nd Sess. (1850–51). President of the Navy Board, Commodore Charles Stewart, letter to Secretary of the Navy Will. A. Graham, 1 January 1851, 3.

33. S. Doc. No. 12, 31st Cong., 2nd Sess. (1850–51). Report of Secretary of the Navy to the President, 9 January 1851, 7, 10.

34. S. Doc. No. 10, 32nd Cong., 1st Sess. (1851–52). Report of Secretary of the Navy, 22 December 1851, 5.

35. Ibid.

36. Ibid., 7.

37. S. Doc. No. 10, 32nd Cong., 1st Sess. (1851–52). Report of Secretary of the Navy to the Senate, 22 December 1851, 4, 5, 7.

38. Valle, *Rocks and Shoals*, 32–34.

39. *New York Times*, 15 January 1852, "XXXIId, Congress, First Session, Bills Reported."

40. Langley, *Social Reform*, 200.

41. *New York Times*, 20 January 1852, "Flogging."

42. Naval History and Heritage Command, Dictionary of American Naval Fighting Ships, www.history/navy/mil/danfs.

43. Ex. Doc. No. 10, 32nd Cong., 1st Sess. (1851–52). Commandant New York Navy Yard, W. D. Salter letter to Secretary of the Navy, William A. Graham, 21 July 1851.

44. S. Exec Doc 12, 31st Cong., 2nd Sess. (1850–51). Excerpt from Captain Salter 10 December 1850 letter.

45. S. Exec Doc 12, 31st Cong., 2nd Sess. (1850–51). Commanding Officer USS *Brandywine*, Capt. Charles Boarman letter to Commodore Storer, 5 December 1850.

46. S. Exec Doc 12, 31st Cong., 2nd Sess. (1850–51). Commodore Storer letter to Secretary of the Navy William A. Graham, 7 December 1850.

47. Langley, *Social Reform*, 194, note 79.

48. *New York Times*, 6 December 1853, "Flogging Sailors."

49. *New York Times*, 6 December 1854, "Public Documents, Reports of Secretary of the Navy, etc."

50. George Minot, ed. *The Statutes at Large and Treaties of the United States of America from December 1, 1851 to March 3, 1855*, vol. 10 (Boston: Little, Brown, 1855), 627.

51. Langley, *Social Reform*, 203.

52. Farquhar, "Inducements for Retaining Trained Seamen," 176.

53. Ibid., 184.

54. Ibid.

55. William S. Dudley, "A Museum Reborn," *Naval History*, February 2012, 48–49.

56. Farquhar, "Inducements for Retaining Trained Seamen," 186.

57. Ibid., 188.

58. Peter Moskos, *In Defense of Flogging* (New York: Basic Books, 2011), 2.

Chapter 3. Shipboard Punishments Post Flogging (1862–88)

1. Valle, *Rocks and Shoals*, 276.
2. Annual Report of Bureau of Equipment and Recruiting for Fiscal Year 1886 in Annual Report of Secretary of the Navy for Fiscal Year 1886, 291. National Archives Records Administration in Washington, D.C., Record Group 80. Hereafter NARA Washington, D.C., RG 80.
3. Ibid., 288.
4. Report labeled *Monocacy* punishments, 30 June 1867, NARA Washington, D.C., RG 125, Records of the Office of the Judge Advocate General (Navy), 1799–1953, Personnel Reports from Commanding Officers, Box 2.
5. Report labeled *Michigan* punishments, 30 June 1867, NARA Washington, D.C., RG 125, Records of the Office of the Judge Advocate General (Navy), 1799–1953, Personnel Reports from Commanding Officers, Box 2.
6. Report labeled *Shenandoah* punishments, 30 September 1867, NARA Washington, D.C., RG 125, Records of the Office of the Judge Advocate General (Navy), 1799–1953, Personnel Reports from Commanding Officers, Box 8.
7. Report labeled *Chocura* punishments, 30 June 1868, NARA Washington, D.C., RG 125, Records of the Office of the Judge Advocate General (Navy), 1799–1953, Personnel Reports from Commanding Officers, Box 6.
8. Ibid.
9. Report labeled *Jamestown* punishments, 30 September 1870, NARA Washington, D.C., RG 125, Records of the Office of the Judge Advocate General (Navy), 1799–1953, Personnel Reports from Commanding Officers, Box 6.
10. Report labeled *Wachusett* punishments, 30 March 1874, NARA Washington, D.C., RG 125, Records of the Office of the Judge Advocate General (Navy), 1799–1953, Personnel Reports from Commanding Officers, Box 19.
11. Report labeled USS Torpedo Steamer *Alarm* punishments, 31 December 1875, NARA Washington, D.C., RG 125, Records of the Office of the Judge Advocate General (Navy), 1799–1953, Personnel Reports from Commanding Officers, Box 6.
12. *Regulations for the Government of the Navy of the United States, 1876*. Washington, D.C.: Government Printing Office, 1877, 106–7.
13. Ibid.
14. Charles H. Lauchheimer, 1st Lt., USMC, "Naval Law and Naval Courts," U.S. Naval Institute *Proceedings* 32, no. 1 (1897): 121.
15. Report labeled SS *Alliance* punishments, 30 June 1888, NARA Washington, D.C., RG 125, Records of the Office of the Judge Advocate General (Navy), 1799–1953, Personnel Reports from Commanding Officers, Box 23.
16. Farquhar, "Inducements for Retaining Trained Seamen," 201.
17. Ibid.
18. Ibid.
19. Ibid., 202.
20. Ibid., 201.
21. *Regulations for the Government of the Navy of the United States, 1876*. Washington, D.C.: Government Printing Office, 1877, 103.

22. Farquhar, "Inducements for Retaining Trained Seamen," 186.
23. Annual Report of Bureau of Equipment and Recruiting for Fiscal Year 1875 in Annual Report of Secretary of the Navy for the Fiscal Year 1875, 86. Navy Department Library.
24. Annual Report of Bureau of Equipment and Recruiting for Fiscal Year 1876 in Annual Report of Secretary of the Navy for the Fiscal Year 1876, 107–108. Navy Department Library.
25. Annual Report of Bureau of Equipment and Recruiting for Fiscal Year 1877 in Annual Report of Secretary of the Navy for the Fiscal Year 1877, 122. Navy Department Library.
26. Ibid.
27. Ibid.
28. Annual Report of Bureau of Equipment and Recruiting for Fiscal Year 1883 in Annual Report of Secretary of the Navy for Fiscal Year 1883, 239. Navy Department Library.
29. Ibid., 85.
30. Annual Report of Bureau of Equipment and Recruiting for Fiscal Year 1886 in Annual Report of Secretary of the Navy for Fiscal Year 1886, 291. Navy Department Library.
31. Ibid.
32. Annual Report of Bureau of Equipment and Recruiting for Fiscal Year 1888 in Annual Report of Secretary of the Navy for Fiscal Year 1888, 66. Navy Department Library.

CHAPTER 4. ORIGINS OF THE NAVAL PRISON SYSTEM (1870–88)

1. Navy JAG History, 1, http://www.jag.Navy.mil/history.htm
2. Register of Prisoners Under Sentence of General Court-Martial ("Court-Martial Prisoners"), Jan 1877–June 1892, NARA Washington, D.C., RG 125, Records of the Office of the Judge Advocate General (Navy), Entry 32, Single Bound Volume.
3. S. C. Lemly, "The Prisoners of the United States Navy," *Proceedings of the Annual Congress of the National Prison Association of the United States* (Pittsburgh: Shaw Brothers, Printers, 1899), 206.
4. *Boston Daily Globe*, 19 May 1897, "In the Naval Prison, How the Offenders of the United States Navy Are Cared For."
5. Annual Report of Secretary of the Navy for the Fiscal Year 1868, Headquarters Marine Corps, 19 October 1868 letter. Navy Department Library.
6. Records Collection of the Office of Naval Records and Library, Correspondence, 1798–1918, NARA, Washington, D.C., RG 45, Letters Received from Commandants of Navy Yards and Naval Stations, 1848–86, League Island Navy Yard Book of 1879 letters (vol. 276 of 332), no. 97. Note: This book was misfiled with the Mare Island books.
7. Langley, *Social Reform*, 152.
8. H.R. Doc. No. 61, 41st Cong., 2nd Sess. (1870). Letter from the Secretary of War to the House of Representatives, 13 January 1870, 2.

9. Ibid., 1.

10. Ibid., 4.

11. H.R. Doc. No. 73, 42nd Cong., 2nd Sess. (1872). Letter from the Secretary of War to the House of Representatives, 16 January 1872, 1, 7.

12. Ibid.

13. H.R. Doc. No. 1 Part 2, 44th Cong., 2nd Sess. (1876). Report of the Secretary of War, 20 November 1876, 19.

14. H.R. Doc. No. 550, 57th Cong., 1st Sess. (1902). Letter from the Secretary of the Treasury to the House of Representatives, 15 April 1902, 1–3.

15. H.R. Doc. No. 1 Part 3, 43rd Cong., 3rd Sess. (1872). Commodore C. R. P. Rodgers' "Report of Examination of the Naval Prison at Lewes, England," London, 27 April 1871, 454.

16. Ibid.

17. Ibid.

18. Ibid.

19. 43rd Cong., 1st Sess. (1873) Report of Secretary of the Navy, 29 November 1873, 61.

20. Ibid.

21. Davis, *A Navy Second to None*, 13.

CHAPTER 5. MAKESHIFT NAVAL PRISONS (1888–1908)

1. "Lieut. S. C. Lemly," *The Illustrated American: A Weekly News-Magazine*, 24 December 1892, 22.

2. Lemly, "The Prisoners of the United States Navy," 206.

3. Ibid.

4. *Boston Daily Globe*, 19 May 1897, "In the Naval Prison, How the Offenders of the United States Navy Are Cared For," 7.

5. Annual Report of the Chief of Bureau of Yards and Docks for Fiscal Year 1889 in Annual Report of Secretary of the Navy for Fiscal Year 1889, 57. Navy Department Library.

6. Alexander McCrack, Lt., USN, "Desertion and the Bertillon System for Identification of Persons," U.S. Naval Institute *Proceedings* 16, no. 3 (1890), 361.

7. Ibid.

8. Ibid., 362.

9. Ibid.

10. H.R. Doc. No. 2, 58th Cong., 2nd Sess. (1903). Annual Report of the Navy Department for the Year 1903, Miscellaneous Reports, 9–11.

11. Ibid.

12. A. S. Williams, Capt., USMC, "Desertion and Its Prevention," U.S. Naval Institute *Proceedings* 30 (1904), 769–78.

13. Ibid., 775.

14. H.R. Doc. No. 2, 58th Cong., 2nd Sess. (1903). Annual Report of the Navy Department for the Year 1903, Miscellaneous Reports, 9–11.

15. Annual Report of Judge Advocate General (Navy) for Fiscal Year 1908 in Annual Report of Secretary of the Navy for Fiscal Year 1908, 95. Navy Department Library.

16. Ibid., 97.
17. H.R. Doc No. 2, 65th Cong. 2nd Sess. (1918). House of Representatives, Sub-committee of Committee on Naval Affairs for Investigation of Conduct and Administration of Naval Affairs, Estimates Submitted by Secretary of the Navy, 19 December 1917, 17–18.
18. Captain Boston Navy Yard, Capt. E. O. Matthews, letter to Commandant, Commo. W. P. McLaren, 13 November 1888, NARA Waltham, RG 181, Book of Boston Navy Yard Press Copies of Letters Sent 1888–1892, 8, 102.
19. Commander of the Post, Capt. H. L. Cochrane, USMC, letter to Captain of the Yard, Capt. E. O. Matthews, 5 March 1889, NARA Waltham, RG 181, Book of Boston Navy Yard, Press Copies of Letters Sent 1888–1892, loose copy of letter at page 134.
20. Ibid.
21. Commander Marines, Maj. Robert L. Meade, letter to Commandant Boston Navy Yard, Commo. J. N. Miller, 12 December 1895, loose copy of letter at page 138, NARA Waltham, RG 181, Book of letters to Secretary of the Navy, October 21st 1895–July 2nd 1896, E-67, Box 7.
22. Commander Boston Navy Yard Marines letter to Commandant Boston Navy Yard, 12 December 1895, and Commandant Boston Navy Yard 1st endorsement to Secretary of the Navy, 13 December 1895, and Secretary of the Navy 2nd endorsement to Boston Navy Yard Surgeon, 17 December 1895, and Boston Navy Yard Surgeon 4th endorsement, 20 December 1895, all loose at page 138, NARA Waltham, RG 181, Book of letters to Secretary of the Navy, October 21st 1895–July 2nd 1896, E-67, Box 7.
23. Annual Report of Judge Advocate General (Navy) for Fiscal Year 1897 in Annual Report of Secretary of the Navy for Fiscal Year 1897, 75; NARA Washington, D.C., RG 80.
24. Ibid.
25. Lemly, "Prisoners of the United States Navy," 206–9.
26. Ibid., 209.
27. *Boston Sunday Globe*, 1 January 1893, "They Have an Easy Time, Inmates at the Naval Prison in Charlestown," 1.
28. *Boston Daily Globe*, 31 March 1898, "Naval Prison Crowded," 4.
29. *Boston Sunday Globe*, 20 April 1891, "Flynn Will Visit Boston, For Six Months He Will Languish in the Naval Prison," 1.
30. *Boston Daily Globe*, 31 March 1898, "Naval Prison Crowded," 4.
31. Chief Engineer letter to the Commandant Boston Navy Yard, 20 March 1901, NARA Waltham, RG 181, Boston Naval Shipyard Letters sent to Secretary of the Navy, Feb. 13, 1901–June 4, 1901, 243.
32. Secretary of the Navy John D. Long letter to Commandant Boston Navy Yard, Rear Adm. William T. Sampson, USN, 15 April 1901, NARA Waltham, RG 181, Boston Naval Shipyard Letters sent to Secretary of the Navy, Feb. 13, 1901–June 4, 1901, 307–10.
33. Commandant Boston Navy Yard, Rear Adm. W. Sampson, letter to Secretary of the Navy, 27 May 1901, NARA Waltham, RG 181, Boston Naval Shipyard Letters sent to Secretary of the Navy, Feb. 13, 1901–June 4, 1901, 479–81.

34. Boston Navy Yard Chief Engineer letter, 30 November 1901, NARA Waltham, RG 181, Book of Boston Navy Yard Press Copies of Letters Sent 1888–92, 3–10.
35. *Boston Daily Globe*, 12 April 1902, "Naval Prison Ship Arrives," 7.
36. *Boston Daily Globe*, 25 October 1907, "By Courtmartial, Apprentice Clark Charged with Assault," 17.
37. *Boston Daily Globe*, 7 August 1908, "Escape from Naval Prison," 14.
38. *Boston Daily Globe*, 25 April 1909, "Detached from Naval Prison," 1.
39. *Boston Daily Globe*, 27 April 1909, "Succeeds Capt. Carpenter," 11.
40. *Boston Daily Globe*, 12 October 1910, "Menace Navy Yard, Prisoners in a Liberty Dash," 8.
41. *Boston Daily Globe*, 18 July 192, "Naval Prisoner Escapes," 4.
42. Letter Number 2, NARA Washington, D.C., RG 45, Letters Received from Commandants of Navy Yards and Naval Stations, 1848–86, Mare Island Book of 1866 letters (vol. 165 of 332), Records Collection of the Office of Naval Records and Library, Correspondence, 1798–1918.
43. Ibid., Letter Number 145.
44. Ibid., Letter Number 144.
45. Letter Number 94, NARA Washington, D.C., RG 45, Letters Received from Commandants of Navy Yards and Naval Stations, 1848–86, Mare Island Book of 1867 letters (vol. 172 of 332), Records Collection of the Office of Naval Records and Library, Correspondence, 1798–1918.
46. Letter Number 150, NARA Washington, D.C., RG 45, Letters Received from Commandants of Navy Yards and Naval Stations, 1848–86, Mare Island Book of 1868 letters (vol. 180 of 332), Records Collection of the Office of Naval Records and Library, Correspondence, 1798–1918.
47. Letter Number 104, NARA Washington, D.C., RG 45, Letters Received from Commandants of Navy Yards and Naval Stations, 1848–86, Mare Island Book of 1867 letters (vol. 172 of 332), Records Collection of the Office of Naval Records and Library, Correspondence, 1798–1918.
48. Letter Number 93, NARA Washington, D.C., RG 45, Letters Received from Commandants of Navy Yards and Naval Stations, 1848–86, Mare Island Book of 1870 letters (vol. 204 of 332), Records Collection of the Office of Naval Records and Library, Correspondence, 1798–1918.
49. *San Francisco Bulletin*, 13 July 1868, "Mare Island Navy Yard Items," 2.
50. John S. Wallace, "The Mare Island Navy Yard," *Scribner's Monthly: An Illustrated Magazine for the People*, April 1872, 649.
51. Library of Congress photo HABS No. CAL.48-MARI 1CA-19, Plan of Naval Prison U.S. Navy Yard Mare Island, CAL., circa 1870.
52. Miscellaneous Report of Judge Advocate General (Navy), 28 November 1906, in Annual Report of Secretary of the Navy for Fiscal Year 1906, 114–15; NARA Washington, D.C., RG 45.
53. Ibid.
54. Ibid.
55. Letter Number 93, NARA Washington, D.C., RG 45, Letters Received from Commandants of Navy Yards and Naval Stations, 1848–86, Mare Island Book

of 1872 letters (vol. 223 of 332), Records Collection of the Office of Naval
Records and Library, Correspondence, 1798–1918.

56. Ibid., Letter Number 112.

57. Ibid., Letter Number 196.

58. Letter Number 102, NARA Washington, D.C., RG 45, Letters Received from
Commandants of Navy Yards and Naval Stations, 1848–86, Mare Island Book
of 1876 letters (vol. 256 of 332), Records Collection of the Office of Naval
Records and Library, Correspondence, 1798–1918.

59. Letter Number 206, NARA Washington, D.C., RG 45, Letters Received from
Commandants of Navy Yards and Naval Stations, 1848–86, Mare Island Book
of 1872 letters (vol. 206 of 332), Records Collection of the Office of Naval
Records and Library, Correspondence, 1798–1918.

60. Letter Number 72, NARA Washington, D.C., RG 45, Letters Received from
Commandants of Navy Yards and Naval Stations, 1848–86, Mare Island Book
of 1873 letters (vol. 231 of 332), Records Collection of the Office of Naval
Records and Library, Correspondence, 1798–1918.

61. Ibid., Letter Number 202.

62. Ibid., Letter Number 205.

63. Ibid., Letter Number 204.

64. Letter Number 28, NARA Washington, D.C., RG 45, Letters Received from
Commandants of Navy Yards and Naval Stations, 1848–86, Mare Island Book
of 1874 letters (vol. 240 of 332), Records Collection of the Office of Naval
Records and Library, Correspondence, 1798–1918.

65. Commanding Officer Marine Barracks 4 March 1874 endorsement to Letter
Number 28, NARA Washington, D.C., RG 45, Letters Received from Commandants of Navy Yards and Naval Stations, 1848–86, Mare Island Book of 1874
letters (vol. 240 of 332). Records Collection of the Office of Naval Records and
Library, Correspondence, 1798–1918.

66. Commandant Mare Island Navy Yard 7 March 1874 endorsement to Letters Number 28 and Number 27, NARA Washington, D.C., RG 45, Letters
Received from Commandants of Navy Yards and Naval Stations, 1848–86, Mare
Island Book of 1874 letters (vol. 240 of 332), Records Collection of the Office
of Naval Records and Library, Correspondence, 1798–1918.

67. Ibid., endorsement to Letter Number 41.

68. Ibid., endorsement to Letter Number 61.

69. Letter Number 102, NARA Washington, D.C., RG 45, Letters Received from
Commandants of Navy Yards and Naval Stations, 1848–86, Mare Island Book
of 1876 letters (vol. 256 of 332), Records Collection of the Office of Naval
Records and Library, Correspondence, 1798–1918.

70. *San Francisco Bulletin*, 22 December 1890, "Mare Island Navy Yard, The Large
Amount of Work to Be Done Will Probably Prevent Any Change of Officials–
Other Notes," 1.

71. 52nd Cong., 1st Sess. (1891–92). Bureau of Yards and Docks Annual Report,
14 October 1891 in Secretary of the Navy Annual Report, 3 December 1891,
96–97.

72. H.R. Doc. No. 3, 58th Cong., 3rd Sess. (1904). Miscellaneous Reports in Annual Report of Secretary of the Navy for the Year 1904, 93.

73. Annual Report of Judge Advocate General (Navy) for Fiscal Year 1908 in Annual Report of Secretary of the Navy for Fiscal Year 1908, 86. Navy Department Library.

74. Ibid.

75. Ibid., 86.

76. Ibid., 87.

77. Ibid., 98.

78. Letter from CINC U.S. Naval Forces on Asiatic Station, Rear Adm. Thomas L. Meade, to Secretary of the Navy, John D. Long, of 18 June 1900, NARA Washington, D.C., RG 45, Subject File U.S. Navy 1775–1910, RP Prisons, Shore and Ships, Box No. 605, 1872–1908, Naval Prison at Cavite, P.I., Folder 8.

79. Ibid.

80. Ibid.

81. Letter from Secretary of the Navy to Commandant Norfolk Navy Yard, 14 June 1901, and letter from Chief of Bureau of Navigation to Secretary of the Navy, 7 April 1902, NARA Washington, D.C., RG 45, Subject File U.S. Navy 1775–1910, RP Prisons, Shore and Ships, Box No. 605, 1872–1908, "Prisons, Miscellaneous Material Relative to," Folder 7.

82. Bureau and Offices of the Navy Department Memorandum, 9 July 1903, NARA Washington, D.C., RG 45, Subject File U.S. Navy 1775–1910, RP Prisons, Shore and Ships, Box No. 605, 1872–1908, "Prisons, Miscellaneous Material Relative to," Folder 7.

83. Commandant Portsmouth Navy Yard letter to Secretary of the Navy, 11 July 1903, NARA Washington, D.C., RG 45, Subject File U.S. Navy 1775–1910, RP Prisons, Shore and Ships, Box No. 605, 1872–1908, "Prisons, Miscellaneous Material Relative to," Folder 7,

84. Potter and Nimitz, *Sea Power*, 387–88.

85. Judge Advocate General (Navy), Capt. E. H. Campbell, USN, letter to Secretary of the Navy, 21 June 1908, NARA Washington, D.C., RG 45, Subject File U.S. Navy 1775–1910, RP Prisons, Shore and Ships, Box No. 605, 1872–1908, "Prisons, Miscellaneous Material Relative to," Folder 7.

86. Acting Secretary of the Navy, J. E. Pillsbury, letter to CINCPACFLT, 26 June 1908, NARA Washington, D.C., RG 45, Subject File U.S. Navy 1775–1910, RP Prisons, Shore and Ships, Box No. 605, 1872–1908, "Prisons, Miscellaneous Material Relative to," Folder 7.

87. Acting Secretary of the Navy letter to Commandant Portsmouth Navy Yard, 2 July 1908, 7, NARA Washington, D.C., RG 45, Subject File U.S. Navy 1775–1910, RP Prisons, Shore and Ships, Box No. 605, 1872–1908, "Prisons, Miscellaneous Material Relative to," Folder 7.

CHAPTER 6. THE NAVY FINALLY GETS A REAL PRISON (1908–14)

1. 52nd Cong., 1st Sess. (1891–92). Bureau of Yards and Docks letter, 14 October 1891, in Annual Report of Secretary of the Navy, 3 December 1891, 96–97.

2. *New York Times,* 21 January 1893, "Prison for Naval Convicts."

3. Ibid.

4. Potter and Nimitz, *Sea Power,* 376.

5. Quoted in Potter and Nimitz, *Sea Power,* 376.

6. Lemly, "The Prisoners of the United States Navy," 213.

7. Ibid., 211–17.

8. Ibid., 217.

9. *Portsmouth Herald,* 28 June 2012, "Historic Portsmouth, Captured Spanish Admiral Takes a Walk," B4.

10. Ibid.

11. *Portsmouth Herald,* 3 October 1902, "Coming to Portsmouth, Naval Prison Likely to Be Removed from Boston, Believed Change to Be Made in the Near Future, Secretary Moody of the Opinion that Prison Should Be Located Here," 3.

12. Ibid.

13. *New York Times,* 17 October 1902, "Power of Courts-Martial."

14. *Boston Daily Globe,* 18 October 1903, "Portsmouth Protest," 4.

15. *Boston Daily Globe,* 27 November 1904, "Naval Prison at Portsmouth," 8.

16. John P. Adams, "The World's Biggest Bang," *Yankee Magazine,* July 1973, 114–19.

17. Annual Report of Judge Advocate General (Navy) for Fiscal Year 1906 in Annual Report of Secretary of the Navy for Fiscal Year 1906, 116. Navy Department Library.

18. Commanding Officer Portsmouth Naval Prison letter to Secretary of the Navy, 14 July 1908, Annual Reports of the Commanding Officer, compiled 1908–1928, ARC 1807646, NARA Waltham, RG 181, Portsmouth General Collection.

19. Annual Report of Judge Advocate General (Navy) for Fiscal Year 1908 in Annual Report of Secretary of the Navy for Fiscal Year 1908, 66. Navy Department Library.

20. Ibid., 87.

21. Verge, *A History of the U.S. Naval Prison,* 9–10.

22. Ibid., 10.

23. *New York Times,* 20 November 1908, "Magness Goes to Jail."

24. Ibid.

25. *Portsmouth Herald,* 28 January 1909, "Father to Be Executed, Son Released from Prison, Charles Crook Under Sentence for Deserting from Navy, Allowed to Go Home to Care for Brother and Sister," 5.

26. Seaman Arthur Y. Monahan's Request for Clemency letter to Secretary of the Navy, 28 September 1913, NARA Waltham, RG 181, Portsmouth General Correspondence.

27. *Boston Daily Globe,* 29 January 1910, "Shot Down by Guard," 1.

28. *New York Times,* 29 January 1910, "Jail Breaker Killed."

29. *Portsmouth Herald,* 25 January 1909, "Man Rescued by Prisoners, Workman Who Was Buried in Coal at the Navy Yard," 8.

30. Ibid.

31. Ibid.

32. Ibid.
33. Annual Report of Judge Advocate General (Navy) for Fiscal Year 1916 in Annual Report of Secretary of the Navy for Fiscal Year 1916, 13. Navy Department Library.
34. Verge, *A History of the U.S. Naval Prison at Portsmouth*, 13.

Chapter 7. The Naval Prison System Matures (1914–17)

1. Statement of Commander Winslow, Assistant to Bureau of Navigation, 20 March 1908, at Hearings Before the United States House of Representatives Committee on Naval Affairs on Estimates Submitted by Secretary of the Navy, 7.
2. *Boston Daily Globe*, 14 March 1909, "Prison Ships Now Crowded, Many Prisoners from Fleet's Long Tour," 11.
3. H.R. Doc. No. 1059, 62nd Cong., 3rd Sess. (1913). Letter from Acting Secretary of the Navy to the House of Representatives, 31 January 1913, 2.
4. *Christian Science Monitor*, 17 August 1911, "New Idea Naval Detention Camp," 14.
5. *Portsmouth Herald*, 28 August 1912, "Maj. Charles Hatch, U.S.M.C., Has Worked Out Problem of Treating Court Martial Prisoners," 6.
6. Ibid.
7. Annual Report of Judge Advocate General (Navy) for Fiscal Year 1913 in Annual Report of Secretary of the Navy for Fiscal Year 1913, 8–9. Navy Department Library.
8. H.R. Doc. No. 1059, 62nd Cong., 3rd Sess. (1913). Letter from Acting Secretary of the Navy to the House of Representatives, 31 January 1913, 26.
9. Verge, *A History of the U.S. Naval Prison*, 11.
10. Quoted in Verge, 10.
11. Ibid., 11.
12. *New York Times,* 11 September 1911, "Admiral Harber Retired."
13. Judge Advocate General (Navy) letter to Commandant, U.S. Marine Corps, 28 May 1914, NARA Waltham, RG 181, Portsmouth General Collection.
14. H.R. Doc. No. 1059, 62nd Cong., 3rd Sess. (1913). Letter from Acting Secretary of the Navy to the House of Representatives, 31 January 1913, 2.
15. H.R. Doc. No. 1059, 62nd Cong., 3rd Sess. (1913). Letter from Acting Secretary of the Navy to the House of Representatives, 31 January 1913, 26.
16. Ibid., 27.
17. Annual Report of Judge Advocate General (Navy) for Fiscal Year 1913 in Annual Report of Secretary of the Navy for the Fiscal Year 1913, 12. Navy Department Library.
18. Josephus Daniels, *The Wilson Era: Years of Peace (1910–1917)* (Chapel Hill: The University of North Carolina Press, 1946), 317.
19. *Boston Daily Globe*, 25 April 1914, "Night Trip of Navy Prisoners," 2.
20. Judge Advocate General letter, 12 August 1914, NARA Waltham, RG 181. Portsmouth General Collection.
21. Ibid.
22. Annual Report of Judge Advocate General (Navy) for Fiscal Year 1915 in Annual Report of Secretary of the Navy for Fiscal Year 1915, 3. Navy Department Library.

23. Ibid.

24. Ibid., 3–6.

25. Annual Report of Judge Advocate General (Navy) for Fiscal Year 1916 in Annual Report of Secretary of the Navy for Fiscal Year 1916, 157. Navy Department Library.

26. Ibid., 164, 165.

27. Annual Report of Judge Advocate General (Navy) for Fiscal Year 1917 in Annual Report of Secretary of the Navy for Fiscal Year 1917, 130. Navy Department Library.

28. Ibid.

29. Ibid., 123.

30. Ibid.

31. Ibid., 117.

32. Ibid., 129.

CHAPTER 8. SECRETARY OF THE NAVY JOSEPHUS DANIELS (1912–20)

1. Jonathan Daniels, *The End of Innocence* (Philadelphia: Lippincott, 1954), 20.

2. Josephus Daniels, *The Wilson Era: Years of Peace*, 112.

3. Ibid., 126.

4. Joseph L. Morrison, *Josephus Daniels: The Small-d Democrat* (Chapel Hill: The University of North Carolina Press, 1966), 51.

5. Quoted in Morrison, *Josephus Daniels*, 49.

6. Ibid., 51.

7. Ibid., 77.

8. E. David Cronon, *The Cabinet Diaries of Josephus Daniels, 1913–1921* (Lincoln: University of Nebraska Press, 1963), 504.

9. Josephus Daniels, *The Wilson Era: Years of Peace*, 386.

10. Josephus Daniels, *The Navy and the Nation: Wartime Addresses by Josephus Daniels, Secretary of the Navy* (New York: George H. Doran Company, 1919), 302, 305.

11. *Christian Science Monitor*, 8 April 1914, "Ordering the Navy to be Temperate," 22.

12. Josephus Daniels, *The Wilson Era: Years of Peace*, 257, 274–76, 239.

13. Ibid., 273.

14. *New York Times*, 19 August 1913, "Findings Disgust Daniels."

15. Geoffrey C. Ward, *A First-Class Temperament: The Emergence of Franklin Roosevelt* (New York: Harper & Row, 1989), 224–25.

16. *New York Times*, 3 May 1916, "Fiske Disputes Daniels."

17. Davis, *A Navy Second to None*, 210.

18. Tracy Barrett Kittredge, *Naval Lessons of the Great War: A Review of the Senate Naval Investigation of the Criticisms by Admiral Sims of the Policies and Methods of Josephus Daniels* (Garden City, NY: Doubleday, Page, 1921), vii.

19. Quoted in Kittredge, *Naval Lessons*, 4.

20. Ibid., 6.

21. Jonathan Daniels, *The End of Innocence*, 304. This quote is attributed to Senator Boise Penrose during the Senate investigation of the charges against Daniels.

22. Ibid.

23. Potter and Nimitz, *Sea Power*, 464.
24. Josephus Daniels, *The Wilson Era: Years of Peace,* 256–58.
25. Quoted in David Pietrusza, *1920: The Year of the Six Presidents* (New York: Basic Books, 2007), 63.
26. Potter and Nimitz, *Sea Power*, 464.
27. Kittredge, *Naval Lessons*, 98, 354–56.
28. *Boston Daily Globe*, 23 December 1915, "Twenty-Five Released," 8.
29. Secretary of the Navy Daniels letter to Commandant, Navy Yard, Portsmouth, N.H., 20 February 1917, NARA Waltham, RG 181, Portsmouth General Correspondence.
30. Thomas Mott Osborne personal letter to Secretary of the Navy Josephus Daniels, 20 February 1917, Osborne Family Papers Collection, Syracuse University Bird Library, Syracuse, New York.
31. Ibid.
32. Judge Advocate General (Navy) letter, 23 June 1917, NARA Waltham, RG 181, Portsmouth General Correspondence.
33. Secretary of the Navy Daniels letter, 4 December 1914, NARA Waltham, RG 181, Portsmouth General Correspondence.
34. Josephus Daniels, *The Navy and the Nation*, 79.

Chapter 9. Osborne prior to Portsmouth (1859–1917)

1. Chamberlain, *There Is No Truce*, 31–33.
2. Ibid.
3. Ibid., 33–34.
4. Sherry H. Penny and James D. Livingston, *A Very Dangerous Woman: Martha Wright and Women's Rights* (Amherst: University of Massachusetts Press, 2004), 86.
5. Ibid., 223
6. Ibid., 32–49.
7. Quoted in Penny and Livingston, *A Very Dangerous Woman*, 57.
8. Ibid., 57.
9. Chamberlain, *There Is No Truce,* 33.
10. Ibid., 34.
11. Ward, *A First-Class Temperament*, 195.
12. Quoted in ibid., 130.
13. Ibid.
14. Ibid., 128.
15. Robert Cowley, ed. *What If? 2* (New York: Simon & Schuster, 2001), 240–41.
16. David Connelly, narrator, *TMO @ the Castle*.
17. Rothman, *Conscience and Convenience*, 154.
18. Ibid., 155–57.
19. Ibid., 119.
20. Ward, *A First-Class Temperament*, 444–45.
21. Ibid., 445.
22. Chamberlain, *There Is No Truce,* 138.
23. McLennan, *The Crisis of Imprisonment*, 408.

24. Tannenbaum, *Osborne of Sing Sing*, 135.

25. Chamberlain, *There Is No Truce,* 307.

26. Ibid., 329.

27. Tannenbaum, *Osborne of Sing Sing*, 203. Tannenbaum and Chamberlain devote several chapters to the details of these charges, the investigation, and Osborne's defense.

28. Chamberlain, *There Is No Truce,* 347–57.

29. Ibid., 347.

30. Ibid., 359.

31. *Boston Daily Globe*, 22 November 1916, "Move to Abolish All Naval Prisons," 10.

CHAPTER 10. REFORM COMES TO PORTSMOUTH

1. Robert H. Connery, *The Navy and Industrial Mobilization in World War II* (Princeton: Princeton University Press, 1951), 266.

2. Gary Weir, *Building American Submarines 1914–1940* (Washington, D.C.: Naval History and Heritage Command), 114.

3. A. I. McKee, "Development of Submarines in the United States," *Historical Transactions 1893–1943* (New York: Society of Naval Architects and Marine Engineers, 1945), 347.

4. Ibid.

5. Portsmouth Naval Shipyard, *Cradle of American Shipbuilding* (Portsmouth Naval Shipyard: Government Printing Office, 1978), 48.

6. Jonathan Daniels, *The End of Innocence*, 249; Chamberlain, *There Is No Truce,* 367.

7. *New York Times*, 4 December 1916, "Condemns Navy Prison."

8. *New York Times*, 17 January 1917, "Osborne Begins Term on Navy Prison Ship."

9. *Boston Daily Globe*, 17 January 1917, "Thomas Mott Osborne Will Break Stone," 1.

10. *Boston Daily Globe*, 19 January 1917, "Osborne May Be Put in Ice Cutting Crew," 16.

11. *Boston Daily Globe*, 21 January 1917, "Osborne in a Role of a Coalheaver," 9.

12. *New York Times*, 30 January 1917, "Had to Punish Osborne" and *Boston Daily Globe*, 30 January 1917, "Reports on Naval Prison," 11.

13. Rothman, *Conscience and Convenience,* 119.

14. *Christian Science Monitor*, 11 July 1919, "Naval Discipline in War and Peace," 4.

15. Chamberlain, *There Is No Truce,* 367.

16. Verge, *A History of the U.S. Naval Prison,* 13.

17. *New York Times*, 31 July 1917, "Osborne's Prison Plans."

18. Chamberlain, *There Is No Truce,* 19.

19. Osborne, *Prisons and Common Sense,* 7–8.

20. Thomas Mott Osborne, "The Prison of the Future," in *The Handbook Series, Prison Reform*, compiled by Corinne Bacon (New York: H. W. Wilson, 1917), 305–6.

21. Thomas Mott Osborne, "Abolishing a Human Scrap-Heap," *Literary Digest* 57 (June 15, 1918): 33.

22. *Naval Welfare News*, Naval Prison, Portsmouth, NH, 17 September 1917, vol. 1, no. 3.

23. *Boston Daily Globe*, 19 November 1917, "Sec Daniels Visits Portsmouth Station," 2.

24. Josephus Daniels, *The Navy and the Nation*, 77.

25. Thomas Mott Osborne Personal Diary for 1917 (The National Diary). Hereafter Personal Osborne Diary for 1917.

26. Judge Advocate General (Navy) letter, 31 July 1917, NARA Waltham, RG 181, Portsmouth General Correspondence.

27. Medical Officer Naval Prison letter to Commandant Portsmouth Navy Yard, 15 September 1917, NARA Waltham, RG 181, Portsmouth General Correspondence.

28. Commanding Officer Naval Prison memorandum to Commandant Portsmouth Navy Yard, 21 September 1917, NARA Waltham, RG 181, Portsmouth General Correspondence.

29. Ibid.

30. Chamberlain, *There Is No Truce*, 17.

31. Rothman, *Conscience and Convenience*, 119.

32. Osborne, "Abolishing a Human Scrap-Heap," 33.

33. William Adams Slade, "Books and Boys in Portsmouth Prison," *The Survey* (December 27, 1919).

34. Osborne, *Within Prison Walls*, 163.

35. Osborne, *Prisons and Common Sense*, 55–56.

36. Tannenbaum, *Crime and Community*, 418.

37. Ibid., 420.

38. Ibid., 425.

39. Ibid., 423.

40. Slade, "Books and Boys in Portsmouth Prison."

41. Commanding Officer Naval Prison letter, 22 January 1918, NARA Waltham, RG 181, Portsmouth General Correspondence.

42. Ibid.

43. Ibid.

44. Don Best, "Our Commander," *Naval Welfare News*, 3 September 1917, vol.1 no. 1.

45. Slade, "Books and Boys in Portsmouth Prison."

46. Tannenbaum, *Osborne of Sing Sing*, 430.

47. Annual Report of Secretary of the Navy for Fiscal Year 1920, 133. Navy Department Library.

48. Osborne, *Prisons and Common Sense*, 45.

CHAPTER 11. REFORM STRUGGLES AT PORTSMOUTH

1. Chamberlain, *There Is No Truce*, 371.

2. Richard Lewis Alan Weiner, "Ideology and Incumbency: Thomas Mott Osborne and the 'Failure' of Progressive Era Prison Reform" (AB thesis, honors, Harvard University, 1981), 39.

3. Commanding Officer Naval Prison memorandum, 13 September 1917, NARA Waltham, RG 181, Portsmouth General Correspondence.

4. Commandant Portsmouth Navy Yard, Rear Admiral Boush, endorsement, 14 September 1917, to Commanding Officer Naval Prison memorandum, 13 September 1917, NARA Waltham, RG 181, Portsmouth General Correspondence.

5. Chamberlain, *There Is No Truce,* 372,

6. Osborne Personal Diary for 1917.

7. Annual Report of Secretary of the Navy for Fiscal Year 1918, 94. Navy Department Library.

8. Cronon, *The Cabinet Diaries,* 116, 117, 159, 177.

9. Ibid., 203, 238, 250, 317, 464, 529.

10. Osborne Personal Diary for 1917.

11. Bureau of Yards and Docks letter, 15 December 1917, NARA Waltham, RG 181, Portsmouth General Correspondence.

12. Industrial Manager Portsmouth Navy Yard letter, 24 December 1917, NARA Waltham, RG 181, Portsmouth General Correspondence.

13. Ibid.

14. Bureau of Yards and Docks letter, 29 December 1917, NARA Waltham, RG 181, Portsmouth General Correspondence.

15. Metal Trades Council, American Federation of Labor, Portsmouth, N.H., letter, 19 November 1919, NARA Waltham, RG 181, Portsmouth General Correspondence.

16. Industrial Manager Portsmouth Navy Yard letter, 21 November 1918, NARA Waltham, RG 181, Portsmouth General Correspondence.

17. American Federation of Labor, Portsmouth, N.H., letter, 20 January 1919, NARA Waltham, RG 181, Portsmouth General Correspondence.

18. Assistant Secretary of the Navy telegram, 20 August 1919, NARA Waltham, RG 181, Portsmouth General Correspondence.

19. Assistant Secretary of the Navy telegram, 22 September 1919, NARA Waltham, RG 181, Portsmouth General Correspondence.

20. Commanding Officer Naval Prison memorandum, 10 December 1919, NARA Waltham, RG 181, Portsmouth General Correspondence.

21. Tannenbaum, *Osborne of Sing Sing,* 281.

22. *New York Times,* 24 December 1922, "Prison Entertainments."

23. Commanding Officer Naval Prison letter to Secretary of the Navy, 28 February 1918, NARA Waltham, RG 181, Portsmouth General Correspondence.

24. Commanding Officer Naval Prison letter, 28 March 1918, NARA Waltham, RG 181, Portsmouth General Correspondence.

25. Secretary of the Navy Daniels letter, 7 April 1918, NARA Waltham, RG 181, Portsmouth General Correspondence.

26. Thomas Mott Osborne personal letter to Franklin Delano Roosevelt, 5 April 1919, Osborne Family Papers Collection, Syracuse University Bird Library, Syracuse, NY.

27. Commanding Officer Naval Prison letter, 18 September 1917, NARA Waltham, RG 181, Portsmouth General Correspondence.

28. Commanding Officer Naval Prison letter, 3 March 1918, NARA Waltham, RG 181, Portsmouth General Correspondence.

29. Headquarters Marine Corps 2nd endorsement, 13 March 1918, to Commanding Officer Naval Prison letter, 3 March 1918, and Secretary of the Navy letter, 13 April 1918, NARA Waltham, RG 181, Portsmouth General Correspondence.

30. Judge Advocate General (Navy) telegram to Chief Bureau of Navigation, 17 December 1917, NARA Waltham, RG 181, Portsmouth General Correspondence.

31. Commandant Portsmouth Navy Yard, Rear Admiral Boush, letter, 3 January 1918, NARA Waltham, RG 181, Portsmouth General Correspondence.

32. Commanding Officer Naval Prison letter, 17 March 1918, NARA Waltham, RG 181, Portsmouth General Correspondence.

33. Commanding Officer Naval Prison letter, 25 March 1918, NARA Waltham, RG 181, Portsmouth General Correspondence.

34. Ibid.

35. Ibid.

36. Commander H. L. Wyman letter to Commanding Officer Naval Prison via Commandant Navy Yard, 2 April 1918, NARA Waltham, RG 181, Portsmouth General Correspondence.

37. Ibid.

38. Commanding Officer Naval Prison letter, 12 April 1918, NARA Waltham, RG 181, Portsmouth General Correspondence.

39. Ibid.

40. Ibid.

41. Commanding Officer U.S. Marine Barracks, Navy Yard, Portsmouth, N.H. letter, 14 August 1918, NARA Waltham, RG 181, Portsmouth General Correspondence.

42. Ibid.

43. Commanding Officer Naval Prison letter, 22 August 1918, NARA Waltham, RG 181, Portsmouth General Correspondence.

44. Supply Officer, Navy Yard, Portsmouth, N.H. letter, 8 January 1920, NARA Waltham, RG 181, Portsmouth General Correspondence.

45. Supply Officer, Navy Yard, Portsmouth, N.H. memorandum, 23 September 1919, NARA Waltham, RG 181, Portsmouth General Correspondence.

46. Ibid.

47. Supply Officer, Navy Yard, Portsmouth, N.H. memorandum, 6 October 1919, NARA Waltham, RG 181, Portsmouth General Correspondence.

48. Commanding Officer Naval Prison letter, 5 October 1919, NARA Waltham, RG 181, Portsmouth General Correspondence.

49. Thomas Mott Osborne, "Common Sense in Prison Management," *Journal Criminal Law* 8 (1918).

50. L. Faucher, de la reforedes prisons (1838), 64 in Michel Foucault, *Discipline and Punishment: The Birth of the Prison* (New York: Pantheon Books 1979), 62.

51. Verge, *A History of the U.S. Naval Prison,* 21.

52. Supply Officer, Navy Yard, Portsmouth, N.H. letter, 8 January 1920, NARA Waltham, RG 181, Portsmouth General Correspondence.

53. Ibid.

54. Commandant Halstead letter, 10 January 1920, NARA Waltham, RG 181, Portsmouth General Correspondence.
55. Commanding Officer Naval Prison letter, 18 June 1919, NARA Waltham, RG 181, Portsmouth General Correspondence.
56. Commandant Portsmouth Navy Yard, Rear Admiral Boush, 1st endorsement, 29 June 1919, to Commanding Officer Naval Prison letter, 18 June 1919, NARA Waltham, RG 181, Portsmouth General Correspondence.
57. Commanding Officer Naval Prison letter, 31 July 1919, NARA Waltham, RG 181, Portsmouth General Correspondence.
58. Commandant Portsmouth Navy Yard, Rear Admiral Boush, letter, 2 August 1918, NARA Waltham, RG 181, Portsmouth General Correspondence.
59. Commanding Officer Naval Prison memorandum, 5 September 1919, NARA Waltham, RG 181, Portsmouth General Correspondence.
60. Ibid.
61. Commanding Officer Naval Prison letter, 21 June 1919, NARA Waltham, RG 181, Portsmouth General Correspondence.
62. Commandant Portsmouth Navy Yard, Rear Admiral Boush, memorandum, 4 September 1918, NARA Waltham, RG 181, Portsmouth General Correspondence.
63. Commandant Portsmouth Navy Yard, Rear Admiral Boush, memorandum, 20 June 19.19, NARA Waltham, RG 181, Portsmouth General Correspondence.
64. Allan Berube, *Coming Out Under Fire: The History of Gay Men and Women in World War II* (New York: The Free Press, 1990), 130.
65. Rothman, *Conscience and Convenience*, 124.
66. Secretary of the Navy letter to Commandant Navy Yard Portsmouth N.H., 27 March 1918, NARA Waltham, RG 181, Portsmouth General Correspondence.
67. Commanding Officer Naval Prison letter, 6 April 1918, NARA Waltham, RG 181, Portsmouth General Correspondence.
68. Commandant Portsmouth Navy Yard, Rear Admiral Boush, endorsement, 17 April 1918, to Commanding Officer Naval Prison letter, 6 April 1918, NARA Waltham, RG 181, Portsmouth General Correspondence.
69. Ibid.
70. Secretary of the Navy letter, 2 May 1918, NARA Waltham, RG 181, Portsmouth General Correspondence.
71. Commanding Officer Naval Prison letter, 17 June 1918, NARA Waltham, RG 181, Portsmouth General Correspondence.

Chapter 12. What's Going on at Portsmouth Prison?

1. Commanding Officer Naval Prison letter, 15 September 1917, NARA Waltham, RG 181, Portsmouth General Correspondence.
2. Commanding Officer Naval Prison 2nd endorsement, 10 December 1917, to Secretary of the Navy letter, 30 October 1917, NARA Waltham, RG 181, Portsmouth General Correspondence.
3. Commanding Officer USS *New Jersey* letter, 16 October 1917, NARA Waltham, RG 181, Portsmouth General Correspondence.

4. Commanding Officer Naval Prison letter, 10 December 1917, NARA Waltham, RG 181, Portsmouth General Correspondence.

5. Ibid.

6. Seaman Second Class Slim Morton personal letter to Seaman Speed, 17 February 1918, NARA Waltham, RG 181, Portsmouth General Correspondence.

7. Fireman John F. Cody personal letter to Fireman Edso, 10 February 1918, NARA Waltham, RG 181, Portsmouth General Correspondence.

8. Commander Squadron Two, Patrol Force U.S. Atlantic Fleet letter to Commander-in-Chief, U.S. Atlantic Fleet, 15 April 1918, NARA Waltham, RG 181, Portsmouth General Correspondence.

9. Commander-in-Chief, U.S. Atlantic Fleet letter to Secretary of the Navy, 30 April 1918, NARA Waltham, RG 181, Portsmouth General Correspondence.

10. Commanding Officer Naval Prison letter, 3 July 1918, NARA Waltham, RG 181, Portsmouth General Correspondence.

11. Ibid.

12. Ibid.

13. Secretary of the Navy Josephus Daniels letter, 23 May 1918, NARA Waltham, RG 181, Portsmouth General Correspondence.

14. Commanding Officer Naval Prison letter, 1 July 1918 [mistakenly dated 1912], NARA Waltham, RG 181, Portsmouth General Correspondence.

15. Ibid.

16. Quoted in Pietrusza, *1920: The Year of Six Presidents*, 134

17. Josephus Daniels, *The Wilson Era: Years of Peace,* 318.

18. Cronon, *The Cabinet Diaries,* 303.

19. Ibid.

20. Judge Advocate General (Navy) letter to Secretary of the Navy, 8 December 1919, NARA Waltham, RG 181, Portsmouth General Correspondence.

21. *New York Times*, 23 November 1919, "Made Whiskey in Navy Jail."

22. Judge Advocate General (Navy) letter to Secretary of the Navy, 8 December 1919, NARA Waltham, RG 181, Portsmouth General Correspondence, 4.

23. Ibid., 10.

24. Chief Bureau of Investigation (Frank Burke) letter to Judge Advocate General (Navy), 6 October 1919, NARA Waltham, RG 181, Portsmouth General Correspondence.

25. Judge Advocate General (Navy) letter to Secretary of the Navy, 8 December 1919, NARA Waltham, RG 181, Portsmouth General Correspondence.

26. *New York Times*, 16 December 1918, "Daniels Frees Prisoners."

27. *New York Times*, 28 December 1918, "Woman Sues T. M. Osborne," 18.

28. *Boston Daily Globe*, 2 February 1922, "Defense Opens for Osborne, 12.

29. *New York Times*, 8 February 1922, "Thomas M. Osborne Wins."

30. *New York Times*, 27 December 1919, "Expect Osborne Back."

31. *New York Times*, 2 January 1920 "New Legislature Meets."

32. *New York Times*, 6 January 1920, "Will Investigate Navy Prison Charge."

33. *New York Times*, 9 January 1920, "Osborne Courts Inquiry," 22.

34. Quoted in Pietrusza, *1920: The Year of Six Presidents*, 134.

35. Captain J. K. Taussig letter to Secretary of the Navy, 4 February 1920, Osborne Family Collection, Syracuse University Bird Library, Syracuse, NY.

36. Ibid.

37. Pietrusza, *1920: The Year of Six Presidents*, 135.

38. Kittredge, *Naval Lessons of the Great War*, 180–81.

39. Lawrence R. Murphy, *Perverts by Official Order: The Campaign Against Homosexuals by the United States Navy* (New York: Hawthorne Press, 1998), 63–64, 121–51.

40. Ward, *A First-Class Temperament*, 477–80.

41. Ibid., 478.

42. Ibid., 480.

43. Quoted in Pietrusza, *1920: The Year of Six Presidents*, 53.

44. Ward, *A First-Class Temperament*, 483.

45. Pietrusza, *1920: The Year of Six Presidents*, 160–61.

CHAPTER 13. INVESTIGATION INTO CONDITIONS AT PORTSMOUTH PRISON

1. Chamberlain, *There Is No Truce*, 389.

2. Murphy, *Perverts by Official Order*, 158.

3. Commanding Officer Naval Prison 3rd endorsement, 24 February 1920, to Judge Advocate General (Navy) letter, 8 December 1919, NARA Waltham, RG 181, Portsmouth General Correspondence.

4. Ibid.

5. J. S. Scott Hartje personal letter to Osborne, 28 September 1919, NARA Waltham, RG 181, Portsmouth General Correspondence.

6. John N. Watterfield personal letter to Osborne, 18 August 1918, NARA Waltham, RG 181, Portsmouth General Correspondence.

7. James Caruso personal letter to Osborne, 26 December 1919, NARA Waltham, RG 181, Portsmouth General Correspondence.

8. Jerry Elmendorf personal letter to Osborne, 17 April 1918, NARA Waltham, RG 181, Portsmouth General Correspondence.

9. William Seifert personal letter to Osborne, 21 November 1918, NARA Waltham, RG 181, Portsmouth General Correspondence.

10. Report of Board (Roosevelt, Dunn, and Halstead) Appointed to Report on General Conditions at the Portsmouth Naval Prison to Secretary of the Navy, 26 February 1920, NARA Waltham, RG 181, Portsmouth General Correspondence.

11. *New York Times*, 3 March 1920, "Osborne Cleared by Inquiry."

12. Secretary of the Navy letter, 13 March 1920, NARA Waltham, RG 181, Portsmouth General Correspondence.

13. Chamberlain, *There Is No Truce*, 381.

14. Judge Advocate General (Navy) letter, 4 December 1919, NARA Waltham, RG 181, Portsmouth General Correspondence; Assistant Secretary of the Navy 1st endorsement, 15 December 1919, to Judge Advocate General letter, 8 December 1919, NARA Waltham, RG 181, Portsmouth General Correspondence.

15. Morrison, *Josephus Daniels*, 130–31.

16. Ward, *A First-Class Temperament*, 549.
17. Ibid., 473.
18. Cronon, *The Cabinet Diaries*, 492.
19. Osborne personal letter to Josephus Daniels, 25 February 1920, Osborne Family Papers Collection, Syracuse University Bird Library, Syracuse, NY.
20. Josephus Daniels personal letter to Osborne, 28 February 1920, Osborne Family Papers Collection, Syracuse University Bird Library, Syracuse, NY.
21. Osborne personal letter to Mr. Ellery Sedgwick, 1 March 1920, Osborne Family Papers Collection, Syracuse University Bird Library, Syracuse, NY.
22. Cronon, *The Cabinet Diaries*, 503.
23. Ibid.
24. *New York Times*, 9 March 1920, "Osborne Again Resigns."
25. Osborne personal letter to Austin MacCormick, 17 March 1920, Osborne Family Papers Collection, Syracuse University Bird Library, Syracuse, NY.
26. Osborne personal letter to Josephus Daniels, 5 March 1920, Osborne Family Papers Collection, Syracuse University Bird Library, Syracuse, NY.
27. Osborne personal letter to Franklin Delano Roosevelt, 5 March 1920, Osborne Family Papers Collection, Syracuse University Bird Library, Syracuse, NY.
28. Cronon, *The Cabinet Diaries*, 504.
29. Ibid.
30. Ibid.
31. Chief of Bureau of Navigation letter, 3 March 1920, NARA Waltham, RG 181, Portsmouth General Correspondence.
32. Commanding Officer Naval Prison letter, 16 March 1920, NARA Waltham, RG 181, Portsmouth General Correspondence.
33. Quoted in Chamberlain, *There Is No Truce*, 382.
34. *Christian Science Monitor*, 9 June 1920, "Mr. Osborne Finished Report," 10.
35. Ward, *A First-Class Temperament*, 553.
36. Quoted in *New York Times*, 25 October 1920, "Assails Roosevelt on Naval Scandal."
37. Quoted in ibid.
38. Quoted in Ward, *A First-Class Temperament*, 550.
39. Quoted in Murphy, *Perverts by Official Order*, 159–61.
40. Ibid., 163.
41. Ibid.
42. *New York Times*, 26 October 1920, "Roosevelt Charges Libel, Orders Suit."
43. Ibid.
44. Annual Report of the Judge Advocate General (Navy) for Fiscal Year 1919 in Annual Report of Secretary of the Navy for Fiscal Year 1919, 326. Navy Department Library.
45. Annual Report of the Judge Advocate General (Navy) for Fiscal Year 1920 in Annual Report of Secretary of the Navy for Fiscal Year 1920, 134. Navy Department Library.
46. Ibid., 492–93.

47. Annual Report of Secretary of the Navy for Fiscal Year 1920, 133. Navy Department Library.
48. Ibid., 132.

CHAPTER 14. OSBORNE'S RESULTS AT PORTSMOUTH

1. Osborne, "Abolishing a Human Scrap-Heap," 33.
2. Annual Report of Secretary of the Navy for the Fiscal Year 1920, 134. Navy Department Library.
3. Chief of Bureau of Navigation letter, 13 September 1913, NARA Waltham, RG 181, Portsmouth General Correspondence.
4. Commanding Officer Portsmouth Naval Prison, *Annual Reports for the Years Ending June 30, 1916–1923,* NARA Waltham, RG 181, Portsmouth General Collection.
5. Influenza of 1918, Spanish Flu and the US Navy. http://www.history.Navy.mil/library/online/influenza_main.htm
6. Medical Officers Report with Commanding Officer Portsmouth Naval Prison, *Annual Report for the Year Ending June 30, 1919,* NARA Waltham, RG 181, Portsmouth General Collection.
7. David Connelly, narrator, *TMO @ the Castle.*
8. Chamberlain, *There Is No Truce*, 17.
9. Bates, "Honor System for Inmates," 110, 112, 116.
10. Osborne, *Prisons and Common Sense*, 88.
11. Osborne, *Society and Prisons, Some Suggestions for a New Penology* (New Haven: Yale University Press, 1916), 140.
12. Judge Advocate General (Navy) letter to Secretary of the Navy, 8 December 1919, NARA Waltham, RG 181, Portsmouth General Correspondence.
13. Tannenbaum, *Osborne of Sing Sing*, 291.
14. Austin MacCormick personal letter to Osborne, 22 February 1920, Osborne Family Papers Collection, Syracuse University Bird Library, Syracuse, NY.
15. Ibid.
16. Quoted in Tannenbaum, *Osborne of Sing Sing*, 316.
17. Ibid., 317.
18. Ibid., 319.
19. Franklin Ondley Jr. personal letter to Osborne, 22 February 1920, Osborne Family Papers Collection, Syracuse University Bird Library, Syracuse, NY.
20. Josephus Daniels, *The Wilson Era: Years of Peace*, 318.
21. Osborne, *Prisons and Common Sense*, 96.
22. Osborne personal letter to Josephus Daniels, 18 February 1920, Osborne Family Papers Collection, Syracuse University Bird Library, Syracuse, NY.
23. Tannenbaum, *Crime and the Community*, 427.
24. Weiner, "Ideology and Incumbency," ii–iii.
25. Tannenbaum, *Osborne of Sing Sing*, 433.
26. Rothman, *Conscience and Convenience*, 10.
27. Tannenbaum, *Osborne of Sing Sing*, viii.

CHAPTER 15. PORTSMOUTH POST OSBORNE

1. *Christian Science Monitor*, 11 March 1920, "Prison Commander Named," 5.
2. Hickory Hill and Homeport, www.rosslynredux.com/artifacts/hickory-hill -homeport/.
3. Historic American Newspapers, Burlington, Vermont, 3 Jun 1920, 5, http:// chroniclingamerica.loc.gov/lccn/sn86072143/1920-06-03/.
4. Ibid.
5. Osborne personal letter to Austin MacCormick, 17 March 1920, Osborne Family Papers Collection, Syracuse University Bird Library, Syracuse, NY.
6. *New York Times,* 15 April 1920, "Naval Orders."
7. *New York Times,* 12 April 1921, "Prison Committee Meets."
8. *New York Times,* 16 May 1920, "Says Cruelty Bars Reform in Prisons."
9. Quoted in Verge, *A History of the U.S. Naval Prison*, 20–21.
10. *New York Times,* 7 June 1920, "Osborne Inspects Naval Prison."
11. *New York Times*, 14 June 1920, "Osborne Cheered by 1,200 Convicts," 14.
12. Commandant Halstead memorandum, 26 August 1920, NARA Waltham, RG 181, Portsmouth General Correspondence.
13. Commandant First Naval District (Dunn) 3rd endorsement, 2 July 1920, to Commanding Officer Naval Prison, Commodore Wadhams, letter, 29 June 1920, NARA Waltham, RG 181, Portsmouth General Correspondence.
14. Commandant Halstead memorandum, 12 August 1920, NARA Waltham, RG 181, Portsmouth General Correspondence.
15. Commander J. H. Sypher letter to Secretary of the Navy, 4 May 1921, NARA Waltham, RG 181, Portsmouth General Correspondence.
16. Ibid.
17. Ibid.
18. Pietrusza, *1920: The Year of Six Presidents*, 194.
19. Murphy, *Perverts by Official Order*, 249
20. Ibid.
21. Ibid., 264–73.
22. This description is taken from a Marine Corps newspaper excerpt in Box 273, folder 64, of the Osborne Papers at Syracuse University. The newspaper name and date are missing.
23. *New York Times*, 23 June 1921, "Denby Reverses So-Called Soviet Policy in the Navy."
24. Quoted in *New York Times*, 23 June 1921.
25. *New York Times*, 19 May 1921, "Twenty Years Old, Eleven Times Wed."
26. Tannenbaum, *Osborne at Sing Sing*, 264.
27. Chamberlain, *There Is No Truce*, 389.
28. *Boston Daily Globe*, 22 July 1922 "Prison Reform Killed at Portsmouth," 3.
29. Commanding Officer Naval Prison Order HD-No. 25, 3 August 1921, NARA Waltham, RG 181, Portsmouth General Correspondence; Commanding Officer Naval Prison Order HD-No. 21, 28 July 1921, NARA Waltham, RG 181, Portsmouth General Correspondence; Commanding Officer Naval Prison Order

————. "Common Sense in Prison Management." *Journal Criminal Law* 8 (1918).

————. "The Prison of the Future." In *The Handbook Series, Prison Reform*, compiled by Corinne Bacon. New York: H. W. Wilson, 1917.

Newspapers

Boston Daily Globe

Boston Sunday Globe

Christian Science Monitor

Naval Welfare News (also *The Mutual Welfare News*), Portsmouth Naval Prison

New York Times

Portsmouth Herald

Providence Journal

San Francisco Bulletin

SECONDARY SOURCES

Books

Allen, Gardner W. *A Natural History of the American Revolution*. Boston: A Scholar's Bookshelf, 2005.

Bacon, Corrine, ed. *The Handbook Series, Prison Reform*. New York: H. W. Wilson, 1917.

Barnes, H. F. *The Story of Punishment*. Montclair, NJ: Patterson Smith, 1972.

Beaumont, Gustave de, and Alexis de Tocqueville. *On the Penitentiary System in the United States and Its Application in France*. Carbondale: Southern Illinois University Press, 1979.

Berube, Allan. *Coming Out Under Fire: The History of Gay Men and Women in World War II*. New York: Free Press, 1990.

Blomberg, Thomas G., and Karol Lucken. *American Penology: A History of Control*. New York: Aldine De Gruyter, 2000.

Chamberlain, Rudolph W. *There Is No Truce: A Life of Thomas Mott Osborne*. New York: MacMillan, 1935.

Connery, Robert H. *The Navy and Industrial Mobilization in World War II*. Princeton: Princeton University Press, 1951.

Cowley, Robert, ed. *What If? 2*. New York: Simon & Schuster, 2001.

Daniels, Jonathan. *The End of Innocence*. Philadelphia: Lippincott, 1954.

Davis, George T. *A Navy Second to None: The Development of Modern American Naval Policy*. New York: Harcourt Brace, 1940

Fidell, Eugene R., and Dwight H. Sullivan. *Evolving Military Justice*. Annapolis, MD: Naval Institute Press, 2002.

Foucault, Michel. *Discipline and Punishment: The Birth of the Prison*. New York: Pantheon Books, 1979.

Freedman, Estelle B. *Maternal Justice: Miriam Waters and the Female Reform Tradition*. Chicago: Chicago University Press, 1996.

Jardin, Andre. *Tocqueville*. Baltimore, MD: John Hopkins University Press, 1988.

Keve, Paul W. *Prisons and the American Conscience: A History of U.S. Federal Prisons*. Carbondale: Southern Illinois University Press, 1991.

Kilpatrick, Carroll, ed. *Roosevelt and Daniels*. Chapel Hill: University of North Carolina Press, 1952.

Kittredge, Tracy Barrett. *Naval Lessons of the Great War: A Review of the Senate Naval
   Investigation of the Criticisms by Admiral Sims of the Policies and Methods of
   Josephus Daniels*. Garden City, NY: Doubleday, Page, 1921.

Langley, Harold D. *Social Reform in the United States Navy, 1798–1862*. Urbana:
   University of Illinois Press, 1967.

Lott, Arnold S., Lt. Cmdr., USN. *A Long Line of Ships: Mare Island's Century of Naval
   Activity in California*. Annapolis: United States Naval Institute, 1954.

Lowry, Thomas P. *The Story the Soldiers Won't Tell: Sex in the Civil War*. Mechanicsburg,
   PA: Stackpole Books, 1994.

Mancini, Matthew. *Alexis de Tocqueville*. New York: Twayne Publishers, 1994.

McKelvey, Blake. *American Prisons: A Study in American Social History Prior to 1915*.
   Montclair: Patterson Smith, 1968 [c1936].

McLennan, Rebecca M. *The Crisis of Imprisonment: Protest, Politics, and the Making of the
   American Penal State, 1776–1941*. Cambridge: Cambridge University Press,
   2008.

Minot, George, ed. *The Statutes at Large and Treaties of the United States of America from
   December 1, 1851 to March 3, 1855*. vol. 10. Boston: Little, Brown, 1855.

Morrison, Joseph L. *Josephus Daniels: The Small-d Democrat*. Chapel Hill: University of
   North Carolina Press, 1966.

Moskos, Peter. *In Defense of Flogging*. New York: Basic Books, 2011.

Murphy, Lawrence R. *Perverts by Official Order: The Campaign Against Homosexuals by
   the United States Navy*. New York: Hawthorne Press, 1998.

Penny, Sherry H., and James D. Livingston. *A Very Dangerous Woman: Martha Wright
   and Women's Rights*. Amherst: University of Massachusetts Press, 2004.

Pietrusza, David. *1920: The Year of Six Presidents*. New York: Basic Books, 2007.

Portsmouth Naval Shipyard. *Cradle of American Shipbuilding*. Portsmouth Naval Shipyard: Government Printing Office, 1978.

Potter E. B., and Chester W. Nimitz. *Sea Power: A Naval History*. Englewood Cliffs, NJ:
   Prentice Hall, 1960.

Regulations for the Government of the Navy of the United States, 1876. Washington, D.C.:
   Government Printing Office, 1877.

Robinson, Louis N. *Penology in the United States*. Philadelphia: John C. Winston, 1921.

Rothman, D. J. *Conscience and Convenience: The Asylum and Its Alternatives in Progressive
   America*. Boston: Little, Brown, 1980.

———. *The Discovery of the Asylum: Social Order and Disorder in the New Republic*. Boston: Little, Brown, 1971.

Tannenbaum, Frank. *Crime and the Community*. Boston: Ginn and Company, 1938.

———. *Osborne of Sing Sing*. Chapel Hill: University of North Carolina Press, 1933.

Valle, James E. *Rocks and Shoals: Order and Discipline in the Old Navy 1800–1861*.
   Annapolis, MD: Naval Institute Press, 1980.

Verge, Robert J. *A History of the U.S. Naval Prison at Portsmouth, New Hampshire*. Portsmouth: U.S. Naval Print Shop, 1946.

Walker, Samuel. *Popular Justice: A History of American Criminal Justice*. New York: Oxford
   University Press, 1980.

About the Author

During his thirty-year naval career CAPT. RODNEY K. WATTERSON, USN (Ret.), was involved with the design, construction, and maintenance of submarines. After retiring from the Navy, he served as a plant manager and director for Textron Automotive Industries and went back to school to pursue a lifelong love of history.